BLACK LIGHTNING
THE LEGACY OF THE LOCKHEED BLACKBIRDS

Revised edition of *The Archangel and the Oxcart*

**Other Books
by
Jeannette Remak and Joseph Ventolo, Jr.**

A-12 Declassified
XB-70 Valkyrie Ride to Valhalla
XB-70 the Return to Valhalla

Watch for

To Slip the Surly Bonds
by
Jeannette Remak, coming 2018.

BLACK LIGHTNING

THE LEGACY OF THE LOCKHEED BLACKBIRDS

Jeannette Remak and Joseph Ventolo, Jr.
Revised edition of *The Archangel and the Oxcart*

SPEAKING VOLUMES, LLC
NAPLES, FLORIDA
2017

Black Lightning
The Legacy of the Lockheed Blackbirds

Copyright © 2017 Phoenix Aviation Research

Revised edition of *The Archangel and the Oxcart*

All rights reserved. No part of this book may be reproduced or transmitted in any form or by any means without written permission.

Speaking Volumes, is committed to publishing works of quality and integrity. We are proud to offer this book to our readers; however, the information, and the words are the author's alone.

ISBN 978-1-62815-733-8

We dedicate this book to the OXCART program; to its pilots and crews, support staff and managers, USAF and CIA personnel, and to the wives and families who stood by, silently. Moreover, we dedicate our written words to the eternal memory of those who gave their lives for the ultimate mission: that the United States of America could live on under the *bright light* of their protection.

Acknowledgments

We are sure that there are some mistakes that got past us and both Joe and I own those unintentional errors. We would like to extend out thanks to the following individuals for their help in writing this book. Without them, this book would still be just a dream.

We would like to thank Erica Mueller for all her patience, amazing work. Thanks Erica, you are awesome!!

Robert Andrews, T.D. Barnes-President –Roadrunners Internationale Association, CIA History Office, Alan Tate and the ENTIRE CIA Office of Privacy and Information, Dr. William Elliot, PhD., Charles Frey, Bill Lindsay, Ron Kloeski, Frank Murray-Roadrunners Internationale Association Archivist/OXCART pilot, Hank Meiridieck, Phoenix Aviation Research, Domenic Proscia-Vaughan College of Aeronautics, Mary Anne Ruggiero, Sharlene Weeks and the Weeks family, Robert Williams, Marti Ventolo.

Special Research: Mr. James Petty

To our furry companions who kept us sane, Shanghai Remak,
the late and beloved M. Mae Ventolo, and Amber Ventolo.
If we forgot anyone, please forgive us and know that you are in our hearts.

A very special thank you to Ron Girouard. Ron's work with the OXCART patches that are so rare, is beyond the call of duty. We also thank Ron for his inspirational help in the Weeks project and jumping in at the last minute with more material. Couldn't have done it without you, buddy!

Please visit the Roadrunners Internationale site:
www.roadrunnersinternationale.com

And last but never least, our undying thanks to the A-12 pilots and their magnificent Blackbirds, the teams at Lockheed and all involved in the OXCART/SENIOR CROWN program. All should be treated as a national treasure of the United States. They should stand with their program creators and crews as a shining achievement in the struggle to protect and defend the United States of America in the desperate times of the Cold War. And please:

Always remember;

FREEDOM

IS A GREAT RESPONSIBILITY

AND

FREEDOM ISN'T CHEAP.

Preface

World War II ended only to be followed by another war, the Cold War between the Soviet Union and the United States. The Cold War spawned the arms race followed by the nuclear and space races, pitting the USSR against the United States and its allies. Following an undeclared proxy war, a war known as the Korean War, between the Cold War adversaries, the United States needed to know what the Soviet Union was up to inside its closed borders. After losing 10 Boeing RB-47 bombers and 75 crew members during ferret flights into the Soviet denied territory, the United States sought to develop a plane able to fly beyond the reach of Soviet radar or interception by Soviet missiles.

The Land Advisory Panel, a civilian Intelligence Systems Panel, advising the USAF and CIA on aerial reconnaissance, recommended the CL-282 design proposed by the Lockheed Skunk Works. General Curtis LeMay of Strategic Air Command (SAC) walked out of a CL-282 presentation, saying that he was not interested in an airplane without wheels or guns. Consequently, the panel approached President Eisenhower about having the Central Intelligence Agency build the plane for fear of the military operating the CL-282 during peacetime could provoke a war.

Codenamed Project AQUATONE, the CIA established a pilot training facility at Groom Lake in Area 51, Nevada for flight testing what became the Lockheed U-2 that earned the nickname, Angel. Eight months later, by 1 August 1955, CIA pilots, sheep-dipped out of the Air Force, are flying the U-2 at Area 51. Ten months later, on 20 June CIA pilot Carl Overstreet conducts the first overflight of Soviet denied territory that the Soviets tracked by radar contrary to CIA expectations. Under Project RAINBOW, the CIA unsuccessfully attempts to make the U-2 stealthy to radar. Unable to accomplish the stealth attempt, the CIA estimates a two-year life expectancy of the U-2 before the Soviets would shoot down the plane.

In 1957, Project GUSTO selected the Lockheed "Archangel" design for the U-2 successor. The CIA required the successor to the U-2 to fly at 90,000 feet, cruise at Mach 3, and to incorporate state-of-the-art techniques in radar absorption or deflection. Over the ensuing months, the Skunk Works studied various configurations called "Archangel-1," "Archangel-2," and so forth—a carryover from the original moniker of "Angel" given to the U-2 during its development. At Area 51, the A-12 in its final version flew 2,850 development and training missions before deploying during Operation BLACK SHIELD. In 1957, it flew operationally over Southeast Asia during the Vietnam War.

On the Internet, Google two questions: "The first operational stealth plane was what?" "What is the fastest and highest flying manned jet aircraft ever flown." The first answer you get, it is the US Air Force's F-117A stealth fighter. The second answer you receive is it is the US Air Force's SR-71 Blackbird reconnaissance plane. Both answers are wrong. Even identifying the F-117A aircraft as a fighter plane is incorrect. The F-117A is admittedly a "cute" little plane that looks to be a fighter, but it is a bomber with a fighter plane designation nonetheless. The correct answers to the two questions remain shrouded under the CIA's veil of secrecy for near half a century.

During March 2016, the Central Intelligence Agency declassified and released a report titled: CIA, Directorate of Science and Technology (DST), History of the Office of Special Activities (OSA) From Inception to 1969. This report officially confirms the CIA as founding the mythical, highly classified Area 51 in Nevada. Now, the co-authors of this book, Jeannette Remak and Joe Ventolo are allowed to answer the two questions and do so along with much more in this book containing the newly declassified information denied to their earlier book, "A-12 Declassified", the first definitive book on the Lockheed A-12 Blackbird. While the many SR-71 books have mentioned the A-12, there has never been a source of A-12 information as complete in one place before. The book describes the aircraft and the programs in detail.

Author, Jeannette Remak is the former Aircraft Historian (Ret) at the Intrepid Sea Air Space Museum, New York City, has a Master's degree in Aviation Mechanics. Her aviation background and her thorough research have broadened her knowledge on the subject to a much higher level than that of those who participated in the CIA's Project OXCART and Operation BLACK SHIELD under the highly classified and rigidly compartmentalized environment at the time. Remak is the established "go to" person by historians, museum curators, authors, academia, and even those who participated in the programs at the time. She knows which components contain asbestos and the composites. She knows how to preserve the titanium airframe, the type paint to use to maintain the A-12 articles now retired in museums. Remak's resourcefulness earned her honorary membership in the Roadrunners Internationale association of members of the CIA, Air Force, and support contractors who worked the CIA Archangel and associated projects at Area 51 and while deployed to Kadena, Okinawa during Operation BLACK SHIELD.

The book's co-author, Joe Ventolo, former curator of the National Museum of the USAF, is Remak's partner in Phoenix Aviation Research. It was this research that produced this book containing the most in-depth history of the little-known CIA's role in creating a means of overflying denied territory and bringing home the intelligence needed to keep the United States safe. Ventolo presented the case for saving the A-12s at the Roadrunners International Convention. His support for the A-12s and the Project OXCART veterans is total and unswerving.

Much of the world knows the role that aviation played in the CIA's Air America covert flights where the US Air Force could not fly. In this book, the CIA activities in Area 51 spawn a new component within the CIA at Langley. The CIA formed its Directorate of Science and Technology, the DS&T, as one of five major components. Remak addresses the many questions about why, who, what, where, and when. When finished with this book, the reader will realize that it was the CIA who secretly designed a plane to overfly Russia, constructed of titanium purchased by the CIA from Russia.

Using slide rule technology, the people selected by the CIA produced America's first stealth plane, a plane that to this day is the fastest and highest flying manned jet aircraft ever. Using titanium to design an aircraft that produced high temperatures during flight required inventing virtually everything about this plane. Unlike the Air Force's SR-71 Blackbird that followed the

CIA's A-12, the CIA lost two pilots, an almost 20 percent fatality rate, and two F-101 Voodoo chase pilots. These losses contributed to producing for the Air Force a follow-on plane that never lost a crew member. Each of the six BLACKSHIELD pilots earned the CIA's highest medal, the Intelligence Star for Valor, one awarded posthumously to the pilot's widow.

This is a book that one will read cover to cover and then keep for future reference. Jeannette Remak and Joe Ventolo have written the bible for the CIA's A-12 Archangel.

TD Barnes
Former Area 51 Special Projects
President Roadrunners Internationale
Former Executive Director Nevada Aerospace Hall of Fame

Table of Contents

Prologue 1

Forward *"And eyes to see with. . . ."* 3

Early Reconnaissance: 7

The Cold War 12

Black Lightning 39

The Archangel and the Kingfisher 73

The A-11- The Almost Archangel 77

Building an Enigma 138

Learning to Fly 169

Skylark, Silver Javelin, Black Shield 192

Cygnus Heads Home 229

Black Birds of Another Design 236

End of a Phenomenal Era 256

Epilogue 273

Appendices 276

Index 317

Bibliography 324

Prologue

The story of the A-12 Blackbird and the CIA program OXCART, plainly stated, is an odyssey into Cold War dynamics. In 1981, only small bits and pieces of this program began to come out of the black halls of the CIA. Many in the upper echelons of Government did not know that the A-12 Blackbird and OXCART even existed, so deeply buried was the program. To this day, many cannot make the distinction between the A-12 and the SR-71. It leaves a question as to why it has taken so long for this program to come out into the open. If it were not for the work of diligent historians and buffs, it may have never come into the light, and the A-12s now in museums, would have been known as the "SR-71," as the authors have seen on many occasions. This book will fill in many of the blanks for both the A-12 and the OXCART program. Interviews with survivors of the program, and more recently the release of classified documents, have shown that the OXCART program was not a rose lit, golden edged, story that many have purported it to be. Research has found that it was, in fact, a merciless, political entity born of the Cold War desperation to cover denied territory of the enemies of the United States and her allies. So mercilessly political, that – contrary to the reasons given at the time – it wasn't the airplane's vulnerability that flawed the program; instead it was budgets and egos that ultimately downed OXCART and the venerable A-12. The A-12 Cygnus, as she is known by the pilots who flew her, broke more speed records, covered more denied territory, and spawned more aeronautical institutions than the SR-71 ever did in its long career. That is not to say the SR-71 wasn't a reconnaissance star in her own right. The USAF, being the sole proprietor, changed the mission of the SR-71 to one of post nuclear strike reconnaissance by adding sensors to her long list of accoutrements. The rift between the CIA and the USAF – caused by the fact that the USAF felt itself left out of the glory of OXCART, regardless of the support that it gave to the program—eventually caused the downfall of the SR-71 program. Jealousy from the top of the USAF food chain, and ignorance of the real mission of the SR-71 by bureaucrats and budget offices, caused the loss of this magnificent aircraft and reconnaissance program. However, let it be known: The A-12 sisters; the YF-12, which was the interceptor that the USAF wished for, was a derivative of the A-12, and the MD-21 was also an offshoot which carried the D-21 drone on the back of a modified A-12. They were the Mother/Daughter configuration and the possible answer to high-speed pilotless aerial reconnaissance way before its time. The venerable SR-71, the queen of speed, photographic and electronic intelligence sensors, had a huge legacy in the world of aerial reconnaissance to be sure. The creations of Kelly Johnson and the Lockheed Skunk Works remain absolute gems in the crown of the United States winning the Cold War.

Forward

"And eyes to see with. . . ."

The flagstones for aerial reconnaissance were laid way back in World War I by the British, French, and the Germans. Not until the war was in its fourth year, did the United States step in to help end the stalemate. However, the United States had a few lessons to learn about aerial reconnaissance when compared with her European counterparts. The Germans and the British, along with the French, were working at the vanguard of the issue while the United States was slow to jump on board the reconnaissance train. It wasn't until the fever of WWII aerial campaigns hit that the United States started to really look around and see what the rest of the world was doing with aerial reconnaissance. The British had fine-tuned their war efforts with reconnaissance concepts that helped make American daylight bombing campaigns a reality, and put the final twist on the Third Reich. Men like Robert Lovett, who served as a naval aviator and became the special assistant to the fledging Air Corps, explored what was going on elsewhere in the world of aviation technology. Lovett traveled extensively and interviewed many scientists in an effort to find out just where the United States stood, technologically. He learned that not only was the United States hopelessly behind in aviation techniques and science, it was also unable to count on the support of a capable aviation industry should a war break out. Lovett saw it as his personal duty to see that the Air Corps should have enough aircraft, and that there be nothing lacking in the United States industrial base. He sought to upgrade the industrial base and Army Air Corps equipment and practices so the United States could catch up with contemporary aviation technology.

In later years, the United States also had men like Richard Leghorn, who stepped in at a critical time and helped develop the concepts of aerial reconnaissance at the beginning of the Cold War. Colonel Osmond Ritland, the commander of the USAF Ballistic Missile Division, was responsible for selecting the location of the AREA 51— "The place that didn't exist," and so much more. Richard Bissell of the CIA, who began with the U-2 and CORONA project and brought the A-12 into existence, Kelly Johnson and his Lockheed Skunk Works team, were legends in their own time. Of course, there are also the pilots of OXCART, who hung it out way over the line and pushed the envelope so hard the seams were ready to split. Some of them gave their lives for the OXCART Program. Without these individuals, the United States would have been hard pressed to hold its own in the dangerous skies of aerial reconnaissance and Cold War policy.

The Cold War was a silent, deadly battlefield. Many of our brave airmen and naval aviators, lost their lives being pursued and shot down by Russian MiGs, while taking the images the United States so desperately needed. The RB-57 Canberras, the P-3s, RB-29s, and the P2V Neptunes were not quite fast enough to keep from being MiG meat. Some even tried to fly under the radar but eventually were caught. The Russians were merciless in protecting their skies. Russian MiGs would go after the USAF's huge RB-29s and take them down; nothing was too big or too fast for the Russians. The United States finally saw that something had to be done to stop the hell-bent Russians and get the information needed to protect the United States and her allies from the threat of the Soviet aggression via missile construction and development.

In August 1949, when the Soviet Union detonated its first atomic device, the Stalin regime proudly proclaimed it had put the USSR on an equal footing with its Western adversaries. It came as a surprise to most Americans that the USSR had caught up with the United States so quickly. Perhaps less surprised, but no less concerned, President Truman saw that America's advantage over the Soviet arsenal had narrowed.

After General of the Army, Dwight D. Eisenhower, became the 34th President of the United States, the Soviets raised the bar again. In August 1953, the USSR detonated a "semi - thermonuclear device". On November 23, 1955, the Soviet Union again raised the bar by testing its first real thermonuclear device, dropping a 16 megaton hydrogen "bomb" at the Semipalatinsk Test Site in Kazakhstan. By then, Eisenhower had already concluded that his administration had to develop a radical, new kind of reconnaissance program. That led him to propose an "Open Skies Program" to the Soviet Union. The proposal stated that it would be possible for both countries to "overlook" each other's back yards to see what was being tested in the way of nuclear devices. The Soviets rejected Ike's proposal out of hand.

As the Cold War contest grew, the Soviet Union's successful launch of the world's first Earth satellite on October 4, 1957, convinced Eisenhower that it was urgent for him to take action right away. Sputnik, the 180 lb. ball of metal, tubes, and wires that orbited the earth, threw Americans for a loop. Sputnik's little beeps made an already nervous population more uneasy, knowing that a Soviet satellite flew over their American heads. The Central Intelligence Agency knew that the conventional spy on the ground could not find hidden missile bases in the heart of Siberia. It was going to call for more and different reconnaissance action.

The Eisenhower Administration was urgently searching for better ways to find out what was going on deep within the borders of the USSR and thus to shore up the US intelligence gap. The CIA tasked to find a way to look beyond those borders, needed to find new ways of developing the answer. A new kind of aircraft was the obvious answer. President Eisenhower made it quite clear that he wanted *no military personnel* in the cockpit, *nor anything related to the military*, flying over the denied territory of any hostile nation. That, he knew, would be tantamount to a declaration of war. Hence, "sheep dipping" of military pilots was quietly invented as the CIA started its design programs for reconnaissance aircraft. Eisenhower knew the gamble they all were taking, and the time had come to define the requirements to find the aircraft to do the job.

The step was taken and AQUATONE was created. Born in Building 42 of the Lockheed Burbank facility, the U-2 "Dragon Lady" came from out of the Kelly Johnson "Skunk Works" and made history at the "place that didn't exist," known then as "The Ranch", also known to us as AREA 51. However, it was not long before the Dragon Lady was compromised. The thing that Eisenhower and the CIA feared most happened on May 1, 1960. Francis Gary Powers and his U-2 were knocked out of the sky over Soviet Russia by a SAM missile. The nightmare had begun. Eisenhower had to "fess up" to the Russians and the world and admit that the United States was flying over denied territory. It wasn't just a political mortification for Eisenhower; it jeopardized many of the political issues confronting the United States at the time. However, worst of all, it gave the Soviets and Premier Khrushchev the upper hand. While the CIA had already been looking for the U-2 successor, after May 1,1960, it became imperative to do so immediately. Project GUSTO was launched. It didn't take long before GUSTO changed to OXCART thanks to Kelly Johnson, once again, OXCART would bring the A-12 Cygnus to life.

Based on the decision to authorize OXCART, the whole nature of aviation and spying on unfriendly nations was changed. No longer would the crews of slower aircraft have to risk their lives over dangerous territory. The time had come for the dark angels to take to the skies. With the birth of the Lockheed A-12 Blackbird, came the first real endeavor to over fly denied territory and remain untouchable. The creation of the A-12 was a true revolution in the art of aerial reconnaissance. It gave the United States the ability to see "over the wall" of nations like North Korea and other critical places where conventional aircraft feared to tread. The CIA, the pilots of OXCART, and the USAF, melded together to form one of the most powerful, dangerous, and enlightening eras of the Cold War, redefining the world of aerial reconnaissance and high speed, high altitude flight. The satellites of the CORONA project were aloft but not fully successful, and the U-2 had been "caught out," but the A-12 had been born and the "Archangel" would transform the world of aerial reconnaissance. With a swift wing, a heart pounding with the pulse of the Pratt & Whitney J-58's, Cygnus had given the United States new "eyes" to see with.

Early Reconnaissance:

In the spring of 1945, the war in the European Theater of Operations was coming to an exhausted end. The United States, as one of the vanquishers of the Third Reich, was tackling the job of going through the vast amount of material generated by the German military infrastructure. Information and material retrieved from repatriating Soviet Union POWs, was perceived as spoils of war, and gave the United States a larger view of what her erstwhile ally, the Soviet Union, was up to. Much of that material was quickly becoming outdated, according to the Soviet POWs' who were interviewed, at the end of the war. Even in the late 1940s, the U.S. remained convinced of the need to obtain aerial reconnaissance any way it could. Yet, the U.S. was still "in the woods" about finding a way to do it during the fragile peace of the Cold War.

It was obvious to all the combatants of WW II that aerial reconnaissance had not only contributed to the Allied victory, but had completely changed the look of the battlefield. Now that the war had finally ended, new challenges began to emerge. The United States realized that its military policy on aerial reconnaissance needed to be changed just as quickly. The USAAF and the Navy needed to have their tools sharpened and their attitudes revamped. To show just how poorly the United States was equipped, by the end of the war it was relying almost entirely upon the Navy and its long range PBY Catalinas (which were usually used for rescue) to do double duty as aerial reconnaissance "platforms." The Navy Catalina, re-designated PGB-1W, carried the AN/APS-20B search radar in the large radome and had limited fighter capability with a detection range of 65 miles against low flying aircraft, and 200 miles against shipping. This was considered state-of-the-art in aerial reconnaissance by the U.S. It seemed that the military, while worrying about how to do the job, was re-using current aircraft in the inventory for the role of reconnaissance, without devising a program to develop new equipment. However, while this was a critical issue, we need to remember that America was also bearing up under the exhausting pressures of a war that had drained it of men and materials.

To show how anxious the U.S. military was to provide accurate aerial reconnaissance, in the summer of 1942 during the war in Europe, the Army Air Forces loaned the Navy a number of B-24 Liberator bombers. These B-24s used the naval designation of F-7 or F-7A, mainly because they carried cameras. The conversion totaled about 182 aircraft, each of which carried 11 cameras mounted in the bomb bay and rear fuselage. All of this was done with the hope that the Kamikaze attacks that had inflicted so much damage on U.S. Navy ships during the war would be quelled by the promise of "Project Cadillac" and the use of a larger, tighter, radar system. "Cadillac" was successful enough and really became the first of the AEW (airborne early warning system) aircraft for the U.S. Navy. However, the promise of "Cadillac" was not then available, it did not enter service until 1946, months after the war ended.

The F-7As had also been used in the South Pacific for photo-mapping the Japanese held islands before any allied attacks. Infrared and color photography were a rarity, but on occasion the Liberators used such photography to pick out camouflaged targets. On February 4, 1944, two B-24s from the VMD-254, which was the U.S. Marine Corps Photo Reconnaissance Squadron, made a 12-hour night flight from the Solomon Islands to photograph the island of Truk in preparation for a carrier strike later that month.

Later, on April 18, 1944, to be exact, bailed (aircraft loaned from one service to another) Liberators from the VD-3 Naval Reconnaissance Squadron made a 13-hour round trip flight to photograph Saipan, Tinian, and Agrihan Islands, in preparation for invading the Marianas Islands. The VD-3 squadron was accompanied by the USAAF B-24 Liberators, which were bombing the island as a diversionary tactic. B-24Js were also converted to carry six bomb bay cameras, and were used for reconnaissance of Japanese homeland in the closing months of the Pacific war.

Another program to upgrade the aerial reconnaissance capability for the military was sponsored by the U.S. government and undertaken by the Massachusetts Institute of Technology. This program, known as "Cadillac II," used 32 B-17G Flying Fortresses fitted out as airborne combat reconnaissance information centers, to fly as countermeasures against Kamikaze suicide attacks. This system could be considered a precursor of the modern "Joint Stars" concept of forward control from the air.

Putting radar on an aircraft was not as easy as it sounded. The first problem was to guarantee that there would be no bombing runs on friendly targets appearing on the radarscope; processing the incoming information from the radar proved to be a monumental issue. The information needed to be unscrambled and sorted, which took precious time away from planning and implementing the missions. It was obviously a time sensitive procedure. For example, a convoy on its way to a rendezvous, picked up by aerial reconnaissance, would have arrived at its destination before anything could be done about stopping it. The lag in processing photographs taken by a reconnaissance flight was a critical limitation.

More American wartime aircraft were being used for double duty. The Boeing B-29 Superfortress was fitted out for photoreconnaissance and re-designated F-13. The F-13s of the Third Photo Group, under Col. Elliot Roosevelt, arrived at Steeple Mort in Cambridgeshire, England, in September of 1942, and left for North Africa two months later. This group also used B-17s modified as F-9s. Lockheed's P-38s (F-4s) were soon converted to P-38Gs/Hs, also known as F-5As. On and on it went with the aircraft designation changes, so that many U.S. aircraft were sporting two designations along with their two jobs.

By the end of 1944, three reconnaissance groups were operational in the Mediterranean Theater. Meanwhile, the 8th and 9th Air Forces in England had 20 reconnaissance squadrons equipped with F-5s, and F-6s (photo reconnaissance versions of P-51 Mustangs) along with the De Havilland Mosquito MK XVI s which served with the 25th Bombardment Group in Norfolk, England.

A modified B-24D Liberator code named *"Ferret"*, made an electronic intelligence mission over the Aleutian Islands to acquire information on the Japanese radar system at Kiska. The name "Ferret" really referred to *Ferret* flights. *Ferret* flights would go in and the "turn on the lights" of the Japanese radar and electronic communications installations. A *Ferret* flight would over fly the area and cause the enemy radar to paint it. These *Ferret* flights also ran under the *nom de plume* "Weather Gathering" or "Training flights." The name "*Ferret*" stuck and was used on later missions of this type.

The Mediterranean Theater was slow in using the B-24 Liberators for reconnaissance. The 16th Reconnaissance Squadron flew in support of Allied landings on Sicily and in Southern Italy, pinpointing no fewer than 450 enemy radar sites. The 16th Reconnaissance wing also pioneered the use of the RC-156 Jammer system designed at the Harvard Radio Research Laboratories. The project was known as "Carpet" and it was meant to close any gaps that might appear when "Window" (thousands of aluminum strips that were dropped from Allied aircraft to obscure a bomber's radar echoes) was being used.

Toward the end of WWII, there were three types of dedicated photoreconnaissance aircraft under development by the United States. The first was the Northrop F-15A "*Reporter*," developed from the P-61 Black Widow night fighter with a twin engine and twin boom design. The first "*Reporter*" was flown June 1945, but only 36 were built at the War's end. The original contract for 175 aircraft was canceled, and the F-15A *Reporter* never went operational.

The second aircraft developed was the Republic X-12 (XR-12), previously designated the *XF-12 Rainbow*. Designed in 1943 to very precise requirements drawn up by the Army Air Forces' photographic section of the Air Technical Service Command, this very large aircraft was almost 94 feet long and had a wingspan of over 129 feet. It was powered by four 3500 hp Pratt & Whitney R-4360 WASP major radial engines, which gave the *Rainbow* a top speed of over 425 mph and a ceiling of over 40,000 ft. The first of two prototypes flew on February 4, 1946. However, since the war was at an end, the project was no longer considered urgent. The second prototype aircraft did not fly until 1947. The XF-12 *Rainbow* was also being tested as a long range, trans-Atlantic airliner.

A third reconnaissance design was the XR-11 (formerly XF-H) which, like the *F-15A Reporter*, was a twin engine, twin boom monoplane. The XR-11 was a large aircraft with a wingspan of 101 feet and a length of more than

65 feet. The airframe was streamlined, with every joint smoothed and sanded. The airframe was then sprayed with a shiny nylon based clear coat. Dried and polished, the carefully prepared finish did add slightly to the 400+ mph speed of the aircraft.

The first XR-11 prototype flew July 7, 1946, with Howard Hughes at the controls. The aircraft had propeller trouble and crashed into the Beverly Hills area of California. Hughes was severely injured but mended well enough to fly the second prototype on April 5, 1947. A victim of post war economy, altered requirements, and progress into the jet age, the XR-11 even with the 40,000 ft. ceiling and its 400 mph speed was no longer immune to interception in the air, so it—along with the F-15A Reporter and the XF-12 Rainbow, two other propeller-driven designs—was no longer a candidate for the reconnaissance role.

During WWII the United States had thrown everything it could into building a successful aerial reconnaissance fleet. However, times had changed very quickly after the close of the second "war to end all wars." Prototypes and Jerry-rigged aerial reconnaissance systems on existing aircraft were not going to be sufficient for the upcoming Cold War, a war that that would last more than 40 years.

The Cold War

In the early years of the Cold War, there were aircraft capable of reconnaissance roles, albeit, many of the aircraft and systems were left over from WWII. The close of the war brought change. The USSR was no longer an ally. Instead, Soviet Russia had now become the quintessential enemy. To combat this new enemy, the United States needed to rethink its current position for protection of the homeland.

As the Soviet Union and the United States continued to grow further apart in their diplomatic relations, the basic ideologies that had bound them together during WWII became a distant memory. The race for the stronger military and better weapons consumed both the USSR and the U.S. The USSR was trying desperately to keep the quality of its military up to wartime standards, something that was in jeopardy. This was not for lack of talent, but for lack of resources. The U.S., on the other hand, was still on the 'high' of the closing of WWII. While America was secure in its military strength, it was not content unless it knew what the Soviets were up to. There were too many things left unresolved at the close of the war.

While the U.S. was quickly scooping up V-2 Rockets and homeless German rocket scientists, the Russians were gathering up any left over Third Reich scientists that the United States didn't get. The military hardware technology war between the former WWII allies had begun in earnest. The Soviets were not only trying to build a better rocket, they were also looking to upgrade their military aviation and strategic reconnaissance capabilities.

The number of strategic bombers being built for the USSR was of prime interest to the United States for some time, the Soviets had been trying unsuccessfully to build a long range bomber. They wanted to grab any U.S. B-29 that they could get their hands on so that they could measure and examine it. They succeeded in 1944, when a B-29 Superfortress of the USAAF 58th Bomb group had to make an emergency landing in Russian territory after attacking a Japanese target in Manchuria. By the end of 1944, the Russians had gotten three more B-29s much the same way. The Russians quickly learned all they could from those B-29s, copying the aircraft's every detail. The head of the Tupolev Design bureau, Andrei Tupolev, attempted to recreate the fuselage, while engine designer, Arkadiy Shvetsou, tried to copy the Wright R-3350 engines. No matter how they tried, they could not recreate the B-29s rear turret for the gunner. The construction of the Russian TU-4, as it came to be known, started in March of 1945.

The first of three prototypes were readied for flight testing within two years. Reports of the Russian advances reach the United States, but details of the developments were vague. U.S. Intelligence sources knew little more than the fact that work was in progress. The U.S. did not realize what was really happening until 1948 when three Tupolev TU-4 prototypes were brought out at the annual Tushino Air Show in Moscow. This surprised the U.S. If the Russians were developing a long range bomber, then it was possible that they were working at bases in the Soviet Arctic or from the Kamchatka Peninsula in the Far East. In the 1930s the Soviets had made an effort to develop a long range air route to the United States via the Arctic. It was evident that the Soviets knew more about the Arctic than anyone else did at the time. That left open a point of vulnerability for the United States mainland.

The threat of the TU-4 finally hit home for the U.S. To combat the perceived threat, the 46th Reconnaissance Squadron of the USAAF, was sent to Ladd Air Base in Alaska in March of 1946. The squadron was equipped with 120 B-29s including a couple of F-13s (RB-29) fitted for reconnaissance, which would come under the control of the 311th Reconnaissance Wing. These aircrafts were assigned to the USAAF Strategic Command, established in March 1946. The 28th Bomb Group stationed at Grand Island Army Air Field, Nebraska, was sent to Elmendorf Air base in Alaska for a six month training exercise in the Arctic conditions. The detachment of the 311 Reconnaissance Wing was equipped by SAC with B-17s (F-9) photo-mapping aircraft and based at Thule Air Base, Greenland for aerial mapping of Greenland.

The 311 Reconnaissance Wing was involved with "Operation Eardrum". The Reconnaissance Wing received two F-13s (RB29s), which were equipped with photographic and electronic reconnaissance equipment. The first two aircraft #44-651583 and #44-61999 were delivered to the 7th Geodetic Control Squadron at Mac Dill Air Base Florida. A month later, the squadron was transferred to 16th Photo Squadron for intelligence gathering flights. The F-13 officially became the RB-29 in June of 1948.

It is obvious that once the United States got a whiff of what was happening with the Soviets, they looked to tighten the "front gate" in the north. However, they were doing it with aircraft made for dual purposes. Was that really going to be enough to reverse the damage done by the Russians and their attempt to build a long range bomber?

The USAF Created

The United States gained two new services in the shuffle of government after the war. The United States Air Force was created in 1947, after a long hard battle for recognition and autonomy. *The National Security Act of 1947 (Public Law 253)* finally established the USAF on July 26, 1947, after an often brutal political struggle. The USAF became official on September 18, 1947. Along with this new service, the National Security Act also dispensed funding for the Navy, Army, and Air Force, and allowed the newly created Secretary of Defense to coordinate the efforts of all the services. This Act also provided each service with its own Secretary to command each branch. That new secretary was answerable to the Secretary of Defense. The Public Law 253 also created the Central Intelligence Agency.

The Demise of the OSS and the Establishment of the CIA

The CIA actually got its start from the OSS (Office of Strategic Services). The OSS initially started service on June 13, 1942. The Coordinator of Information Office was replaced by the new OSS. At its inception, the OSS was a military office. Its history began with the statement:

> *"The Office of the Coordinator of Information established by Order of July 11, 1941, exclusive of the foreign information*

activities, transferred to the Office of War. Information by Executive Order June 13, 1942 shall hereafter be known as the Office of Strategic Services. In addition, it is hereby transferred to the jurisdiction of the Joint Chiefs of Staff.

The Office of Strategic Services shall perform the following duties:

Collect and analyze such strategic information as may be directed by Joint Chiefs of Staff. Plan and operate such services as may be directed by the Joint Chiefs of Staff. The head of the Strategic Services will be appointed by the President of the United States and shall perform his duties under the direction of the U.S. Joint Chiefs of Staff. William J. Donovan is hereby appointed as Director of Strategic Services."

This officially put the OSS in the espionage business with no civilian government authority to answer to, and only the military to control it. After the defeat of Germany in 1945, with President Roosevelt gone, new president Harry Truman didn't feel it was necessary for the OSS to continue. President Truman had no love for William Donovan, then head of the OSS and the father of the soon to be established CIA. Truman and Congress, were deeply concerned that some day in the future, an organization like the OSS might be used against the United States. Truman also felt that the U.S. wartime intelligence success was built more on the busting of codes, to which the OSS had very little participation. SIGINT (Signals Intelligence), which was the mainstay of the Army and Navy, who were also service rivals, was credited with the success.

Truman could have tried to turn the OSS into the Central Intelligence Service, doing clandestine operations, collection and analysis services overseas. However, many felt that Truman's dissolving of the OSS was done in haste and ignorance. Clark Clifford, Truman's aide, complained that Truman "prematurely, abruptly and unwisely disbanded the OSS." Truman wanted only to think of rebuilding after the war and fervently wished that all *"secret organizations like the OSS would disappear"*. However, Truman acknowledged his mistake when he approved reassembly of many of the OSS services in the new Central Intelligence Agency.

Congress, however, saw Truman's earlier decision to disband the OSS as acceptable to them. Most legislators felt that the OSS was marked for termination and that was fine. Many of the units were not needed during peacetime, and it would be redundant to keep them on. The OSS was regarded as a temporary war agency to be used only for national emergencies such as a war. Congress was more than ready to disband and forget it. When Truman got the report from Congress on the OSS, he was shocked. The document said that the OSS was "bumbling, had lax security "and complained that (William Donovan, OSS head) had proposed intelligence systems reforms that had *"all the earmarks of a Gestapo system."* The report recommended abolishing the OSS. The Research and Analysis branch, would then be salvaged and turned over to the State department.

Early in 1945, Congress passed legislation requiring the White House to seek specific Congressional funding for any new agency operation longer than twelve months. This kept any presidential wish to preserve the OSS or create a permanent intelligence agency just that, a wish. That legislation, when signed into law, would not allow Donovan to create an "American Gestapo". Donovan insisted that the intelligence branch should report directly to the President and not to his advisors. The White House concluded that the solution was to create a new peacetime intelligence office without Donovan. Many White House advisors also believed the nation needed some sort of intelligence office, but not the type that Donovan had formulated, agreed with this.

By August 1945, the Bureau of Budget (BoB) started planning the liquidation of the OSS, along with other non-essential war agencies. The BoB assumed that it could stretch the procedure out over a long period of time to preserve the OSS assets, while releasing those not needed in peacetime. However, by August 27th or 28th of 1945, Truman and principal advisors, Harold

Smith, S. Roseman, and the Director of War Mobilization and Reconversion, John Synder, suddenly recommended the dissolution of the OSS immediately. Within a week, the BoB had readied the paper for presidential signature. Executive Order 9621, which was signed on September 20, 1945, officially dissolved the OSS, effective October 1, 1945. This gave the Research and Analysis offices to the State Department, and everything else to the War Department.

Orders also directed the Secretary of War to liquidate all OSS assets, whenever he deemed it compatible with national interest. In one fell swoop of a pen, William Donovan was disenfranchised from all that he had done to create the first intelligence organization in the United States. The OSS now belonged to history and the War Department. Donovan later found out that the October 1st date was no longer valid and this gave Donovan less than two weeks to dismantle everything he had worked for.

As the changes progressed, the OSS transformed into the CIG (Central Intelligence Group). The newly appointed CIG had two missions in life: strategic warning and covert action. The CIG did not exist for very long.

Twenty months into its reign, it was disbanded in favor of the new "Central Intelligence Agency" (CIA). In 1949, the Central Intelligence Agency Act was passed. This completed the 1947 National Security Act that instituted the concept of the CIA, and put it firmly in place. With both new services, the USAF and the CIA, now engaged the outlook for the United States and its intelligence capability began to look much stronger.

Meanwhile, now under the aegis of the new U.S. Air Force, the 72nd Reconnaissance Squadron also carried out photo reconnaissance missions and ELINT missions over the Soviet Arctic and the Far east. Their RB-29s were equipped with oblique cameras that enabled them to photograph Russian territory while remaining in international air space. The long range photography, however, revealed little of use. By the end of 1948, some of the RB-29s were stripped of weapons and other unnecessary equipment, so they could climb to higher altitudes and make penetration flights over the Soviet Union on behalf of the CIA. President Truman authorized those flights.

The first over flight was made on August 5,1948. The 72nd Reconnaissance Squadron RB-29s took off from Ladd Air Force Base and made surveillance flights over Siberia and landed at Yokota Air Base in Japan. The total time in the air was 19 hours and 40 minutes. There were some longer flights, some up to 30 hours, which soon became routine with aircraft operations at 35,000 feet or more, on missions covering 5000 miles. The RB-29s were seriously challenged when the Soviet MiG 15 fighter entered into Soviet Air Force in 1948, The USAEC (United States Atomic Energy Commission) was worried that the United States had little or no intelligence on the USSR's nuclear program. The USSR had done research on atomic weapons as early as the 1930s. In February of 1939, the Russian scientists learned about the magic of nuclear fission from reading the scientific journals of foreign countries. By the 1940s, the Soviets had created their first chain reaction, using U235 or natural uranium, with a moderator of heavy water (deuterium oxide). Russia was in the race for atomic energy. In June of 1940, a Uranium Commission was established by the Soviet Academy of Science. The premise was to research the "Uranium problem". Soviet dictator Josef Stalin, started a small scale project to sturdy uranium under the scientist Igor Kurchatov. In 1943, Kurchatov drew up a research plan with three objectives:

a. Achieve a chain reaction using natural uranium
b. Develop isotope separation
c. Study design of U-235 and plutonium bomb.

The United States performed its first nuclear test on July 16, 1945. President Truman then told Stalin the U.S. had a new weapon of unusual destructive power. Stalin's cold reply was to try it out on the Japanese, and then proceeded to push Kurchatov harder in the research. That is just what Truman did: he "tried out" the first atomic bomb to be used as a weapon, on August 6, 1945 over Hiroshima, Japan. After receiving no response to a surrender request, Truman authorized the AAF to carry out its second atomic mission on August 9, and struck the Japanese city of Nagasaki. The Emperor of Japan agreed to his nation's surrender on August 14, 1945. The formal surrender took place on September 2, 1945.

Nuclear Jitters

The United States developed a long range nuclear detection program in 1947. The newly created USAF used an airborne monitoring system that was capable of detecting and pinpointing a nuclear detonation on the Soviet mainland or in the Arctic. The USAF employed the WB-29 weather reconnaissance aircraft, which flew at 18,000 ft. between Japan and Alaska, to detect any unusual amount of radioactive debris. The aircraft was fitted with a collection filter, which picked up radioactive particles that had been carried eastward from the Central Asia area. Analysis of the debris by United States atomic physicists, which included Robert J. Oppenheimer of the "Manhattan Project", confirmed the detection of atomic particles.

The cat was out of the bag. Russia, indeed, had a nuclear device. The Russian test, named JOE I, was announced to the U.S. by President Truman on September 23, 1949. The U.S. had missed the date of the USSR's big test. It wasn't until the middle of 1953, that the United States found out that the test actually took place on August 29, 1949, with the test site being somewhere in the Ural Sea area. It was becoming obvious that American intelligence procedures were not quite adequate.

News of the nuclear test was compounded by the fact that the Russians had blockaded Berlin from June 23, 1948, until May 29, 1949. That put real weight to the need to "see" just what was going on in the USSR. The American commitment to the security of Europe increased with nothing else to fly except aircraft left over from WWII inventory, the U.S. none the less, attempted to extract the secrets of the USSR using the aerial reconnaissance tools at hand.

The United States entered the 1950s and the Cold War with the realization that the world, and the USSR especially, had changed drastically. Aerial reconnaissance became a major issue. U.S. over flights of other nations were no longer considered "tame" measures. It had become "hostile" reconnaissance flights over denied territory. Territory to which the USSR had denied access to its former U.S. and European allies.

Deadly Reconnaissance

In April 1950, a PB4Y-2, from the Naval Patrol Squadron, took off from Wiesbaden, Germany, and headed out over the Baltic sea on a reconnaissance mission. The plan was to gather intelligence on Soviet Naval installations. Somewhere off the port of Libou, Russian Lavochkin LA-9, LA-11 and MiG 15 fighters intercepted the flight. The Russians shot the PB4Y-2 out of the sky, claiming that it was an RB-29 penetrating Soviet air space. The soviets also claimed that the fight had ignored instructions to land. This was not the first time something like this had happened. On October 22, 1949, an LA-9 intercepted an RB-29 over the Sea of Japan, fired a warning shot over the RB-29, and chased it out of the area. However, the PB4Y-2 incident was viciously different. It was clear that the Russians would not tolerate any intrusion and any intelligence gathering by aircraft of non-Soviet denomination. All comers would be shown no mercy.

The Korean War

The 1950s not only brought the issue of U.S./Soviet intelligence issues to the forefront, it also brought the Korean War. North Korea crossed the 38th Parallel and invaded South Korea on June 25, 1950. It was at this point that the serious deficiencies in the U.S. reconnaissance system, both strategic and tactical became clearly apparent. With 180,000 Chinese troops already in North Korea having come from Manchuria, U.S. intelligence claims of only 60,000 Chinese troops became a myth. That error in intelligence became apparent when the Chinese started beating back the U.S. and Allied UN forces. However, by then, it was too late. There were two reasons for the failure in intelligence in North Korea:

a. The Chinese Communist forces could move across the country in small groups at night, to reach areas of assembly. There were no Allied spies on the ground in North Korea; hence the movement went undetected.
b. The shortage of aerial reconnaissance assets, and the fact that there were no detailed maps of the North, became a problem when it came to interpreting what aerial photos there were.

Even the USAF's headquarters in the Philippines could not deploy effective reconnaissance. The USAF relied on the RB-17s of the 204th Photo Mapping Flight, at Clark Air Base, Philippines, for gathering information to carry the load.

The U. S. Strategic Command unit at Kadena Air Base, Okinawa, brought some help on board. The Lockheed RF-80 Shooting star of the 8th Tactical Reconnaissance Squadron was sent in. In August 1950, the Douglas RB-57s, based at Yokota, Japan brought a night reconnaissance capability. Next to arrive was the 45th Tactical Reconnaissance Squadron with P-51 Mustangs. The P-51s were not utilized, however, due to operational shortages. The role for the 45th Tactical Reconnaissance Squadron was designed as a visual battlefield reconnaissance group. Thus, the nightmare of aerial reconnaissance grew for the U.S. in Korea.

On the other side of the U. S. Military, the Army and the North American T-6 carried out reconnaissance on behalf of the 8th Army at a great risk to both men and machine. At one point, an RB-29 crew, out on a "recce" run, said that there were seventy-five Chinese aircraft parked on North Korea's Antung airfield. He flew on what was known as a "2000 Overflight Mission." By the next morning, on the return flight, all were gone. It was an indication that the Chinese were getting involved in the Korean air war. In November 1950, six Russian MiGs crossed the Yalu River and ran straight into a P-51 flight. The next incursion occurred on November 9th, 1950 when MiGs attacked and damaged RB-29. From that point on, the RB-29s were forbidden to fly into the territory, alone or otherwise. The job was passed on to the Lockheed RF-

80A Shooting Stars. On and on it went, as the Korean "Police Action" raged in the skies over Korean. Another reconnaissance disaster occurred on November 9, 1951. An unescorted RB-45C Tornado was attacked by nine MiG-15s near Haja, North Korea and barely escaped due to the poor gunnery skills of the enemy. The RB-45C Tornados were no longer permitted to make penetration flights into Northwestern Korea, then known as "MiG Alley". One by one, aircraft were being pulled from reconnaissance duty because they were too slow, did not fly high enough or couldn't outrun a MiG.

A Cold War Story

Mele Vojvodich, who was soon to become an OXCART pilot, could attest to the fact that he was a frustrated fighter pilot. In 1950-51, Vojvodich was assigned to SAC, flying the F-84, while trying to get in to the fight in Korea. He kept volunteering but the cards were never in his hand. Not until he finally volunteered for reconnaissance duty. Vojvodich didn't know anything about reconnaissance duty, but he figured it was the only way to go, he'd learn. It was a chance to get into the fight and that was what he really wanted. Vojvodich finally reached Korea in 1952, after a short course in picture taking at Shaw Air Base in South Carolina. He arrived at Kimpo Air Base in Seoul, Korea and was assigned to the 67th tactical Reconnaissance Wing. Thinking he could hedge his bet, Vojvodich immediately went to the 4th Fighter Wing commander and told the commander, "I want to shoot down MiGs". His request was met with," You're the guy we're looking for! We'll work it!" Well, it didn't work because Vojvodich's commander at the 67th Reconnaissance Wing, Colonel Russell Berg, (who would later be Brig. Gen. Berg and served as Staff Director for HQ for the National Reconnaissance Office 1967-69), put the kibosh on it. It seemed that there was someone prior to Vojvodich who had just pulled the same stunt. Like it or not, Vojvodich was not going to shoot anything except photos, at least for now.

Between 1952 and 1953, Vojvodich flew the RF-86, a reconnaissance version of the F-86 Sabre jet. During the time Vojvodich flew with the 67th RW, there were some 50 to 60 missions, many of them across the Yalu River, a hot bed of Korean Army activity. Vojvodich had the chance to fly what was known as the "Classic Mission". This meant Vojvodich over flew and photographed MiG airfields at Fen Cheng, Tatum Kao, and Antung among other places in the People's Republic of China, just about every week. As a reconnaissance pilot, he flew on what was known as a "2000 Overflight Mission". That meant that Vojvodich flew with no less than 24 to 48 F-86 Sabre jets from the 4th Fighter Wing, who acted as his escort. At least that was what the escort pilots were supposed to be doing. The escort pilots used the reconnaissance pilot as "fish bait" because they knew every time they went up the reconnaissance guy would draw fire from the enemy fighters. This set up the escort party for a chance at a MiG kill. Everyone in the 4th fighter wing was ready to go for escort service since it was their chance at a MiG kill.

As missions were planned, a reconnaissance briefing was given for approximately 100 pilots who were itching for a chance to shoot down enemy planes. The 2000 Mission flights were made up from three fighter pilots flying on Vojvodich's wing, and the rest would be looking for MiGs to chew on further up on the Yalu River. The early 1953 mission would find the entire 2000 Flight crossing the river at Mukden, which was way up north. Without fail, 24 to 48 MiGs would jump the flight and the stinker of all dog fights would begin.

Vojvodich told his commander that he wasn't getting any photos because of all the action the escorts were mixing up. His commander asked for his suggestion. Vojvodich's answered "I think we ought to let the F-86s go up there and patrol up and down the river, get involved with a dogfight with the MiGs and then two of us, one wingman and myself, will penetrate and head up north." Vojvodich's idea worked like magic. He remembered one flight as actually funny in hindsight anyway.

In March of 1952, Vojvodich took possibly the longest flight he ever had taken, three hours and fifteen minutes. His F-86 escort was low on fuel and had returned to Kimpo Air Base, in Seoul, Korea. Vojvodich was up there all alone. However, he still thought that there were at least some escort planes still hanging around the Yalu River, maybe as far as Harbin, Manchuria.

Vojvodich was reaching Mukden at 50,000ft., in his RF-86F-30. This aircraft had four additional wing tanks for extra fuel, and was moving along at Mach 0.9, when Mele looked to his left wing and HELLO! there were 4 MiG-15s just waiting for him. Vojvodich recalled "Here I am at 250 miles from home base at Kimpo, low on fuel and I'm surrounded by the enemy!" The MiGs did not fire and suddenly the MiGs threw open their air brakes and descended under Vojvodich's wing. The MiGs just flew along and looked at Vojvodich for a little while. The enemy flight then headed down to Mukden and Vojvodich really suspected something was not right. Ten minutes late, Vojvodich turned to overfly Mukden and he saw 24 friendly aircraft on his tail. It was possible that the first four MiGs were low on fuel and decided to let Vojvodich off. Mele said that his escort pilots must have called into the Air Defense Center, prior to sighting him and reported an F-86 was missing. They all thought that Vojvodich was nuts when he made a turn to Mukden to head back to Antung. In his rear view mirror, he saw 24 MiGs closing on him at 55,000 ft., just 4,000 to 5,000 ft. above and behind him. Vojvodich made his turn and the MiGs ceased their chase. Mele thought, "Boy! This is going to be a desperation act. You better do something quick." Mele rolled over in a Split S with the RF-86 and while in the dive, he got to Mach 1.05. Looking in his rear view mirror, he saw the MiGs were out of control trying to catch him. All of them, were trying to hit Mach.95, and ended up fishtailing and firing cannons like mad. As Mele recalled," The good thing about being in a dogfight with 24 airplanes is that only one of them can get on your tail at a time and all of them were behind me."

Vojvodich broke radio silence and yelled like a madman, thinking the leader of the 2000 Flight would show up from the Yalu river and save him. Mele flew to the deck and right over the Antung airfield at 100 feet! He gave the Chinese pilots something to wonder about! Mele then headed out to the Yellow Sea, which was pretty close, knowing it was his only chance to stay alive.

He figured that if he had to eject, the Navy would be close by to pick him up. The MiGs faded out once he passed the coast of the Yellow Sea. On vapor, Vojvodich flew back to altitude and called his Kimpo air field base, telling them he was flaming out. True to tower form, the answer was; "You're number six on the flameout pattern." In essence the tower couldn't care less what his problem was they had aircraft with the same problem right ahead of him. Think of LaGuardia airport when you are trying to land at rush hour. He figured they were kidding. Kimpo had a 6000 foot runway, which was 100 feet wide. All the F-86s were coming back at once from their missions. They were all on "flameout". Vojvodich finally got a slot and made it safely to the hangar.

That wasn't the end of the story. Vojvodich's commander, Colonel Russ Berg, met him when he landed. Berg asked him "where the heck were you?" Mele was 45 minutes late and it had been reported that he was shot down over the Yellow Sea. Mele replied to Berg, "Colonel Berg, you won't believe it. Let me show you." He grabbed his map and laid it out on the wing of his aircraft and showed his boss his flight path, which covered Harbin, Manchuria and the surrounding areas including the airfields. Berg was shocked. He told Mele that both of them were due to be court marshaled. Berg quickly told him to "grab that film". Vojvodich never reported his mission. He remembered that he never got the chance to fill out a Form 5. The raw film was retrieved from the camera of the RF-86, put into a staff car, along with Berg and himself sitting in the back, and headed for downtown Seoul.

Colonel Berg was at the wheel of the staff car, driving Mele and himself to downtown Seoul to see their boss, General Glenn O. Bocus, Commander of the 5th Air Force. Mele, who was feeling pretty good right about now, decided that he deserved a well earned smoke. He lit up his pipe, while sitting in the back seat of that staff car. Smoking happily way, he dropped the ashes in to what seemed to be the ashtray on the door handle. Unbeknownst to Mele, there was no ashtray in that door compartment. He was actually dumping ashes into the back seat of the car! Somewhere about halfway to downtown Seoul, the back seat started to get hot. Mele finally asked Berg to pull over. Berg asked him why and Mele broke the news that the back seat was on fire. To add to this confusion, when they did pull over a Korean woman, who was working the rice paddies nearby was carrying two buckets of water on her shoulders. As soon as Mele opened the back seat door, he flew out of the car. The poor Korean lady seeing Mele's service revolver was totally rattled. Mele grabbed the two buckets from the poor woman and doused the back seat.

Getting back into the staff car and Mele, climbing back into the soggy back seat, they proceeded to General Bocus's office. However, the fire had not been completely put out and this time restarted with flames. It seemed to Mele and the good Colonel, who had just about enough of him, that they pull into a Korean fire station with smoke pouring out of the back of the car! The Korean firemen pulled out their machine guns as if they would shoot the fire out. It took a bit of time, but finally the message got through and they soon put the fire in the back seat out.

After all the hysteria of the burning car, Vojvodich and Berg arrived at General Bocus's office with the film intact. When Lt. General Bocus finally got to see the film that Mele had taken on his flight, it was truly awesome. Colonel Berg was doing his best to brief the General, but was really flustered. Mele jumped in and took over the briefing explaining what he had found. The main concern was the fact that Russia had planted Ilyushin–28 Beagle aircraft in Manchuria, so that they could possibly strike as far inland as Japan. The film had confirmed that they were there in Harbin, Manchuria. Bocus looked at the wet film processor, where the film was rolling off, showing the Beagles and the MiGs as plain as day. The General congratulated Vojvodich, as a result of this flight, Berg was made a General and Vojvodich got the medal. This was all in the day's work of a reconnaissance pilot. Vojvodich later found out that most of the pilots that had flown the 2000 Mission were up for the USAF Silver Star. Mele Vojvodich was up for five Silver Stars. However, Lt. General Bocus said to pick the nastiest of the missions and upgrade all of that to the Distinguished Service Cross (DSC). While Mele went back to the states, he never left reconnaissance far behind. He went on to become a pilot for the OXCART program.

Heavy losses and more configurations

From 1951 through 1952, the RB-29 Reconnaissance forces suffered heavy losses due to the MiG 15s chasing them. The flak shot at the RB-29s wasn't helping the matter either. This made daylight operations treacherous. Emphasis was switched to night bombings, which brought out more problems in U.S. bombing techniques and equipment. As the Korean War raged on, the U. S. aerial reconnaissance effort continued to falter.

Between 1950 and 1954, the USAF ELINT (electronic intelligence) Operations began to use the Convair RB-36D Peacemaker for reconnaissance duty. The aircraft, which had a wingspan of 230 feet, was one of the largest aircraft ever built. It had many variations, but the RB-36D carried 14 cameras, which weighed about 3390 lbs., in the forward bomb bay. The second bay contained 80 T-86 flashbulbs. An extra 3000 gallon fuel tank was installed in the third bay. Electronic Counter Measures(ECM) were installed in the fourth bay. The RB-36D carried standard gun armament with an AN/APQ24 radio navigation unit for target locating. It had a crew of 18, that later increased to a total of 22 crewmen. The RB-36D Peacemaker was loaded for plenty of photo-taking.

Later on, in July of 1950, the Boeing RB-50 appeared on the flight line. It was delivered to the 91st Strategic Reconnaissance Wing, at Barksdale Air Force Base in California. On August 20, 1950, the 91st SRW also took delivery of the RB-45C Tornado. The RB-36D, flying out of the British base at Sculthorpe, was making over flights of the Soviet Arctic bases. The island of Novaya Zemlya was a reconnaissance target because of the news that the Russians were building what looked like a large nuclear weapon test complex there. The USSR nuclear weapons testing went on from 1958 to 1964.

Russia was also on the trail of finding a fighter able to do the work needed to protect their bases. The Russian Air Ministry sent out an urgent specification for an "all weather fighter" to be fitted with long range radar for search missions.

The "Isumro Emerald" Air radar, already in use, was proving not to be enough. By 1956, the Yakovlev YAK-25 Flashlight (NATO Code Name), was a fighter with improved radar and came into service adding to the Soviet fighter squadrons.

The RB-50s and the RB-45s were flying "FERRET" missions over the Soviet Union. The JOE II atomic bomb was being tested at a Russian Central

Asian site, during September of 1951. The only way the United States was gaining any success in picking up information on what the Russians were doing was finding gaps or holes in the Soviet research radar. Listening in on the Soviet stations from covert stations in Europe, the Middle East and the Far East accomplished this.

The United States continued to fly "Ferret" missions out of Rhein-Main Air Base in Germany, Mildenhall along with Lakenheath in England. In the Far East, it was Misawa and Iwakuni in Japan, Kadena in Okinawa and Sangley Point in the Philippines. Other bases were included in both Norway and Libya. "Ferreting" was a nasty business and the Ferret crews were very much aware that should they go down during a mission, there was no hope of a rescue. The only real survival chance for a Ferret crewmember was cloud cover. A "severe clear" sky could mean death because it made the Ferret flight easy to see.

The aircraft used the American reconnaissance were building up quickly. By 1953, there were four heavy strategic reconnaissance wings built up by the USAF, the 5th, 28th, 72nd and 99th and they were all packing B-36s. The earlier B-36 now had developed into the RB-36F and the RB-36H of which there were 24, RB-36Fs and 73 RB-36Hs.

By May of 1953, a contract was awarded to both Convair and Republic Aircraft for modifications to 10 B-36Ds that would be turned into the mother/carrier aircraft and 25 RF-84s to be turned into parasite aircraft. The designations were changed to RB-36Ds and RF-84Ks. December 1954, brought the 91st Strategic Reconnaissance Squadron and the 407th Strategic Wing together at Grand Falls, Air Force Base. More squadrons were being activated in January of 1955. The 71st Strategic Reconnaissance Wing began operations at Larson Air Force Base, Washington. Two squadrons, 25th and the 82nd Strategic Reconnaissance Squadrons and their F-84s were combined with the RF-84s of the 91st Strategic Reconnaissance Wing.

More B-36Ds were delivered to the 99th Strategic Reconnaissance Wing at Fairchild Air Force Base. Even with all this moving around and influx of additional aircraft, the reorganization only lasted one year. The 91st Strategic

Reconnaissance Wing changed out its aircraft and got a new designation in 1956, remaining a part of the 71st until July 1957.

The USAF added another reconnaissance unit to the list. The 55th Strategic Reconnaissance Wing was actually a SAC unit primed for ELINT (electronic intelligence) missions using the RB-50. The 55th SRW was sent to Yokota, Japan and there became Detachment 2. They used the RB-50G, which was especially configured for the ELINT role, while other RB-50B and D versions were used for photo mapping and photo reconnaissance. The RB-50Gs from the 343rd SRW out of Japan, took off for a mission to Vladivostok, USSR on a ELINT mission. This aircraft carried a total crew of eleven. Six crewmembers, called RAVENS, were dedicated to listening to Russian intelligence. The date was July 29, 1953, and it turned out to be one of the most gruesome reconnaissance missions of the Cold War.

At approximately 6:15 A.M. on June 29, 1953, an RB-50G from the 55th Reconnaissance Wing, tail number #15829 by the name of "Little Red Ass" was at 20,000 feet, just southeast of Vladivostok, when the aircraft was attacked by Russian F-15 MiGs. The MiGs shot out two engines on the RB-50 which drove her into a death dive into the Sea of Japan below. Captain John Roche called for the crew to bail out. Some 20 hours later, a US. Navy Destroyer, the USS Picking (DD605) picked up Captain Roche and pilot Captain O'Malley who died awaiting rescue. The other 13 crew members were MIA, picked up by the Soviets, while 7 crew died with the aircraft. Only Captain Roche survived.

The USAF claimed that their RB-50 flight was a routine navigation-training mission and insisted it was shot down over international waters. The Soviets refused to bat an eye at the protest. When the USAF gave the Russians a bill for $2.7 million for replacement of the RB-50, the Russians then countered with their bill for $1.8 million for an Ilyushin IL-12 that had been shot down by an F-86 Sabre on the last day of the Korean War. All 21 crewmembers of that Ilyushin had been killed.

As noted, the Russians were tolerating no one in their airspace and were always waiting around for something to shoot down. If it "smelled" like an American plane, all the better for the Russians, to them it was meat on the plate to take home. The fact that the Soviets always had ships in the area of a shoot down site, attests to the fact that they wanted to make sure they could pick up any American survivors.

After the shoot down on June 29, 1953, fighters now escorted the RB-50s. This procedure saved an RB-50 in 1954, when MiGs flying over the Yellow Sea attacked the aircraft. The F-86s chased the MiGs off, actually shooting down one of them. Not all reconnaissance flights were successful, however. On July 23, 1954, a Cathay Pacific DC-4 commercial airliner was shot down by Communist Chinese fighters off Hainan Island, China as just another casualty of the hot reconnaissance "war". Three days later, two U.S. Navy AD Sky Raiders of Air Group 5, from the carrier Philippine Sea, was attacked by a pair of Russian Lavochkin LA-7s or LA-9s, capable of 413 mph and 35,343 feet. The Navy destroyed both. The shooting never stopped. By April 1955, Russian fighters got the first victory against an RB-47E Stratojet, from the 55th Strategic Reconnaissance Wing Detachment 2, out of Japan. An RB-47E was shot down over Kamchatka by Soviet MiG17s. Something new had been added by the Soviets; they were now flying the MiG 17 Fresco, which was replacing the MiG 15 Fishbed since early 1954.

National Security was the name of the game in early 1954. Anyone in Washington D.C., who was anyone, was on constant alert against the harbinger of evil known as the Soviet Union. Defense against an unprovoked attack by the Russian Bear was on the minds of the Department of Defense, Congress, the President and the unnerved American public. The threat of a surprise attack by the USSR provoked the need for a committee to oversee the issue. The membership of this committee was the best of the best and the brightest that the U.S. had to offer. No brainpower was spared when it came to studying the problem of defending the U.S. from an attack by the USSR. However, there was something missing and that something was critical intelligence about the USSR. There were two other famous "gaps" in the 1950s, the missile gap and the bomber gap. Both of those gaps fed into the most urgent of gaps, that being good, solid real time intelligence. That was the one thing that the U.S. did not have enough of and sorely needed to find a way to close that yawing fissure, lack of real time reconnaissance.

By November 5, 1954, Edwin Land, (father of the Polaroid Camera), chairman of the "Project 3 Technical Capabilities Panel, (a subgroup under the office of Defense Mobilization Surprise Attack Committee), wrote to Allan Dulles, the director of Central Intelligence Agency, to ask for photo over flights of the USSR and recommend that the CIA, with USAF assistance, should evolve a program for high altitude reconnaissance. The Land Panel proposal, which was titled, "A Unique Opportunity for Comprehensive Intelligence", outlined the risks of a provocation to war that such an intensive program of over flights might bring. Along with the danger involved, should the military engage in this activity, especially in light of the very tense political situation with the USSR?

The paper went on to say that "because it is vital that certain knowledge about industry growth, strategic targets and guided missiles sites be obtained at once, we recommend that the CIA as a civilian organization undertake (with the help of the USAF) a cover program of selected flights."

The war for control of air space raged on throughout the 1950s. the USAF and the Navy were constantly taking the lead for missions over Russia, or China or wherever the call went out that information was needed. The crews were called "Silent Warriors", often not being able to discuss their missions with anyone, including wives and families. The people back home never knew what the missions were about, even when some brave soul lost his life and his family became the recipient of the dreaded notification telegram. It usually wasn't until many years later, and through much research or declassified documents, that the loved one's family even got an inkling of what he had been doing out there. The scorecards of shoot-downs were adding up rapidly in the mid to late 1950s. In July of 1955, a Navy P2V-5 Neptune of the VP-9 Squadron, on a mission off the Aleutian Islands, was viciously attacked by two MiGs and shot down.

In August of 1956, a P4M Mercator, from Navy Squadron VQ-1, was on a night patrol 32 miles of the Chinese mainland. The crew was attacked by enemy fighters over international waters, shot down, and never heard from again. In September 1956, the Russians shot down an RB-50 on a photo-mapping job over the Sea of Japan. In June of 1959, another P4M Mercator from Squadron VQ-1, flying near the western edge of the Korean Peninsula, was attacked and shot down by two MiGs. The list went on, silently, as the crews of the aircraft died, silently. By the middle of 1959, the aircraft and the equipment being used by the U.S. was changing. Modifications were being made to better the systems and make it safer for the reconnaissance crews. The RB-57 Canberras and the RF-101 Voodoos were now taking over the main ELINT task and photo surveillance over China. As the year arrived, no new attacks on U.S. aircraft were carried out and the reconnaissance crews were getting better at their jobs. For example, no Neptunes from the Navy VP-22 units were attacked, however they were intercepted.

The RB-57 CANBERRA

The USAF had also upgraded to the B-57 Canberra workhorse, but that happened almost by accident. The Canberra was selected to equip squadrons of the USAF Tactical Air Command. While design changes were made, production continued. After the first Canberra rolled out in July of 1953, the aircraft manufacturer, Glenn L. Martin Company, received instructions to proceed with production of the revised design, under the designation B-57B. Only eight of them were built to bomber configuration, while the next 67 were produced for a reconnaissance role as the RB-57A. By 1954, the RB-57 was sent to the 363rd Tactical Reconnaissance Wing at Shaw Air Force Base, South Carolina. They were actually used by the 10th and 66th TRW of the USAFE (United States Air Force in Europe) based in Germany and France. Most of the aircraft were left in natural metal, but some were covered with anti-searchlight black matte paint formerly used on the P-61 Black Widow, which rendered them nearly invisible to searchlight beams.

The 10th and 66th Tactical Reconnaissance Wing were also using the RB-57 to replace the RB-26Cs they had been flying. The 10th and 66th Reconnaissance wings were attached to the 4th Allied Tactical Air Force in NATOs central front. Their main job was night photographic reconnaissance, along with target markings. However, a high accident rate caused the Canberra to be grounded in March of 1955. By April of 1957, the 10th RW was trading out its RB-57s for the Douglas RB-66D, the last aircraft was delivered in December. The closing out of the RB-57 was completed by November of 1958. The 66th TRW had changed over to the McDonald RF-101A Voodoo. Many of the remaining RB-57s were sent to Air National Guard units and kept flying until the early 1980s.

The Department of Defense was consistently refining the requirements for the consummate reconnaissance aircraft. A GOR (General Operation Requirement), #53-WC-16507, was posted by the Defense Department. This program, known as *"Black Knight"* asked for a single seat, subsonic, high altitude reconnaissance aircraft capable of carrying a 700 lb payload over 3000 miles at 70,000 ft. Three companies answered the request for designs.

The Martin company proposed a stepped up version of the RB-57 Canberra. Bell Aircraft and Fairchild Aircraft Companies submitted new designs for consideration. While what Martin proposed to the DoD was accepted, it was considered a stopgap measure and not so much advancement, until work on a new design could be started. Martin's design was the Model 294, which actually translated to an RB-57D designation. This aircraft carried the standard B-57B fuselage melded into a new wing with a span that increased from 64 to 108 feet.

The J-57P turbo jet engine, built by Pratt & Whitney, powered the Model 294 design. It was a single seat version equipped with K-38 and two KC-1 split vertical cameras. Six Model 294s were ordered, and seven Model 744 RB 57-Ds that were almost the same as the earlier models except that they had better flight characteristics followed them. The next RB-57D had a flight crew of two, ability for inflight refueling and carried a specialist in the SIGINT/ELINT role. The last design for the RB-57D was a single seater aircraft, used for day and night radar mapping. It was equipped with an AN/APQ56SCR side looking radar. Only one aircraft of this type was delivered. Even with the initial wing problems, the first RB-57D was accepted by the USAF, and delivered to the 4080th Squadron Reconnaissance Wing.

By March 19, 1956, detachments of this unit were sent to Yokota, Japan and Eielson Air Force Base, Alaska. The Alaska detachment handled ELINT operations around the Kamchatka Peninsula for a short time before returning to Ramey Air Force Base in Puerto Rico. The Japan detachment remained at Yokota from October 1956 through September 1957 and was involved in "Operation Sea Lion". This program monitored radiation samples from the Soviet Union nuclear tests and pulled whatever ELINT it could record. The 4025th sent more RB-57Ds in a detachment of four aircraft, to Rhein-Main Air Base in Germany.

Operation Bordertown was set up for ELINT and SIGINT missions along the German border over the Baltic Sea. These flights were usually intercepted by the British Hawker Hunter Aircraft Squadron, which was scrambled to make identifications of inbound aircraft, since the missions of the RB-57Ds were flown in secrecy.

By 1959, progress moved the R-57Ds out of the 4025th SRS as they were deactivated. Many of these aircraft were later purchased by NASA, which would use them in high altitude test flights and terrain mapping tests. They were assigned to the 7677th Radar Calibration Squadron for NASA. Six more of the leftover birds were then assigned to monitor the last of the American atmospheric nuclear tests in 1962.

Three more RB-57Ds were assigned to the 1211th Test Squadron of the U.S. Weather Service at Kirtland Air Force Base, New Mexico and re-designated WB-57s. Finally, the RB-57 wing structural problems put it into retirement. Martin Company had gotten a new USAF contract to rebuild the wings of eight stored RB-57 aircraft with 3000 airframe hours on them. These aircraft were then refitted with a series of ECM equipment and were used in the U.S. Defense role until the 1970s, then placed in storage. The final designation for this aircraft was the EB-57D.

Project Diamond Lil

Project *Diamond Lil* began in 1958, which allowed the U.S. to overfly the Chinese mainland with the RB-57s. These aircraft crews were attached to the "friendly" Chinese Nationalist Air Force. Six Chinese "Nationalist" pilots were trained on the RB-57Ds, by U.S. pilots and sent to Taoyan Air Base in Taiepei. By 1962, the main spar fatigue problems really started to crop up, grounding a sizable portion of the RB-57D fleet. The USAF asked the General Dynamics Corporation, who serviced the RB-57D, if it would be feasible to revamp the existing RB-57 design and produce a new reconnaissance aircraft with the performance payload capacity and extended fatigue life.

A contract was signed to redesign two of the aircraft. The RB-57F, made its first flight after reconstruction in June 23, 1953. The RB-57F was a completely different version of the aircraft, with many components taken from the technology of the B-58 Hustler. The F- Wing was new. It encompassed 3 spar structure and an enormous wing span of 122 feet 5 inches. The wing carried a marked anhedral (wing with a downward bend). The ailerons were set at mid-spar and the wing carried supplemental spoilers. The control surfaces were sealed to reduce drag, and there were no flaps. The larger vertical tail was twice the area of the standard RB-57. Engines were replaced with two 18,000 lb thrust Pratt & Whitney TF33-P-11A turbofan that gave the RB-57F double the power of earlier models. J60-P-9 engines, in detachable pods could be added to hard points under the wings.

When the turbojets were not mounted, the RB-57F could carry external stores on the under wing hard points. Fuselage tanks were taken out to make room for special equipment. All fuel was now carried in the wings. The RB-57F also carried a two ton HTAC camera of high altitude resolution, capable of taking photos of targets at oblique range of up to 60 miles. Special ELINT/SIGINT equipment was carried in the redesigned nose and plastic wing tip.

The times were changing

The time had come for the U.S. reconnaissance world to reformulate its objective, along with its hardware. It was obvious to Eisenhower's Administration and the Allan Dulles run CIA, that the current methods of gaining intelligence via aerial resources had become an extremely dangerous game. No longer could the "Band Aid fixes" be used to shore up aircraft that had been taken from their original duties to serve as reconnaissance platforms over denied territories.

Eisenhower, having lived through the horror of Pearl Harbor, always had a "Surprise Attack" by the USSR, on his mind. He formed the "Technological Capabilities Panel" in 1954. Since the presidency had no true idea of what was going on behind the Iron Curtain, Eisenhower created this prestigious panel of individuals that were on the cutting edge of technology. Eisenhower gave them the job of finding out if the U.S. could meet the USSR's menace.

The panel consisted of James R. Killian Jr., president of MIT. Killian was also the chairman of the President's Scientific Advisory Board. Dr. Edwin Land was also included in the panel. The panel contained within it a steering committee, military advisory committee, three project teams, and a communications committee. In total, there were about forty of the leading minds in all disciplines, forming a report for the President. On February 14, 1955, the report titled *"Meeting the Threat of Surprise Attack"* was delivered to Eisenhower. Eisenhower ordered that the essential parts of the intelligence portion be given directly to him via Land and Killian, for fear that some of the sensitive satellite reconnaissance material would be leaked.

Eisenhower was also passionate that the CIA and not the USAF, would handle the collected information regarding the air and space reconnaissance. Eisenhower ardently believed that the USAF was totally and completely obsessed with the amplification of the enemy danger, so that they could further enhance their budget requirements to reflect that threat. To be noted, James Killian made a statement regarding the rather amazing estimation the USAF had the Russian bomber fleet, which in fact didn't exist at all, and only enhanced Eisenhower's fear for letting the USAF get involved. Killian stated unconditionally, to Eisenhower, "You must find a way to do it (meaning the U-2 Reconnaissance program) that does not give the primary control to the Air Force." Once again, the USAF was not only behind the times, but also behind the eight ball, when being considered for anything as sensitive as reconnaissance work. Those who owned the air certainly were being kept out of the race when it came to intelligence gathering.

There were two other reasons for shutting out the Air Force from reconnaissance work. It would be less confrontational to have the program run by a civilian agency, as Eisenhower was to find out with the May Day shoot down of the U-2.

Eisenhower also worried that the USAF might somehow rile the Soviets up, which would most definitely increase the tension between the two adversaries, something that Eisenhower didn't want or need. The job went to the CIA hands down. It wouldn't be easy, however. There was no way that the colossal clashes that would develop over the control of both the "take" and the collection method could be avoided. The "turf minded" USAF and the civilian CIA became and would become political, visceral enemies from those very early days.

The best thing that Eisenhower brought to the White House was his heartfelt and military mind's decision not to allow the U.S. to be run by the U.S. Military complex. In essence, Eisenhower did not want to allow his administration to become a full scale build up of military hardware, while the rest of the economy was drained. In Eisenhower's State of the Union address he said:

> *"Our problem is to achieve adequate military strength within the limits of an endurable strain on our economy. To amass military powers without regard to our economic capacity would be to defend ourselves against one king of disaster by inventing another."*

Since Eisenhower's main career was a professional soldier, when it came time for Congress to approve money for the USAF fighters and bombers, or a possible new missile system, Eisenhower "refused to be stampeded" into signing off on just anything Congress put on his desk. Eisenhower's experience as a military general and supreme commander during WWII, told him not to be goaded into believing "dire" consequences by his military commanders about needing the new systems or else. This really did rile the upper echelon of commanders in the various military services. It basically meant that Eisenhower held his ground against the onslaught of military want. General Hoyt Vandenberg of the USAF was in that upper echelon that Eisenhower seemed to always be in a tug of war with. Included in the upper echelon were Congressional leaders like Senator Stuart Symington and Senator Henry Jackson and Lyndon Baines Johnson.

Allan Dulles of the CIA also stood by the "basic defense concept". The idea of having a very strong nuclear force and a strong delivery system (aka USAF) meant that both bombers and missiles should share the mission and be a back check against one becoming more powerful than the other.

Black Lightning

Aquatone

It had become necessary for the CIA and the USAF to re-evaluate their relative positions in collecting intelligence. The methods of WWII, while tried and true, had been overtaken by the fierceness of the Soviet Union in reacting to over flights of their homeland by American surveillance aircraft. In conjunction with the USAF, the CIA pursued the next step in reconnaissance.

The Air Force had come out of the end of WWII as a new service, still basking in the glory of the win. However, it was obvious that the new USAF had not moved on with the rest of the services in dealing with the Cold War. The upper echelon of the USAF chain of command had not come to terms with the "new" type of strategic reconnaissance that was required to keep the USSR at bay. The USAF was still in the WWII mind frame of "the only good target is a destroyed target." Hence, the USAF thinking still stuck to budgetary requirements that came down on the side of buying bombers to destroy the targets, and fighter planes to protect the bombers on the missions. That was not the reality of the new military mission facing the U.S., that being aerial reconnaissance. The year-to-year budgets proved how the USAF repeatedly stuffed their requests to meet their inflated needs. However, the USAF seemingly hadn't learned that they no longer had the same mission that WWII presented them. Perhaps Air Force leadership of the time had forgotten the admonition of the "Father of the Air Force," General Henry H. "Hap" Arnold, to "stop fighting the last war and start planning for the next one."

The Soviet Union situation had demanded all of the Washington D.C. politicos and military to direct their attention to the issues of defense against surprise attack by the USSR. The critical issues of defense had transformed into a high level committee whose membership included only the best of the best military and political minds in the country. This committee met in Washington D.C. for a Cold War Symposium on strategy. The committee would then advise the president. The problem was, while there was no shortage of expertise, there was a big shortage of information on which the strategic policies could be formed. This became known as the "intelligence gap." Because of the logistics on the new "Iron Curtain" and the USSR's contempt of the west, the classical means of gathering intelligence would not work. By the summer of 1954, it was obvious that the present intelligence system in the U.S. had drawn only one conclusion: the only way to get what was needed was "systematic aerial reconnaissance of the USSR."

As mentioned earlier, a special study project directed by the Hoover Commission, asked retired General James H. Doolittle to investigate the CIA policies on covert activities, and deliver a report. In the September 30, 1954, report, Doolittle said "Every known technical scheme should be used and new ones developed to increase intelligence by high altitude photo reconnaissance and other means. No price would be too high to pay for knowledge derived from them." By November 5, 1954, Edwin Land (of Polaroid Land Camera fame), chairman of the "Project 3" panel, also known as the "Technological Capabilities Panel," wrote to CIA director Allen Dulles and asked for photo reconnaissance flights over the USSR, and then recommended that the USAF should also begin work on the problem.

The Land Proposal reported "A unique opportunity for compressive intelligence," and showed the risks of provocation toward war that over flights could produce. There was also the "red flag" of having military involved, in view of the hot political environment with the USSR. The proposal continued, "because it is vital that certain knowledge about industry growth, strategic targets and guided missiles sites be obtained at once, we recommend that the CIA (with USAF assistance) [begin] a covert program of selected flights." This, in itself, was a provocation, of sorts, to the USAF, who owned the role of aerial reconnaissance. To have a civilian agency now "calling the shots", leaving the USAF as second banana, was not going to go down easily.

Of course, the potential aircraft that Land had in mind was the CL-282, which Lockheed and Kelly Johnson had initially proposed to the USAF, was turned down way back in 1952. When the Land Panel, in researching its technological capabilities study, came across the Lockheed proposal, it seemed to be just what the doctor ordered.

In Land's letter to Dulles, he made it clear on the panel's behalf that it was appropriate for the CIA, with USAF help, that it would be perfect for what had been proposed. Land also added that immediate action, via the CIA, should start the covert means to produce the aircraft, and all else needed to set up in a task force. Land also added:

> *"Opportunity for safe over flight may last for only a few years, because the Russians will develop radars and interceptors or guided missiles to counter defense of the 70,000 ft. regime... and that the aircraft itself was so obviously unarmed and devoid of military usefulness that it would minimize affront from the Russians even if through some remote mischance it were detected and identified."*

Edwin Land, from the President's Advisory Council, had reviewed the advances in the field of optics for photographic reconnaissance. The USAF was already years ahead in development of suitable camera systems as a result of their many years of expertise gathered from sponsorship of basic research and development programs. The paper went on to say:

> *"This is particularly true of electronic computation of optical systems. The development of these complicated optical systems would have taken years in Germany by older methods. But now it is about to be accomplished in sixteen working days with the IBM/CDC computers."*

The CIA should use the covert approach to pass funds. Dulles, the CIA chief, and General John Stanford of the USAF, met later and decided that

Dulles would write the memo to the president for approval. The memo, dated November 24, 1954, recommended Presidential approval of the national requirement for reconnaissance over flights, and asked both the CIA and the USAF be directed to get started on the aircraft as soon as possible. Eisenhower approved the memo verbally.

Both Dulles and USAF officials reached the joint organizational and management responsibilities agreement on August 5, 1955. That memo, titled, "Organizational Risk and Delineation of Responsibilities" was given for general direction of project control to the DCI and Chief of Staff of the USAF, to be issued jointly. The Agency appointed project directors, and the USAF appointed deputy project directors, who would be responsible for the conduct of the project throughout, subject to higher authority. The USAF project group, headed by Colonel Russell Berg, would act in the name of the Chief of Staff of the USAF, and SAC (Strategic Air Command) would support its role in operations. The program would be operated so that "It would be clandestine intelligence gathering operation to be conducted in such a way as to minimize the risk of detection".

Even Colonel Richard Leghorn of Wright Patterson AFB, in attempting to study the new reconnaissance mission, was soon to realize that the upper layer of USAF command was not interested in the subject, and that he was not supported. The USAF availed themselves of the services of the RAND Corporation. The RAND Corporation was a think tank that the USAF employed to help them figure out the best way to solve problems. The RAND Corp. delved into the concept of aerial reconnaissance for them. One thing that the USAF didn't care to learn was that in the collection of intelligence, time was of the essence. If you had old intelligence, you lost the game. The USAF also hadn't faced the concept that not only timely intelligence but the speed of acquiring it was also an issue. This is based on the concept that RAND came up with. In an effort to supply a solution, RAND teamed up with the RCA Corporation in a study that went under the name of *"Feed Back"*. By 1954, this study sponsored the idea that the USAF increase their research into the realm of "electro-optical" satellites. This concept would use a television camera to radio images down from the satellite. It was a good idea on paper, but with a resolution of 144 feet, it was hardly the best possible solution to the problem. There was no probable way that this resolution could be used to discern aircraft on the ground or other types of images needed for photo interpretation from a target site. The RAND solution to this issue was to suggest to the USAF that they engage other contractors to develop a higher resolution television system for satellites. This turned out to be yet another time waster for the USAF.

Later in March of 1958, RAND then proposed a new method of collecting intelligence from space. This method had to do with taking standard photos from satellites, dropping the film canisters out of orbit and return them to earth via parachute for recovery. This concept is accredited to RAND physicist Richard C. Raymond. His idea was included in a twenty page report titled "Photographic Reconnaissance Satellites". However, as soon as this report was read, it was withdrawn from consideration because once again, the fickle, USAF and their idea monger RAND became mesmerized with the idea that the "near time" television was the way to go. The USAF, in its "WWII wisdom" dismissed the idea of the capsule drop containing film as archaic and removed the idea from consideration. Once again, the USAF missed the technological boat due to its own close-mindedness and inbred disregard for anything other than its own wants.

The CIA and the USAF had never been on the best of terms. The CIA felt it should control the missions and the aircraft while the USAF felt the same on their end. Jealousy and infighting between the two services and would become a main stay in their relationship. This conflict between the CIA and the USAF, in later years, would be responsible for the loss of one of the most sophisticated aerial reconnaissance systems ever devised.

CL-282

The advent of the CL-282 project brought with it many issues that had to be defined before production could even be considered. The Eisenhower Administration was already deeply concerned about the possibility of a shoot down over denied territory. Eisenhower was so concerned that he informed both services, USAF and CIA, that he did not want a "uniform" in the cockpit. The "uniform" down over denied territory would be an unmitigated disaster. It would take only a year's time before Eisenhower's worst fear became a reality.

The search for the new aircraft would end at the Lockheed Aircraft Company. Kelly Johnson, the renowned designer responsible for the creation of the P-80 Shooting Star in the record time of 143 days for the Army Air Force, was again in the running. Johnson was ready to build the first aircraft and ready to restart the "Skunk Works", the ultra secret part of Lockheed that would produce aircraft designs that would rock the Aviation and Reconnaissance world. That is, when the world eventually found out about them.

Before the A-12 was even a gleam in Kelly Johnson's eye, the CL-282, was a concept never seen before. In late 1952, Major John Seaberg of the USAF New Development Office at Wright-Patterson Air Force Base, Ohio, recognized the aerial reconnaissance situation as urgent. Seaberg laid out a consistent structure for a high altitude reconnaissance aircraft. Since there was no USAF requirement on the books, Seaberg collected all his ideas for the new aircraft and presented it to his boss William Lamar, then Chief of the New Development Office. After Lamar's review, Seaberg wrote the completed official proposal for the concept. March 1953 called for the formal request of a high altitude reconnaissance aircraft. This review took time, until it finally received an approval from Air Research Development Center (ARDC) office for the USAF. After a final review, a figure of $200,000 was set for the design studies. Three aircraft companies were chosen to step up to the challenge of designing the new project MX-2147: Bell Aircraft Company of New York, Fairchild of Maryland and Martin Aircraft of Maryland.

This project officially went into effect with a run date of July 1, 1953, to December 21, 1953. The project also had a new classified name of "Bald Eagle." The idea of seeking out the larger aircraft companies, like Boeing or North American, was unpalatable to Seaberg. He was hesitant to select any of the larger aerospace companies for fear they wouldn't be able to give this special project the same type of attention a smaller company could.

However, only the Bell Aircraft Company and the Fairchild Aircraft Company were asked to put in their proposals after all. Martin was already working on the refit of the B-57 Canberra. Seaberg felt that Martin had the only option available, should other companies prove poorly in their proposals. At the end of the day, Martin and Bell both were chosen. Fairchild's proposal was not in the running.

However, while the design process was going on by mid-March 1954, it was becoming apparent that the new high altitude aircraft may *not* have been what the doctor ordered. Martin aircraft was very heavily involved with the B-57D, which is what essentially took them out of the race. This process again shows the schizophrenic nature of the USAF when it came to making decisions about going into high altitude reconnaissance aircraft, or not. Regardless, the service would be dragged, "kicking and screaming," into the art of high altitude reconnaissance.

The B-57D program, was working on specific modifications already in the works, and it was sure that this program would help the USAF intelligence need in Europe. However, during early May 1954, Major Seaberg was again asked to make another presentation at the USAF headquarters in Washington D.C. At this presentation, Seaberg had been given the go-ahead to proceed with the B-57D project. Almost two weeks later, another proposal appeared on the desk for Seaberg to scrutinize. The new design was from Lockheed and called for a high altitude cruise aircraft. Kelly Johnson, already wise in the ways of how the military procurement process worked, already had some inkling that there just might be something in the offing. Johnson wrote in his diary:

> "*December 1953—we had started an investigation of wing area modifications on the F 104 airplane to get the maximum possible altitude for reconnaissance purposes.*" He continued with, "*February 1954, I was told of Air Force interest that would have developed with the airplane having the characteristics we were finally able to obtain in the F-104A study.*" In *March 1953*, Johnson again wrote, "*I had about*

four men work up Lockheed report #9732, describing the CL-282 high altitude aircraft."

This was a complete report still tying the high altitude airplane to the F104-A. This report was sent to General Bernard Schriever early in March of 1954. He was extremely interested and asked Lockheed to prepare a specific proposal.

The report of the design group said that it contained a design of aircraft with the ability to reach the average altitude of 73,000 ft. and have a combat radius of 1,400 nautical miles. The idea behind the proposal was to have an aircraft that was relatively small and could carry a payload of 600 lbs. The normal takeoff weight would be approximately 13, 700 lbs. in including an additional 4,990 lbs. of fuel, which would be for a common flight. The only real differences were in the square footage of the wing, which was about 500 square feet. The other concern would be the under belly of the fuselage. Since there would be no conventional landing gear, the idea of a ground cart was used on take off. The wing design was, without doubt, completely groundbreaking. Except for all of the above, the configuration would equal that of the F-104, with the exception of forward fuselage modifications. With some more simplification, like the removal of everything on the F-104 design that was not of use, like armament, landing gear, and the usual fighter load accoutrements, the aircraft became lighter. The nice side of the manufacturing problem was that all the F-104 jigs were already in place and were configured for the new aircraft. It wasn't long after that the basic jigs for the F-104 were also being used for the CL-282.

By April of 1954, Johnson presented a letter of proposal to the USAF for thirty planes in which Lockheed would take full responsibility for caring for the aircraft in the field. Major John Seaberg, in the meantime, had heard all about Kelly Johnson's proposal through the grapevine. The timing couldn't have been better. Seaberg was sure that someone in the upper echelon of the Pentagon would soon let Kelly Johnson know of the secret high altitude program that was underway. As Seaberg and staff picked their way through Johnson's proposal, they gave it the temporary design number of CL-282. The final proposal consisted of the XF-104 fuselage, the unconventional trapezoid wings, and the General Electric J-73-3 turbojet engine. The concept for the landing gear actually came earlier to Johnson back in 1930 when he devised something similar for the Lockheed Vega flown by Wiley Post. The fix for the weight issue, which was mandatory since the aircraft would have to reach high altitude, was to have the aircraft would use a jettisonable, wheeled dolly for takeoff. The cockpit would be unpressurized, which would require the pilot to wear a pressure suit. Even though Seaberg and his staff rushed through the design, they concluded that the J-73 would not be the right powerplant for the CL-282. They also stated that the unpressurized cockpit and the range deficiencies would all be part of the issue. Because the J-73 was basically untried in the surroundings that the CL-282 presented, Seaberg and his staff decided that the Pratt & Whitney J-57 would be an enhancement to the CL-282 proposal. Seaberg wrote the evaluation letter in June of 1954, which did not recommend buying the CL-282 design. This was again proof of the fact the USAF really didn't have a handle on what it was looking for and couldn't discern the quality of the Lockheed design.

After Johnson got the word that his concept had been rejected, he added to his personal diary:

> *"May 1954, Air Force was proceeding with the Martin Canberra and they are not too impressed with the CL-282 proposal."*

Later in June, Johnson added;

> *"June 7, 1954, received a letter which turned down our proposal on the basis that it was too unusual that it was a single engine aircraft, and that they were already committed to the Martin Program."*

The USAF told Johnson of their decision to drop the CL-282 from the list of contenders. Johnson did not quit, he decided to find the money to build elsewhere. He went back to Lockheed, took some fifty engineers that were hand chosen, and went to work in a small design room in Plant 6B, adjacent to the Lockheed main building. Johnson put the crews on shifts of forty-five hours per week while he himself spent more than half of his working time on the CL-282 redesign. With the need for secrecy and speed already instilled in his crews, this was the only way that the CL-282 could be completed.

By December of 1954, the members of the Land Commission, a secret division inside of the Killian Technological Capabilities Panel, headed by Dr. Edwin Land, decided to hold a meeting. The meeting was held in one of the member's 1953 Ford so that their privacy would be assured. As they drove around, the discussion turned to the high altitude aircraft concepts of Bell, Martin, and Lockheed. The group was there to decide which of these designs would fit the bill for the current high altitude aircraft the Eisenhower Administration so desperately wanted for the United States. The committee took a one-hour spin around the nation's capital trying to make the decision. Can you imagine a committee of Congress trying the same tactic to make a decision today?

The arguments developed, but by the end of the drive, the commission decided to recommend the Lockheed aircraft to President Eisenhower. Along with the Killian Committee, who also recommended the Lockheed bird, the decisions were sent to the Secretary of Defense, Charles Wilson, and CIA director Allan Dulles. In late November of 1954, both the Secretary of Defense and the CIA director felt that it was necessary to brief the President on the current findings. With Eisenhower's approval in hand, Allan Dulles then brought Richard Bissell, (an economist who taught both Yale and MIT) in to take care of the program for the CIA interests. In the words of Richard Bissell:

> *"Towards the end of 1954 (Nov), I was summoned one afternoon into Allan's office and I was told with absolutely no prior warning or knowledge that one day previously President Eisenhower had approved a project involving the development of an extremely high altitude aircraft to be used for*

surveillance and intelligence collection over 'denied areas' in Europe, Russian and elsewhere. And Allen, after perhaps 15 minutes of explanation on the background of this undertaking told me that in a half hour I was to go over to the Pentagon and present myself in Trevor Gardner's office. When I arrived, General Putt, General Irvine and several others were already gathered there. We were to decide between us how the project was to organize and run. My most vivid recollection of this meeting is of the telephone call put through at the end of the meeting by Trevor Gardner to 'Kelly' Johnson in which he gave him the go ahead on a program to develop and produce 20 aircraft."

"AQUATONE" was agreed upon as the name of the new project that President Eisenhower signed off on. All funding and organization would be controlled through the CIA, and Richard Bissell would be the person running the show for the project. It was Bissell's tremendous talent for organization that would drive AQUATONE and OXCART to fruition. However, to make things a bit easier to manage, some USAF funding was used for the J-57 power plant. In order to hide the special J-57's, they would be mixed in with the contract for the regular J-57 engines that the USAF was using on the F-100 and F-102 Delta Dart aircraft. The USAF agreed to handle the rest of the J-57 issue from their main offices due to sensitivity of the mission.

On December 9, 1954, funding for AQUATONE was signed with money coming from the CIA's secret contingency reserve fund. The top figure for the project was $54 million with Kelly Johnson returning about 15% as the project came in under cost. With today's bloated programs and overruns, this would be totally an unheard of event.

Johnson promised the first aircraft to be ready in less than eight months, after the first metal was cut. The aircraft that would be known as the "Kelly's Angel," or the "Angel of Paradise Ranch," was quickly coming to life. By November 1954, Johnson had assembled his team of twenty-five engineers and some eighty shop personnel and the race was on. The team put in some one hundred hours a week to get the aircraft born in the allotted eight months. Johnson noted in a December 20th diary entry:

> *"Working like mad on the airplane. Initial tunnel tests successful."*

With weight as the big issue, design engineers had a devil of a time getting the airframe into specs. So many things in the design had changed. The bicycle landing gear was one of the heaviest parts added to the airframe. This consisted of a single strut with jettisonable, pogo mounted wheels mid-span on each wing for balance, and it was a most unique concept for this aircraft. The CIA decided in the long run to agree to the initial twenty aircraft to be built in Burbank, and later in the Oildale, California, plant. The aircraft was then sent to a secret place for testing.

Groom Lake

Early 1955 found Johnson and the CIA looking for a place to test the new U-2 aircraft of the AQUATONE project. Kelly Johnson had sent his chief test pilot, Tony LeVier, out into the desert to check numerous places in California, Arizona, and Nevada, for a place to roost the new bird. Tony Le Vier and the Skunk Works foreman, Dorsey Kamerer, took off in a Lockheed owned Beech Bonanza to begin surveying the land. They looked at some fifty locations to no avail. Richard Bissell (now a CIA Special Assistant), Colonel Osmond "Ozzie" Ritland, who was then acting as the Air Force liaison for AQUATONE, rejected all of the fifty sites checked by LeVier and Kamerer. None of the sites met the strict security requirement set out by the CIA.

It was then Colonel Ritland remembered something from his past. While he was involved in nuclear testing for the USAF, Ritland remembered a desolate place called "Groom Lake." Groom Lake was situated just outside the nuclear testing grounds at Yucca Flat, Nevada. Johnson, LeVier, Bissell, and Ritland, piled into the Lockheed-owned Beech Bonanza and flew out to check the site. On viewing it, they all realized that this would be the perfect spot to bring the U-2. However, even though the site was perfect for the program, Johnson was really not too pleased with it. He felt that it was too far from the Burbank plant. Not to mention, it was adjoining the Atomic Energy Commission (AEC) nuclear test site! It had nothing in the way of useful facilities; all the supporting infrastructure would have to be supplied.

Funding for the new base was done clandestinely so that the secrecy of the new site could be protected. It would take all of $830,000 of "black" money to complete the new base. Johnson unhappily settled on the site. Besides, with the atomic testing grounds at the back door, that would settle the issue of "prying eyes." No one in his or her right mind would want to venture into the radiation-contaminated desert. Bissell requested, by presidential action, that the new base be added to the Atomic Energy Commission list. Colonel Ritland addressed three memos. The first to the USAF, the second to the AEC, and the last to the gunnery range that inhabited the site. The memos were endorsed by all three organizations, which guaranteed that the new site would be off limits to the Atomic Energy Commission. By April 1955, Johnson and the CIA had discussed the problems of the new site. Johnson took to calling it *"Paradise Ranch."* Johnson's little inside joke had to do with the concept of not quite letting the Lockheed employees know exactly what was going on there and what they were in for. In May of 1955, Johnson and LeVier returned to *Paradise Ranch* to take a survey and see just what was needed. It took over a month to clear up the shells left over from the gunnery practices that had been run there by the Army. Johnson also laid out the four proposed 3-mile runways on the hard surface. "Silas Mason Company", a fictitious construction company created by Lockheed got the license for the work and "CLJ" another fictitious organization covered for Johnson and Lockheed. This was done so that no one could trace the funding that was going out. Johnson would receive checks at various post office boxes to be sure the checks couldn't be traced.

July 1955 found the CIA, USAF and Lockheed arriving at the new home of the U-2. Another name was added to the Groom Lake history. *"Watertown" or Watertown Strip"* became the home of the new crew for the high altitude aircraft. *"Watertown," aka "Groom Lake,"* is in Alamo Township, Lincoln

County, Nevada. This name was derived from the hometown of CIA director, Allen Dulles. Dulles was dead set against the CIA becoming embroiled in the overhead reconnaissance business. However, he became an advocate when he saw what the U-2 could deliver. With Richard Newton of the CIA assigned the role of Base Commander, *Groom Lake* was now the official home of the U-2. President Eisenhower signed Executive Order 10633 which formally restricted the airspace of the U-2's home on August 19, 1955. No flyover was permitted within a five by nine nautical mile zone.

Another 58,000 acres were officially withdrawn from public access under Public Land Order 1662. It was this rectangular addition to *Groom Lake* that later became known as *Area 51* and appeared on the AEC charts and maps. At the same time that this occurred, NASA had gotten permission to land the X-15 there in case of emergency. This never took place.

"As of March 15, 1955, the wind tunnel testing was settled and the design was considered airworthy," Johnson noted in his May 21, 1955, entry to his diary. Johnson continued with: *"Number one fuselage out of jig. Having a tough time on the wing. Put almost everyone on it."* The drive to finish by deadline was, in a word, intense. On June 29, 1955, Johnson again noted *"Terrific drive to finish the airplane."* By July 15th, he added: *"Airplane essentially completed. Terrifically long hours. Everybody almost dead."* However, from this last dire comment, things really started to progress. A few days later, Johnson noted that the airplane was turned over for inspection and final check. The following day Johnson noted, *"Airplane disassembled and loaded into loading carts."* Johnson and the Skunk Works crew had done it.

July 24, 1955, found the aircraft moved to *Groom Lake* for testing. The move itself was an awesome feat. The crews started at 4:00 AM to start the loading operations. It took approximately three hours to load the aircraft into a waiting C-124. There was an issue for the C-124. It had to land on a wet runway on the accepting end of the flight. After a quick, hurried assessment, the group decided to let as much air out of the tires as possible. It was up to Kelly Johnson to make the final call on whether or not to land the C-124 with its precious cargo. Two hours had passed and the finally the C-124 landed in the dust of the dry lakebed using reverse propellers. The U-2 was finally unloaded and reassembled in the hangars by the Lockheed crews at the new *Groom Lake* home.

U-2 Pilots

By June of 1956, the first group of pilots for the CIA was in final training phase. The CIA met with President Eisenhower to discuss the plans for the new over flight program. The first flight scheduled for July 1 of that year. The program carried the name "*Operation OverFlight*", with the first of two U-2's (U- for Utility) packed off to the Royal Air Force at RAF Lakenheath, England, on April 30, 1956. They were to be undercover as the 1st Weather Reconnaissance Squadron. The personnel was a conglomeration of CIA and Air Force personnel and of course, contracted civilian pilots, better known as "sheep dipped" USAF pilots that had traded in their blue suits and their commissions to fly the new U-2. Not only had these men traded in their blue suits for the privilege of flying the new high altitude reconnaissance aircraft, they entered a whole new realm of flight. Since they would be flying at altitudes above 65,000 feet, new problems in human flight would arise. At these higher altitudes, the human body would experience the problem of body fluids vaporizing unless they were kept under pressure. This higher altitude also put enormous pressure on the pilot's heart and lungs. Knowing that these pilots would have to operate in long over flights required a new process to be devised so that they could remain in flight safely.

Two Air Force doctors, Col. Donald D. Flickinger and Col. Randolph W. Lovelace II, joined the U-2 program to solve the problem. Both Flickinger and Lovelace had made many contributions to human flight during WWII. Lovelace was the inventor of the standard Air Force oxygen mask. Both Flickinger and Lovelace made parachute jumps from B-47s to test the survival gear issued to pilots. Flickinger and Lovelace turned to the David Clark Company of Massachusetts, designer of the flight suits for USAF pilots. The Clark Company soon came up with the new high altitude suit designs for the U-2 pilot. Clark's designer, Joseph Ruseckas, devised a complete life support system. This turned out to be the first pressurized suit for keeping humans alive during high altitude flights for long periods of time. In addition to that, the U-2 cockpit was designed and built by the Firewel Company of Buffalo, NY; it allowed for the pressurization of the cockpit to 28,000 feet. Should the 28,000 foot-level cockpit pressure decrease, the pilot's suit would inflate and he would be able to receive additional oxygen through his helmet.

The early versions of the MC-2 and MC-3 suits were comfortless, so the suits were redesigned. Since the suit had to prevent loss of pressure, it had to fit snug at both the wrists and ankles. The pilot also had to don heavy gloves and wear a heavy helmet, which tended to scrape the pilot's neck. The helmet visor was prone to fogging. Many of the early suit issues were responsible for some of the U-2 accidents. The U-2 cockpit was far from roomy, so it was tight fit to get a pilot into it. The very early U-2's did not have ejection seats; but later on, when ejection seats were installed, most pilots were apprehensive to use them for fear they might lose their legs during an in-flight ejection. To say the least, an ejection was a violent maneuver. Later on in the program, Kelly Johnson added a fully adjustable seat for pilot's comfort.

Pilots had to "suit up" and breathe pure oxygen for at least ninety minutes before the flight. This purged nitrogen from the pilot's blood so he wouldn't experience the "bends" at the pressurized altitude, or during bailout. The need for physical functions like urination also became an issue. In early flights pilots had to use a catheter before putting on his flight suit. It was a painful situation on long flights; later on in the program, an external bladder was used so that the catheter was not needed. Another problem encountered with high altitude flight was dehydration. This problem was solved by allowing the pilots to drink sweetened water from a tube attached to the water supply within the U-2. This was done via a self-sealing hole in the facemask of the helmet. Food was also served this way. It was contained in a squeezable container much like the food for the first Mercury astronauts. With all of these preparations to make the pilot comfortable during a long flight, U-2 pilots averaged about 3 to 6 pounds of weight loss during a long eight-hour flight. Long flights also carried the danger of shoot down or malfunction in flight over denied territory. U-2 pilots were equipped with the "suicide pill" In actuality; this was a glass ampoule (called the L-Pill) that contained liquid potassium cyanide. When the pilot bit down on this "capsule," death would occur in 10-15 seconds. Later on, this suicide pill was changed to a silver dollar sized coin that contained a sharp needle with the same chemical.

First Flight of Article 341

Because of the unusual security issues involved, the aircraft's official designation hadn't been resolved; the Skunk Works of Lockheed simply called her "Angel". The CIA, being the bureaucrats they are, called her "Article," with the first aircraft numbered 341. Article 341 took almost two days to reassemble for static testing. By July 27, the engine tests were run, followed two days later with the taxi tests. Tony LeVier, veteran test pilot for Lockheed, made the first run. LeVier had noticed that the brakes were sluggish when he first applied them after throttling down on the first test run. The second test run was at 70 knots. As LeVier was intently watching the airspeed indicator, he had no clue that he was actually airborne.

His depth perception did not allow him to see the shallowness of the lakebed. At 35 feet high, cruising over the runway, LeVier pulled back the throttle but still was not aware that he was airborne. Tony LeVier tried to keep the aircraft from stalling. LeVier brought the aircraft back to earth and the dry lake bed, bouncing the aircraft and blowing the tires, while rolling out at least a mile before the aircraft stopped. The brakes, now damaged had burst into flame right under the fuel tank. Kelly Johnson recalls:

> *"We were following in the radio trucks and finally got an extinguisher on the brakes. No harm done. Airplane was subjected to a terrific test. Pogo sticks worked real well."*

Weak brakes had become such an issue that LeVier told Johnson it had to be sorted out before another flight could take place.

The testing went on. August 4, 1955, Johnson assembled several members of the Skunk Works team and they waited while LeVier set up to take the first flight in Article 341. The flight would be comprised of "Angel 1," and a C-47 chase plane. By 3:55 that afternoon, LeVier was ready for takeoff. He climbed to an altitude of 8,000 ft. and spent 45 minutes in the air, cycling the systems to find out just what Article 341 had in her. Landing would be a new issue. Both Johnson and LeVier had talked about how the aircraft should be landed. LeVier did not agree with Johnson's approach, and Johnson did not agree with LaVier. Johnson's approach caused the aircraft to skip and bounce, looking as if she never wanted to land. LeVier went back up and tried another approach, which resulted in flare and touchdown landing. Once again, the bird refused to sit. It took three more tries before LeVier finally attempted to "spike" the landing gear onto the runway. This did not achieve the effect that LeVier wanted. Things were getting rather tense between Johnson and LeVier. Aggravation was running high. To further complicate things, a summer rain shower passed over the landing. Finally, LeVier was fed up with the whole thing. He decided to do things his own way, as only a pilot can do. Just days before the first flight, LeVier had attached two strips of tape on the canopy, just parallel to the horizon. While watching these strips, LeVier let the aircraft glide at seventy-five knots into a controlled stall. At that point, the aircraft settled on her tail and main gear in complete accord onto the lakebed. The aircraft pitched forward slightly, then settled into a smooth rollout and a gentle stop after Levier pumped the gust settings on the flaps. The "Angel" had finally after much coaxing, settled on the runway.

There were a total of twenty test flights for the "Angel of Paradise Ranch." Tony LeVier had completed the first phase of the testing for Article 341. However, during this test period, the USAF had given the name U-2 to the aircraft as her formal military name. Interestingly enough, the new "Articles" that were being produced carried hardly any markings except the NACA (National Advisory Committee on Aeronautics) logo. This was done to disguise their true work, that of spying. This was not the first time that the U-2 name was used for an airplane. Back in 1944, the Russians used a biplane with the same nomenclature. N.N. Polikorpov built the aircraft. She served as an air ambulance, light bomber, and enemy territory surveillance aircraft. Nowhere near the height and altitude of the U.S. U-2, this Russian U-2 was capable of 150 kilometers per hour and had a maximum altitude of 10,000 ft. She was listed in the 1945 version of *"Jane's All the World's Aircraft"* as a single engine biplane. An Army Air Forces officer, serving at the Poltana American bombing base in the Ukraine, took a photograph of the Russian U-2.

It had been a long, fast road for the American U-2. The program spread far and wide throughout the United States, Europe, and even into Turkey. Throughout 1957, 1958 and 1959, the U-2 was responsible for some 30 clandestine missions over the denied territory of Soviet Union, and the Chinese Lop Nor missile test range.

The CIA was so concerned about the prospect that the U-2 could be found poking around some rogue nations backyard, the agency developed Project *RAINBOW* in the hopes of finding a way to help subdue the U-2 's radar image. *RAINBOW* was a trapeze set up, built with chord and span wires on the leading edges and ferrite beads on the trailing edges of the wing that supposedly disguised the U-2 on radar. The project also known as "Dirty Bird" was completely unsuccessful! It added weight to the aircraft and ended up reducing the altitude of the U-2. Anyway, the USSR was happily tracking the U-2 regardless of *RAINBOW*. By May 1958, *RAINBOW* was terminated and the CIA was worried that a SA-2 Russian missile would take down the U-2 before they could figure out something else to mask her image on radar. It was not long before their deepest fears would come true.

One of the deepest fears in the Eisenhower White House was that a military uniform would be in the U-2 cockpit when and if the inevitable happened. Eisenhower demanded, at the start of the *AQUATONE* project, that there be no military personnel flying the "U-2 Dragon Lady." In his statement, Eisenhower made it clear that he wanted "no uniforms "in the cockpit. This problem was taken care of by the CIA via "sheep dipping" of Air Force pilots. What that meant was that the pilots chosen would be asked to hang up their blue suits for a while, and serve the "black program" as civilians. When they left the project, they could then resume their Air Force career where they left off. This solved the problem of having any type of military "uniform" in the cockpit.

It is rather startling to think that, before the U-2 was born, the CIA was already planning for her obsolescence. The planners of the program were already working on the inevitable fact that the Soviet Union would either come up with a radar system or an aircraft/missile system fast enough to counter the U-2 at her high altitude. Speed was not the gift of the U-2, but altitude was her best defense. The CIA planners also worked on the fact that sooner or later it was foreseeable that a U-2 would go down over denied territory and the secret cat would be out of the bag. Even with the inevitable in sight, the strength of the U-2 would live on into the future, regardless of the planner's crystal ball predictions. She is the "Dragon Lady," and nothing would stop those sleek wings from flying in service to her country.

CORONA

The United States of the 1950's was a place of deep fears, fears about what the Soviet Union had in the way of military weapons and missiles. Critical information on what was happening in the USSR, was not only scarce, it was often erroneous. The Soviet Union drove that fear home when they launched the Sputnik in 1957. The people of the United States lived with the fearful notion that the Soviets might start dropping bombs from space on them at any minute. This would not stand, and newly re-inaugurated President Dwight David Eisenhower decided that the time had come for the U.S. to find a solution to this situation.

As the U-2 began its operations in 1956, the concept was already in place that it wouldn't be long before her operational life would end. Initially the U-2 program was only to last a couple of years. The United States however, didn't reckon on the Russian radar that picked up the U-2 on the first flight. It took the Russians only days to file a formal diplomatic protest, and within days the mission was told to stand down. This was before the U-2 incident with Francis Gary Powers that the Russian shoot down over Sverdlosk on May 1, 1960. That incident effectively ended the U-2's usefulness over Russian territory. While this was unfolding, another program was just about to become operational. Only 110 days after the Sverdlosk disaster, the "catch" of an exposed film canister was made over Hawaii. This capsule belonged to a new generation of reconnaissance satellites. This satellite had just completed 17 orbits over denied territory and sent the exposed film home to be analyzed. The United States was not out of the reconnaissance race, not just yet.

When the U-2 became operational, the USAF was still working on a new strategic reconnaissance weapons system using various satellites in various configurations. WS-117L (the program designation) began in 1946 when a GOR (General Operational Requirement) was placed with the RAND Company for an orbiting satellite system that would support reconnaissance and define a new technology. In 1953, the USAF Advisory Board in a statement made note of a method to create small, lightweight thermonuclear warheads. It was then the ALTAS ICBM was given the highest development priority available. It was noted that the same propulsion that would be needed to launch an ICBM could also be used to place a satellite in orbit. GOR 80 was another General Operational Requirement that called for "providing continuous surveillance of pre-determined areas of the world to determine the potential status of an enemy's war making capabilities."

The USAF Air Research and Development Command (ARDC) had taken over the RAND program in 1953. It then assigned the program over to the Ballistic Missile Division. The WS-117L program called for the development of systems and subsystems for reconnaissance purposes; basically, the collection of photographs and infrared surveillance material. This program was separated into three segments. In 1956, the project was awarded to the Lockheed Corporation. In 1957, Lockheed Missile and Space Company had already begun work on all three sections for WS-117L, *"Vidicon, Film Recovery and Infrared Observation for Ballistic Missile Early Warning."* Each of these satellites would go on the upper stage of a rocket and would carry its own restartable rocket engine and steering thrusters. All three of these reconnaissance systems would go under the program name *"Pied Piper."* This system set the precedent for every other satellite system to follow. The first in the series of tests was the THOR missile, which would begin in 1958, the second, the Atlas/Agena missile series in 1959, the third and operational series which would begin in 1960.

It was obvious that this program was breaking new ground and quickly fell behind schedule. The program also fell into problems with security. While the U-2 managed to stay under wraps until 1960 with the shoot down, the scope and enormity of this project would not allow security to become an issue. It didn't take long for the press to create the popular stories of "Big Brother" watching from the sky above as they alluded to reconnaissance satellites. At this time, Eisenhower's Presidential Consultant Board was already looking at the feasibility of two reconnaissance programs. The CIA program, a manned reconnaissance aircraft program, which would call for better RCS (reduced radar cross section) and greater speed, was hosting one of them; the second considered was WS-117L. However, since neither of these programs would be ready for 1959, the best of the three that were involved in WS-117L was sorted out of the rest and designated *Project CORONA*. This would be the best of the photographic subsystems.

Richard Bissell, who was already the special assistant to the DCI (Director of Central Intelligence Agency) for planning and development, headed the developments project staff. Along with Bissell, his co-director would be General Osmond Ritland, who also served as Bissell's first deputy in the beginning of the development's project staff. Ritland was then moved to the vice commander of the USAF's Ballistic Missile Division. Bissell's early instructions in the new office were very vague. He was told that there would be the new subsystem that would be branched off from the WS-117L program, and that it would be under covert management. One of the distinct things he was informed of, was that no monies from already established Air Force programs would be available for the new system. This would later prove to be an issue in the means of supplying the THOR missile for the program. Since the USAF owned them all, the CIA was forced to return to the President's office and admit that the money situation was a problem and in fact, it needed more money.

The WS-117L program was an advanced reconnaissance system that was divided into the *SAMOS* (which was also known as *SENTRY*) optical reconnaissance program and the *MIDAS*, which was an early warning satellite. The optical phase of the program projected to recover the film from orbit, via reentry, trajectory and parachute; the film was then retrieved after drop. Lockheed was the prime contractor for the program. Eastman Kodak developed the cameras for the *SAMOS* system. This unique camera was gimbaled for directional shooting and activated by radio command from a ground station.

Since the spilt off from the WS-117L program, the Department of Defense now found it imperative that it was time to restructure its space activities management. On February 28, 1958, with the granting of space management activities ceded to it, the Advanced Research Projects Agency (ARPA) was established. This allowed for the WS-117L reconnaissance program responsibility to be turned over to the USAF. The WS-117L provisional reconnaissance plan, which used the THOR missile as a booster, was dropped totally from the plan.

The cancellation of a military program such as the WS-117L brought with it the problems of notifying the contractors and sub-contractors of the loss of contract with the program. There was a great deal of shock amongst the contractors when they got the word. However, some of these contractors were picked up again as soon as the subsystem program was working. A very limited group, including the USAF, were again told of the new project and cleared to work on *CORONA*.

President Eisenhower approved *CORONA* in 1958. It was pretty much an all out rush to get the new program up and running. The program was brought together with quick decision making, just as quickly called meetings to approve those decisions. It took the Director of Central Intelligence, Robert Gates only three very short paragraphs to consign seven million dollars to the first phase of the new project. In retrospect, there is no possible way today, with the current state of political bureaucracy, that a program like *CORONA* could ever be launched that fast and that quietly. However, the perception seen here is that there was a need to be filled with great speed. It should be noted by today's political machine that these decisions can be made quickly when it is essential to get critical information that is imperative to national security. We all know of the 1993 World Trade Center bombing and the 9-11 World Trade Center disaster that struck the U.S. Perhaps if a little of the *CORONA* momentum could have been used, there would have never been the tragedy of 9-11. It took a little more than two years to go from the first plans of *CORONA* to actually recovering film from orbit. August 18, 1960 saw the first film payload delivered from space and caught by means of a parachute. The first target was a military airbase near Mysn Schmidta on the Chukchi Sea in far northeastern Russia. While the images might have been not the best quality, it didn't take long for those imaging problems to be corrected.

It stuns the mind when we consider the achievements of the CIA/USAF *Project CORONA* and how they were produced so quickly. It amazes one to see how the talent for this project gathered together so rapidly, immense talent to be sure, and how the fruit of this program changed the course in Cold War tactics.

The CIA and the USAF manned *CORONA*. Richard Bissell was the special assistant to the DCI for Planning and development. Brig. Gen Osmond Ritland was the head for the USAF support of *CORONA*; Of course, there were the other technical geniuses like Lockheed Missiles and Space Co., Itek Corp, Fairchild Camera and Instruments, Eastman Kodak, General Electric and Douglas Aircraft. With a team like this *CORONA* was destined for nothing less than greatness. It wasn't an easy trip, however. The technical challenges were huge and there was no time to go the usual route for studies and more testing. Mission failures did happen, but they were reversed and this was all done in the darkest hall that CIA secrecy could provide.

When *CORONA* found its place on the intelligence-gathering map, the successes came fast. The first payload recovered from *CORONA* brought back 3,000 feet of film, which covered a total area of 1,650,000 square miles of Soviet terrain. This total footage was more than the U-2 had collected in 24 of its over flights. That was just the beginning. Consider that during the beginnings of the Cold War, decisions were made bereft of good solid intelligence. This broken down "collection gathering" led to the Missile Gap and the Bomber Gap. The onset of *CORONA* allowed the U.S. to find and maintain a higher form of intelligence that most assuredly kept the Soviet and U.S. nuclear dogs of war at bay. What also should be noted is, that as good as your intelligence photographs might be, they were only as good as the photo interpreters that read them. These men and women would analyze these images and got the information to the services that needed it desperately. There isn't enough praise that can be given to these specialists who analyzed the images from the satellites and U-2 aircraft. These hard won images were used to settle many of the deepest issues of the Cold War.

CORONA was newly announced by the USAF, as the *"DISCOVERER"* series of satellites. The "buckets" of film dropped by the satellite were caught after their drop, via parachute, by specially adapted aircraft known as the Fairchild C-119 Flying Box Car. Should the air catch be missed, the "buckets" could also float in the ocean until pick up could be made by ship. Film was black and white but sometimes infrared and color film were carried for experimental testing. *DISCOVERER* did not make only *CORONA* surveillance flights. The program also made many flights in the name of developing new types of technology and to fix problems in the *CORONA* series. There were two other flights made in support of the MIDAS early warning satellite system. After *DISCOVERER* made its thirty eighth flight, the program was ended and the shroud of concealment would cover all satellite reconnaissance work.

The *KEYHOLE* designation was used to refer to all satellites during photographic reconnaissance work. The KH description would include the type of camera system used. This system came into being in 1962 and started with the fourth camera system used. The first systems to use this new designation were KH-1, KH-2, KH-3, and KH-6. These satellites carried a single panoramic camera or a single frame camera, which was called KH-5. KH-4. KH-4A, KH-4B and used two panoramic cameras set to work thirty degrees apart (one forward and one rear looking). KH-6 was programmed to tilt front and back so it could cover the same land mass twice during a pass and afford stereo coverage. The first satellites used the one-bucket system while later satellites were built with two buckets. KH-4A used multiple buckets and the front and back camera films were packaged separately for missions that used twin panoramic cameras. The *CORONA* payload used a vertical looking, seventy-degree panoramic camera that was produced by Itek using Eastman Kodak film. The camera scanned at right angles to the line of flight. In the early flights, resolution was only 35 to 40 feet. By 1972, *CORONA* was able to produce resolutions of six to ten feet. By the 1960's flights could remain on orbit for nineteen days with precise attitude position and mapping information, gaining coverage of 8,400,000 nautical miles squared per mission. On May 25, 1972, the CORONA program was closed down after this final launch.

CORONA leaves behind an amazing legacy:

*CORONA covered all Soviet medium range, intermediate range and ICBM complexes.

*CORONA covers all Soviet submarine classes from deployment to operational bases.

*Provided inventories of all Soviet bombers and fighters.

*Produced evidence that there were Soviet missiles in Egypt that were protecting the Suez Canal.

*Produced evidence that the People's Republic of China was receiving Soviet nuclear assistance.

*Monitored the SALT I treaty

*Identified the People Republic of China's missile launching sites.

*Produced exact locations of Soviet air defense missile battery

*Produced evidence of construction and deployment of Soviet Ocean going vessels

*Produced evidence of the Plesetsk missile test range north of Moscow.

CORONA (KH-1, KH-2, KH-3, KH-4, KH-4A, and KH-4B), ARGON (KH-5) and *LANYARD* (KH-6) encompass a series of satellite programs that changed the outlook of the Cold War. Without these marvels of reconnaissance, the face of the Cold War would have looked much different.

Francis Gary Powers and the U-2

The CIA estimated that it would take approximately two years before the U-2 would be compromised. That prediction actually turned into four years. The big hit came when Francis Gary Powers and his U-2 were shot down over Sverdlovsk, Russia on May 1, 1960. The incident left Eisenhower with a political black eye. While the White House was under the impression that the pilots of the U-2 program were given the means to end capture by carrying a poison needle, the CIA was not instructing them to do it. The CIA left the decision up to the pilots should the nightmare of a shoot down occur. However, when the White House and the CIA found out that Powers did not do the "honorable thing", there were many in the CIA and White House that showed umbrage at the pilot's supposed "lack of courage." Since the CIA wasn't passing the word to the pilots to begin with, their anger seemed poorly placed. Yet, Eisenhower was still the one that had to face Khrushchev at an upcoming summit and the Soviet Premier was adamant regarding an apology for the over flight. This did not help the summit which imploded, leaving Eisenhower red in the face with humiliation.

Powers doomed flight took off from Peshawar, Pakistan for the Soviet border. The first three hours of the flight were flawless, crossing over Tyuaratam and then heading for Sverdlovsk. According to Powers debriefing, he claimed he was blinded by a flash of light and then felt a heavy explosion from the rear of the aircraft. The U-2 was not hit directly by the SAM SA-2 missile. In fact, due to her fragile nature, the vibration of the explosion shook the aircraft so badly, she broke apart but was not hit by the missile. Powers felt his right wing dip and then the aircraft headed down. Powers actually saw his wings rip right off the fuselage. Powers only chance to escape was to wait until the fuselage flipped over during the dive for the ground so he could fall out of the aircraft to the safety of his parachute.

Powers did not use the poison needle provided to him as he found himself floating down into a farmer's field. He was helped by the locals, who not really knowing what was going on, dumped him into a truck and attempted to drive him to the nearest airport, thinking he was a Soviet pilot. However, it was not long until the Russian police caught up with the truck and took possession of Powers. Soviet Premier Krushchev had a media circus showing the pieces of the shattered U-2 on television. It became worse when the Soviets informed Eisenhower that they had the pilot, too.

While both the White House and the CIA were squirming because of the incident, Powers was also being blamed for not only using the poison needle but also for not pulling the explosive charge in the U-2 which would have destroyed the film and the camera. Powers would suffer enough for all of this. He was being sentenced to ten years in the cruelest of Soviet Prisons, spent two years doing hard labor and was then freed in a prisoner exchange. Powers was ostracized for his actions when he returned the United States. Had he used that poison needle, the outcome would have been much different, Powers could have been considered the consummate hero with all the trimmings. However, Powers, on his homecoming, was subjected to the harshest debriefing the CIA could conger up. After that, Powers went to work for Lockheed as a test pilot, due to the kindness of Kelly Johnson. He later worked as a TV helicopter traffic reporter. He subsequently died in a helicopter crash. As usual, ten years too late, the USAF awarded him the Distinguished Flying

Cross. In this testament of what happened to Powers, it should be noted that all of these men who flew the U-2, the A-12 and all reconnaissance flights, are heroes above and beyond the call of duty. They flew in silence, suffered in silence and gave their lives in silence. No service CIA, USAF or any other should ever treat these men with such disdain as they did Francis Gary Powers.

SUNTAN

The CIA had been in the business of creating aircraft to meet the mission for a short time when they decided that the U-2 needed to have a successor. It was becoming apparent that the U-2 was in jeopardy every time she flew over denied territory. The USAF was also contemplating a supersonic aircraft unbeknownst to the CIA. This was to be *their own* successor for the U-2. The USAF was not pleased with always being the "Bridesmaid" to the CIA's "Bride. It stuck in the USAF's craw that the service who saved the world in WWII with their amazing skills, and that is not to be doubted, would have to play second fiddle to the CIA and their quest for aerial reconnaissance. The Eisenhower Administration had made it quite clear that because of the USAF's stubbornness to enter into the Cold War, they were deprived of the premier spot. The USAF had the chance to step up and be the lead on engine and airframe design. As it has proved over and over again, the USAF was afraid of its own decisions and canceled what could have been a viable aircraft. One has to wonder why the USAF continually shot itself in the proverbial foot when it came to being in the forefront of supersonic flight.

However, the USAF was working on the concept developed by British engineer Randolph Rae. Both the Navy and the USAF were interested in the use of hydrogen fuel as a new way to devise a faster powerplant. As far back as 1949, both the USAF and the Navy were working with North American Aircraft, Aerojet and Glenn L. Martin Company on the building of a prototype hydrogen power plant. There had actually been successful testing of elementary liquid hydrogen rockets. However, the tests did not fair well when it came to funding the project. There were no takers out there to further push the project along. While Rae continued to develop his concept, the USAF was once again going through many twists and turns due to their attempting to develop everything at once. The U-2 was being developed around this time, while the USAF was still dreaming about a supersonic aircraft. The USAF could not make a fair deal with Rae regarding his engine since the USAF was at odds with itself concerning trying to develop both the airframe and the engine. This led to much confusion resulting in bad feelings between Rae and the USAF.

At the same time, Rae had also run into some issues on patent infringement. Finally, around 1955 the USAF contracts were settled. Rae and the Garrett Corporation, which owned his initial engine, were running onto hard times concerning the results of the USAF contract. Once again, the USAF could not come to terms with itself. Rae realized that the contract read the USAF was looking for a long range, high altitude, subsonic aircraft. That was not what the USAF was thinking. The contract read that the USAF was actually looking for a supersonic aircraft, and range was not of significance. This was not what Rae was told.

The schizophrenic nature of the USAF was hiding the fact that the USAF wanted an aircraft that would be a replacement for the CIA U-2. The USAF had not said that up front. The Rae contract virtually fell apart. However, the contract with Rae and Garrett and the USAF funding it produced, was enticing and already payable and both did not want to lose it. During the initial dialogue with Rae in 1954, Rae and Garrett were both invited to join a study to provide designs for airframe under a *Skunk Works* program.

The Garrett/Rae Company would supply to Lockheed the specifics and engine size. Lockheed, however, found that the specifics that Garrett/ Rae provided were not what Lockheed needed. The engine data would provide an engine that would be too small for the project and would not meet the USAF requirements. Both companies went back to work and devised an engine that would be larger and closer to the Mach2.25 number that the USAF was looking for. The USAF re-entered the picture determined that the Garrett Company could not build an engine of the size required. In 1956, Lockheed released a study that showed two different airframes powered by the new Garrett REX III engines built for supersonic flight. This was not good enough for the USAF because the service decided that the REX III engines were doubtful. The USAF in essence did not believe that the Garrett Company could actually build the engines that it designed. By 1956, while the Garrett Company fought the USAF's decision, the USAF closed out all work on the REX III and the CL-325 airframe design of Lockheed, which would have been capable of altitudes of 99,384 feet and M2.5 and range of 2,529 miles. Kelly Johnson of Lockheed had even proposed to build two of the hydrogen-fueled aircraft with more conventional propulsion systems. Johnson also said that he would be able to deliver them within 18 months. Through Kelly Johnson, Lockheed also built its own hydrogen fuel testing facility at it Burbank location.

The U-2 program was being handled by the CIA. The USAF had the chance of being the "Bride" instead of the "Bridesmaid", with the concept of the CL-325. As it was, the USAF was the proverbial handmaiden of the CIA when it came to the building and running of the U-2.: While the USAF still had dissatisfaction at having to deal with the CIA regarding the U-2 program, they had the chance to have their own high altitude, high- speed program. The USAF still expressed the motivations and want to have their own supersonic program.

Johnson and Lockheed went back out to locate another company that would be in a better position to build the hydrogen engines that was the holy grail of the USAF supersonic program. Pratt & Whitney and General Electric were the two companies that got into the running. With two weeks to conclude a presentation on the engines, Pratt & Whitney was chosen as the company to get the study contract. On May 1, 1956, Pratt &Whitney and Lockheed got a six month contract to develop the design work for their engine.

Richard Bissell of CIA, had been shopping the idea around that may be what was needed was a completely new aircraft. Late summer of 1956 found Bissell and his Air Force counter part, Colonel Jack Gibbs, starting the search for a new aircraft, one that would fly faster and higher than the U-2 could. An aircraft that could out run anything on it is tail and would not appear on a radar screen looking like the side of a barn. This aircraft had to escape radar and SA-2 missiles of the Russians. Bissell and Gibbs started to make the rounds of various aircraft contractors to see if what they envisioned was actually feasible. What they wanted was an aircraft that could reach altitudes and speed that would keep the aircraft out of harm's way while it was doing it job of reconnaissance. There were many different and unorthodox designs. One of them was a design by Northrop Corporation for a huge aircraft with a high wing that would reach attitude of 80,000 to 90,000 feet, but only at subsonic speeds and to be sure, the radar paint on the aircraft would equal a large building.

This, was not the answer that Bissell was looking for. Bissell turned to the Scientific Engineering Institute (SEI). The think tank had been working on the U-2's radar problem, and had started to explore the possibility of creating an aircraft that had a smaller radar cross section (RCS). SEI revealed that speed would be the essential item in reducing a radar cross section on an aircraft. This was something that Kelly Johnson and the Lockheed group had already discovered.

Project *SUNTAN* was really the formulation of the A-12. Since 1954, Lockheed and Johnson had been exploring hydrogen–fueled engines and by 1956 Johnson had designed the hydrogen-powered aircraft. Johnson, who was already in partnership with the USAF and CIA via the U-2, promised the USAF that he could deliver a prototype within 18 months. The aircraft was known as the CL-400. It was purported to have a speed of Mach 2.5 and a cruise altitude of around 99,000 ft., with a range of 2,500 miles. The aircraft was flawed however, and too heavy to fly. Yet, *SUNTAN* defined the basic concept of the Mach 3 aircraft.

Bissell, however, was stuck on the idea of building an aircraft that had both high speed and high altitudes, which would make it invulnerable to both missiles and radar. By the time 1957 rolled around Bissell's field trips to the various manufacturers was giving him enough information to be able to go to the Director of the Central Intelligence Agency, Allan Dulles, and ask for the establishment of an advisory committee to begin the selection process for this new aircraft. The process to find members for this committee brought some of the finest minds in the United States together. They were men who began their service to the country during WWII in the aerial reconnaissance field. Among them was Edwin Land (aka Din), father of the Polaroid camera that we know today, scientists like Allan Donovan, George Staves and Eugene Keifer who also served as the special assistant for technical analysis for the CIA. Keifer was the "go to" man when it came to any decisions for film capacity or resolution in regards to the cameras.

Richard Bissell continued on as the special projects manager for the CIA. He appointed a panel headed by Dr. Edwin Land as chairman. This committee ran on from 1957 through 1959. This group of elite engineers and businessmen met at least six times to discuss the future of reconnaissance. Many of the guest presenters included Kelly Johnson of Lockheed, Vincent Dobsen of General Dynamics (of which Convair was a part) along with the assistant secretaries of both the Navy and the Air Force.

In the meantime, Johnson from Lockheed was working on the project that he started with the Air Force. Project *SUNTAN*, the CL-400 as it was named was developed by Johnson to be a high altitude, high speed hydrogen fed aircraft. Things, however, did not go as Johnson had planned. *SUNTAN* had run into a multitude of problems, one being the hydrogen fuel issue. That is not to mention the fact the Johnson himself had already nicknamed the CL-400 the "flying vacuum bottle" or the world's largest thermos bottle, due to its great weight and fuel requirements. The reason for the large body size of the aircraft was that it would carry some 162,850 lbs. of hydrogen fuel. The outer shell of the aircraft would result in a heat friction of above 350 degrees Fahrenheit, while the inside skin would hover around -400 degrees Farenheit! It was an awesome thermodynamic problem that was not going to solve out easily. The USAF did allocate $96 million for the project.

There were two prototypes and one static test aircraft, using the Pratt & Whitney 304 engines. The aircraft called for two engines which weighed in 6270 lbs., and provided 9450 lbs. of thrust at sea level. Johnson was looking for 5940 lbs. of thrust at 100,000 ft. using conventional intakes. For the first time, CL-400 defined the basic characteristics of the essential Mach 3 aircraft.

The CL-400 planform brought the long, sleek missile type nose of the F-104 Star Fighter and a deeply swept wing together to form the beginnings of the A-12.

While *SUNTAN* brought with its program the chance to develop hydrogen fuel, which is something the USAF was looking hungrily at, it seemed like this was a concept that had not met its time. Hydrogen fuel at best was slurry mixture, akin to slush. This zip fuel was not only hard to manufacture, it was hard to contain in storage. Pratt &Whitney, the engine designer for the 304, still used conventional air intakes. These engines were to serve as the pulse and power of the CL-400. Pratt & Whitney had kept hopes alive by opening a liquefaction plant in Florida to help in processing the slurry fuel. However, it was becoming clear to both Pratt & Whitney and Lockheed that this attempt at harvesting hydrogen fuel was going to turn in to a nightmare. Not only was the processing of hydrogen fuel expensive to the point of being cost prohibitive, it was technically extremely difficult to maintain. The facilities for liquid hydrogen fuels were unwieldy. This also required costly and complex tanks which had to be fitted to the aircraft.

It was going to take a lot of engine to lift the CL-400 and a lot of engine to maintain flight levels that the contract proposal called for. By 1958, the program was already eighteen months behind schedule and in deep trouble. It was becoming obvious that Kelly Johnson and the USAF that the CL-400 would not deliver what it had been designed for. There was no way for the aircraft to meet the required range. While none of the CL-400 panned out as planned, the Pratt & Whitney 304 engine found a new life in the U.S. rocket program with the Centaur rocket. This was the first rocket engine using liquid hydrogen to fuel a space vehicle.

The CL-400 did contribute the basic concepts for the Mach 3 aircraft that was to follow. Dated April 21, 1958, Kelly Johnson wrote in his diary for the first time and used the name *"Archangel"* which was later to become the A-12. Johnson also knew that the SUNTAN project was on shaky ground. The 18 month deadline had passed, and the results were not promising, at all. On top of that, the CIA had given President Eisenhower the news that the USSR was also delving into developing a hydrogen fueled aircraft.

The Archangel and the Kingfisher

GUSTO

The CIA was finding itself looking for another proposal on a new high speed, high altitude aircraft. Both the Lockheed and Convair companies were offered a shot at the ultimate aircraft. Convair had their own idea called, "KINGFISHER." Convair locked onto the idea that a parasite aircraft launched from a reconfigured B-58 Hustler might be the way to attain high altitude and high speed. The concept was for the parasite aircraft to reach Mach 4 using a ramjet engine. Lockheed also had two birds under its proverbial hat. One concept was the G2A, a "tailless" subsonic, low RCS (radar cross section) aircraft that was intended to replace the U-2. The G2A was discarded because testing showed that Soviet radar could, in fact, detect the aircraft. That left Johnson and Lockheed with the other design. This was the "Archangel". Proposed was a Mach 3 aircraft with a range of 4600 miles and an altitude of 90,000 ft. to 95,000 ft. Convair and Lockheed went back and forth constantly redefining their concepts hoping for the ultimate aircraft.

In an April 21, 1958, log entry, Kelly Johnson made his first mention of the A-12 as Archangel. Johnson wrote:

> "I drew up the first Archangel proposal for a Mach 3 cruise airplane having a 4,000 Nautical mile range at 90,000 to 95,000 feet."

Three months later in a July 23rd entry Johnson added:

> "I presented this airplane, along with Gusto Model G2A to the program office. It was well received. The Navy mentioned a study they had been asking on the slower, high altitude airplane, on which the program office wanted my comments."

Yet another meeting had occurred with the Land commission on August 14th. The Land Commission presented Kelly Johnson with a layout of the Navy plan. The Navy proposed to a very unique design. The plan called for an inflatable airplane. It would be ramjet powered with a cruise altitude of 150,000 feet. The airplane was carried to the altitude by a balloon. Johnson did some calculations and found that the balloon would have a diameter of one mile. Johnson didn't believe this to be a workable solution to the problem.

August 25th found Johnson and the Skunk Works still refining the *"Archangel"*. Kelly Johnson wrote in his log:

> *"Have contacted Marquandt and Pratt & Whitney and gotten some ram jet data. Have reconfigured the Archangel to include wing tip ramjets as per our proposal on the F-104 to the Air Force in 1954. This appears to give us an airplane, which would cruise at Mach 3.2 at 95,000 to 110,000 feet for the full distance. As of today, it looks like the rubber blimp would have a radius of operation of 52 miles".*

Johnson and his crew spent the next eight days of September the 17th through the 24th feverishly working on their proposal. Johnson would write in his log:

> *"Spent considerable time in Washington and ended up in Boston September 22nd and 23rd to review Archangel Project. I presented a report on evaluation of navy inflatable airplane design and also a revised version of the Archangel design for higher altitude performance, for our particular mission. Convair proposed a Super Hustler which apparently was a Mach 4 ramjet, piloted, turbojet assisted on landing, to be launched from B-58 to do the mission."*

Johnson, true to form, had already analyzed this and continued with:

> "I presented Gusto 2A which was well received and Archangel II. This airplane was 135,000 pound gross weight. Powered by two J-58 turbojets and two 75 inch ramjets, it could do a 100,000 foot mission and a 4,000 mile range. This airplane was not accepted because of its dependence on pertaborane for the ramjet and the over all cost of the system. We left Cambridge rather discouraged with everything."

On the trip back from Boston, Johnson had already figured that he would attempt to break one of the ground rules built into the competition. Johnson wanted to use the engines "in being". What this meant was that he wanted to use the J-58's Pratt & Whitney were wrestling with. One of the reasons that *Archangel II* was so large was the fact that the weight for these engines installed was 15,000 to 18,000 lbs. Johnson scaled them and *Archangel II* down to 17,000 to 20,000 pounds gross weight using the JT12A engine. It appeared to be a viable resolution to the problem.

As the development process went on between the CIA, Kelly Johnson and the Lockheed Skunk Works, Richard Bissell moved forward with his plans. By August 13, 1958, Bissell had sent the first of many top-secret memos to his boss, then Director of Central Intelligence, Allen Dulles. In it, he named five special projects; *CHALICE* (which was *AQUATONE* renamed), *RAINBOW* (which was the U-2 Radar project; *GUSTO* (the soon to be A-12), *KINGFISHER* (the Convair proposal that ran with the GUSTO program) and have course, *CORONA* (the new reconnaissance satellite program). This was the CIA line up for all of its effective tools in the Cold War of Aerial Reconnaissance.

The tug of war went on between Convair, the *KINGFISHER* aircraft, and the Lockheed *Archangel* design. While the differences were obvious, by November of 1959 the decision was made. The winner was Lockheed with the "*Archangel*". Johnson received the funding for the project the next day from the CIA. The dollar amount of the contract was $4.5 million. This covered the dates of September 1, 1959 to January 1, 1960. In September of 1959, the

CIA gave Johnson and Lockheed permission to start on anti-radar structural tests along with other functional modifications. Johnson's team started the plans of a full-scale mockup of the A-11 concept for radar testing.

Let us take a moment to explain the nomenclature of the A-11 and the A-12. The A-11 was the next to last of the series of plans that Johnson had created for the A-12, he had not yet reached the final and definitive design which would turn into the A-12. To keep the reader from being confused and for the sake of history, we will call the A-11 the aircraft prior to the final design of the A-12. In Kelly Johnson's log he wrote of his many attempts to find the right planform he actually went from the A-1 to the A-11, leaving the A-12 to be the ultimate aircraft the CIA would receive.

EG&G (Edgerton, Germeshauser and Grier) would run the cross section test for radar reflection. Johnson was not happy with the original site that was chosen for the pylon, as it was viewable from the local highway. That particular pylon was also not strong enough to support the mockup, so the test site was moved to Area 51. A larger pylon was built at the Area 51 location to allow the A-11 model to be hauled up there. The mockup was brought from the Burbank facility in one of the specially designed trailers. The mockup would verify the A-11 *Archangel's* planform. Fuel additive and composite parts would be included in that verification. However, after some 18 months of testing, and the radar cross section concept was still having issues. It was during this time that the A-11 turned into the *"aircraft that looked like a snake that had swallowed three mice"* according to Johnson. We know her today as the A-12. The theory of the curved airframe to deflect radar was verified and the new planform showed that radar could not gain sight from the rounded edges. This was the first time the word "stealth" was truly used. However, this would soon change in the 1980's when the HAVE BLUES arrived with their many sharply pointed edges; known as the *"Hopeless Diamond"* planform that would also deflect radar. This concept developed by mathematician Bill Schroder and computer scientist Denys Overholser and a little help from Lockheed's awesome aerodynamicist, Ben Rich.

The A-11- The Almost Archangel

A-11—The Aircraft that wasn't but could have been.

The A-11 was almost as elusive as the A-12, though she never really came to be. The A-11 was the planform right before the development of the A-12. It was the evolutionary point that pushed Kelly Johnson into the most remarkable aircraft he ever created. Not only was Johnson thinking of aerodynamic shape, he was thinking about attaining speeds unheard of—Mach 3. At that time period in the late 1950s, the United States had only experienced reaching Mach 1 on October 14, 1947 with "Glamorous Glennis" the Bell X-1 rocket ship. Never had Mach 3 (2000 mph) been truly attempted with an air breathing engine.

The A-11 actually saved the day for the A-12. When President Lyndon Baines Johnson., in error, announced the new high speed aircraft the A-11, he kept the A-12 under wraps for the CIA. This error actually covered the A-12 at a most crucial time for the United States and the CIA.

The A-11 was a different aircraft from the A-12. She looked nothing like the A-12. She had a delta wing of course, but no nacelles that made the A-12 look as Kelly Johnson called her, "A snake that swallowed three mice". She did not carry the two nacelles, one on each wing and had only one vertical as opposed to the A-12's double vertical. The main issue with the A-11 was WEIGHT! Weight was the bane to every aircraft designer's plans. It was through this refinement of the A-11 that the A-12 was created. Let's get back to what the A 11's elusive story really was.

Kelly Johnson's plan for the A-11 configuration didn't just spring up from nowhere. The process started with the drawings of the A-1 through the A-7 and went from the A-8 to the A-11. It was a painstaking process of development. Johnson's personal log is full of notes and line drawings of how he went from the A-1 to the A-11. First the entire concept of a Mach 3 aircraft was mind blowing for the times. The use of titanium as the metal from which to build this creature was also unheard of. Yes, we did have the B-58 using some titanium but that was miniscule in comparison to what Johnson had planned which was close to 93% total value.

The configuration of the A-11 had to support 2000 nautical miles in range at Mach 3 speed with an altitude of 85,100 feet to 100,000 feet. The time frame for this concept was around 1958. Engine technology was making strides but it was an obstacle to climb.

The A-11 had 4 separate elevons on the trailing edge of the delta wing.

The wings start at mid fuselage and the familiar chines of the SR-71/A-12 have not yet been introduced. Below we have a list of the differences between the A-11 and the A-12:

	A-11	**A-12**
Length	116.6 ft.	99 ft.
Span	56.7 ft.	56 ft.
Height	21.03 ft.	18.45 ft.
Zero fuel weight	36,800 lbs.	60,000 lbs.
Mach cruise	M 3.2	M3.2
Range	2000 NM	3000 NM

The A-11 would have been a little larger than the A-12, but the big change was in the fuel and how it would be distributed within the A-11 airframe. The other issue was the fuel itself.

Kelly Johnson was known for coming up with the most diverse of materials for aircraft. For the A-11 many exotic materials were considered for strength, density and elasticity for all temperatures that could go over 1200 degrees. Temperatures up to 800 degrees were put in the titanium alloy basket. Of the titanium alloys chosen, MST 185 and B-120VCA were the ones that looked most promising. Production of the metals was also an issue. B-120 VCA looked like it was the winner as it was practical, holding temperatures up to 800 degrees. Crucible Steel Corporation in Pittsburgh, Pennsylvania was chosen as a manufacturer. B-120VCA was a mix of 13% Vandium, 11% Chromium, 4% Aluminum would add up to the new Beta Titanium alloy. It could be purchased in all stages, cold, aged, worked or annealed. Aging it was a very simple process, all it required was heating from 800 degrees to 1000 degrees for 8 to 100 hours and cooled by air. It had flexibility, it could be brazed and welded. For the A-11 the peak temperatures could range from 500 degrees to 780 degrees.

Wing

The wing for the A-11 was a "solid leading edge arrowhead" with the skin being supported by ribs and stiffeners perpendicular to the swept leading edge. Structurally, the wing box was consisted of multiple beams some 16 inches spaced along the wing chord. The beams were built up of beam caps and located under contour to permit for the passage of surface corrugations. The box surface consisted of an outer skin and an inner corrugated skin. The aerodynamic heating of the structure did result in a temperature gradient, from the outside of the skin to the inside of the airframe. The gradient was accommodated by this type of structure since it gave easily with the expansion and contraction of the skin, causing the buckling or waving between the corrugations. The same process was used in the A-12 wing.

Cabin pressure.

The cabin was pressurized with gaseous nitrogen used from liquid storage for cooling reasons. Nitrogen was needed for pressurization alone, and pilot comfort in descent from very high altitudes. During a 200 kts descent a cabin change could result in 1460 fpm while during a 400kt descent it would go to 8040 fpm.

Air Conditioning:

While in the extremely early stages of investigation, Johnson looked at the air-cycle, ram cooling with variations of machinery and water boilers. It must be understood that while all of this was very highly placed research, none of it was ever built, physically. In the early stages, the engine air bleed was eradicated for cabin use, due to the aircraft performance losses associated with bleed at altitude. It was planned that limited amounts of air bleed would be used for windshield defogging and ram air heating as needed. The temperatures would look something like this:

100 degrees space temperature in the cockpit and equipment bay

135 degrees maximum touch temperature for the trim areas not directly over conductive structure, with minimum possible touch temperatures in all other areas.

Cooling was done entirely by liquid media stored aboard the aircraft (basically nitrogen and water)

Cooling would double as cabin pressure source.

The pilot would be made more comfortable by nitrogen gas, just like on the X-15 rocket plane, in suit ventilation. The use of recirculation system was also looked at with the cabin atmosphere was cooled in two stages one, by passage through the air side of a water boiler then topping off with liquid nitrogen, but at the time weight was a larger issue and it went the way of all things weighty in aircraft.... out.

Emergency escape:

The A-11was provided with both low altitude and high altitude escape. The pilot's ejection seat would release in the normal course of ejecting up and outward with a rocket catapult. This rocket catapult made sure that the ejection seat had clearance to the tail of the aircraft.

Since the aircraft had a long nose, it had the pilot way forward of the tail and since the tail was low aspect ratio, the pilot had every chance of clearing it without incident. The ejection seat was equipped with an emergency kit and bail out oxygen, along with a special shoulder harness and lap belt.

Should a pilot have to escape at a high altitude and high speed, gave Johnson something to think about. With the opening of the parachute and the oscillation of the pilot swinging around during free fall all had to be within tolerable limits. Heat at high mach numbers was also something to think about. The first ten seconds of an ejection is critical. Johnson was considering using the automatic seat belt and shoulder harness release that was used in the Lockheed F-104 Starfighter jet aircraft, which would allow the pilot to remain in the seat till deceleration was over. It would prevent the pilot from being injured in spinning and tumbling, and preventing the premature deployment of the primary chute.

Boron and Zip Fuel and Production Methods

Slurry fuel was a brand new concept back in the 1950s. By 1959, Olin-Matheson and Callery's large plants were hoped to be on line which would allow for picking up the pace for engine development. However, it didn't quite work out that way. It did leave flight testing in the lurch and the shortage of material wasn't helpful either.

Olin-Matheson Chemical Corporation was going to produce HEF-3. Broken down essentially it was ethyldecarborane. Callery Chemical Corp. was going to produce Hi- Cal III that was similar to the HEF-3. These two fuels were relatively easy to maintain and handle compared to the first trials of boron fuels which was the HEF-1 (pentaborane) and HEF-2 (propylpentaborane). Both these fuels were tough customers when it came to handling and storage. The newer fuels HEF-3 and Hi Cal-III was less toxic and could work with the military JP -150. Both the newer fuels were more viscous which would mean there would have to be pumps that could work harder to get them to the engine.

In breakdown these fuels looked like this:

	HEF-2	HEF-3(1961)
Thermal stability	?	Less than 1% Decomposition at various heat levels

HEF-3 and HiCAL–III had a final combustion that was equivalent to boric acid which was a very mild acid, used in some eye washes. There really wasn't much concern over this to say the least.

The unburned fuel is extremely dangerous and could burn human skin if swallowed or touched. The Callery Company had actually lost time due to accidents due to boron vapors escaping.

All of the fuel properties had been checked regarding the A-11 and the material she would be made of. The fuels would not cause any concern with the A-11 which was a major hurdle to cross. Handling the fuels HEF-3 and Hi Cal –III needed some safety measures. It had to be inerted, which meant that it needed to be kept under control with nitrogen gas. There was a mild reaction between the boron and aluminum which could have been a problem with some of the A-11's component parts. At this point in the design of the A-11, the fuel system had aluminum in the tank baffles and the valves which they could replace with another material. Steel, stainless steel and copper could be used. However, rubber and plastic could not. Basically, those materials had to be replaced with Teflon, Kevlar F, and Vitron. Boron fuels could also be used with hydrocarbons such as JP fuels.

Engines

Very early in the Archangel life cycle, there were actually two engines that Johnson was looking at: the Pratt and Whitney J-58 and the General Electric YJ-93 that was already being considered for the XB-70 Valkyrie. Specific thrust comparisons were negliable up to 75,000 ft. where the YJ-93 fell off and the J-58 beat it out. Maximum altitude was a major concern. The engine with the best thrust/ weight ratio that could reach the highest altitude would be the shoe in. The J-58 could handle 3,000 ft. better than the YF-93 and was selected for the A-11.

Of course, the use of boron fuel like the HEF-3 in the afterburner would add an additional 12% thrust. A two dimensional external—internal compression inlet was chosen for the induction system of the A-11. A three dimensional inlet was looked at but it would be more difficult to control. the final selection was made with wind tunnel testing.

Fuel system

Pratt and Whitney designed the J-58. Preliminary testing showed that through very determined fuel scheduling, having to do with rapid heat rise resulted in the thoughts that an uninsulated tank could be used for the A-11. Integral fuel tanks were designed for the A-11which resulted in tanks for the fuselage and the wing. A detailed analysis for the fuselage and wing tanks system showed that fuel tank temperatures would be managed without much trouble. Results showed that 40 minutes was available before 300 degrees was reached, assuming that the initial fuel temperature started at 60 degrees.

Results showed that 40 minutes were available before 300 degrees could be reached, assuming that initial fuel temperatures is 60 degrees. That was more than enough time to use up the wing fuel. The study done to prove these facts also showed that fuel could be routed from the fuselage to the wing tanks during an entire mission if needed.

Another fuel problem other than material compatibility was found. That was the temperature effect on the residual fuel. The plan to purge the tanks totally so that there would be no tank coking was not settled.

Using only hydrocarbon fuel with the A-11 was really going to be a test. Flight testing of the airframe, engine, and equipment along with crew training as well as some tactical missions could be done using just the less exotic fuel, JP -150. To do this the mission radios of the HEF fuel equipped A-11 would need a fuel load of 52,540 lbs. with a takeoff weight of 85,940 lbs. These figures are 6,540 lbs. more than the HEF equipped A-11. The basic airframe could allow the greater weight of fuel at the lesser density because of sufficient fuselage diameter and length that was already established by payload and balance.

Bigger takeoff weights would need a bigger runway, one that could handle the extra weight.

The A-11 in perspective

Kelly Johnson was really pushing the limits of so many different phases of aircraft design, it would be impossible to sit down and dissect all of it for one book. It would take many books. What Johnson brought to the table with the A-11, while there were issues with weight, fuel and other matters with metals used, the concept was truly spectacular. Johnson created the A-12 from the A-11. He managed to put together the best of both worlds and developed the finest aircraft in both speed and altitude ever imagined and still today, remains one of the most amazing pieces of aviation that there ever was. From the A-11, came the A-12, the YF-12, the spectacular SR-71. In one fell swoop, Johnson and Lockheed brought high altitude. high speed reconnaissance flight to the United States to reality.

A-11A and the J-93 engine

While testing was still going on with the A-11, another version was devised by Kelly Johnson. The A-11-A has a smaller wing and tail than the A-11 concept. This was another stage in the design that allowed Johnson to get to the final A-12 aircraft that we know today. Along with the theoretical concept, Johnson had decided to turn to the XB-70 Valkyrie yet again and think about using the General Electric J-93 engine that had been designed expressly for the XB-70.

The General Electric J-93 turbojet engine was used as the conceptual powerplant for the A-11-A. This powerplant was considered as an alternative to the Pratt & Whitney J-58. There were serious concerns that the J-58 was not going to be ready on time. The J-93 was the only other powerplant at the time that could do anything near what the A-12 needed. The thrust to weight ratio of the J-93 to the J-58 was inferior at M3.2 and 90,000 feet for the design condition of the A-12. There were two versions of the J-93, which were used in the analysis: the -5 engine, which used the JP-150, fuel in the primary stage and HEF (High Energy Fuel) in the after burner. Next was the -3 engine, which was using all JP-150. The XB-70, as we know, used JP-6 fuel. The engine used in this test was the upgraded J-93; the turbine inlet temperature was boosted to 100 degrees F. in flight speeds of M.0 to M2.0. At the higher Mach numbers the turbine inlet was cut back to the original value. Both the -3 and the -5 were based on the engine performance bulletins that were in place at the time of the testing. The entire weight of 4,770 lb was used for the -3 and 4,990 lbs. used for the -5. The availability dates for the engines couldn't have made Johnson happy at all, while the -3 would have been ready by Sept 1961, the -5 would be almost 2 years later than the A-12 first flight date.

Johnson added the "chines" (the curved areas of the airframe) to the engine housings, the leading edges of the wings and the fuselage through the airframe. Wind tunnel testing resolved the issue that the new curved edges would solve the problem of RCS. Johnson's concern for the airworthiness of the airframe was also resolved. One of the other numerous problems in solving the curved airframe issue was how to manipulate the titanium into the rounded edges that were needed. Johnson fixed the problem by using "fillets" in triangular shapes. These triangular shapes were epoxy glued onto the airframe. The A-12's chines were created from electrically resistance honeycomb plastic composite with a fiberglass surface that would resist the high heat temperature during flight. The new composite chines would reflect the radar signal rather than absorb it. This also led to the wing "teeth" being fitted into the wings. The metal composite fillets were fixed into the wing via a new epoxy resin.

Perhaps the biggest problem the A-12 faced was the RCS (radar cross section) on the vertical stabilizers. The stabilizers were canted at 15 degrees inward to reduce the reflection. Initially, the test A-12s verticals were made of composite material while the production A-12s were made of metal) however, the USAF and its SR-71 version stayed with the metal not the composite vertical stabilizer.

By the mid- 1960's the A-12 would in fact fit the bill for the new high speed, high altitude aircraft the CIA wanted. However, the new *Archangel* did not please the CIA's Richard Bissell. He was not happy to find out that the new changes had in fact compromised the aircraft's performance. In short, it meant that what Bissell had promised President Eisenhower, in the way of altitude wasn't in the cards anymore. Kelly Johnson was also upset by Bissell's reaction. Johnson proposed to relieve the *Archangel* of 1,000 lbs. in weight and add 2,000 lbs. of fuel back into the load carried. This would bring back the initial target altitude of 91,000 feet. Johnson wrote in his diary:

> *"We have no performance margin left: so this project instead of being 10x as hard as anything we have done, its 12x as hard. The machine matches the design number and is obviously right."*

That comment was the start of the *Archangel* becoming the A-12.

On Jan 26, 1960, Bissell approved the changes and authorized the building of the 12 A-12s. The original quote for the project was $96.6 million. In today's dollars it would cover the cost of about 1/3 of one F-22 Raptor. Yet, this contract was going to cover 12 of the most phenomenal aircraft ever built. The CIA had realized that building the aircraft with the exotic titanium would result in cost overruns. A clause was placed in the contract to cover this eventuality. Over the lifetime of the projects, the A-12 costs were higher than ever expected, sometimes even doubled.

The A-12 was designed to meet a speed of Mach 3.2 (2,064kts or 0.57 miles per second) a range of 4,120 nautical miles and reach altitudes of 84,500 to 91,000 feet. This was faster and 3 miles higher than the U-2. Yet, one of the major problems with the A-12's speed was the enormous heat she generated. Skin temperatures of 900 degrees F. were possible when flying at Mach

3.2. The fuel lubricants and hydraulic fluids that were needed had to be calibrated to support this. In fact, they had to be created, as with almost everything dealing with the Lockheed A-12.

In order to help the process of cooling the aircraft, the A-12 used its fuel as a heat sink to cool various parts of the aircraft components. The engine lubricant used for the engines demanded that they not lose their viscosity at the high temperatures that Mach 3 would bring. Hydraulic fluids became another problem. Johnson, once again, crossed the proverbial "apron" and went over to the white world of the North American Aviation XB-70 Valkyrie bomber, also being built at the same time as the A-12. Johnson used a hydraulic pump from the mammoth XB-70, which also encountered exhaustive high heat at Mach runs.

Titanium became the phrase of the day and it was also the nightmare of the hour for the CIA and the Skunk Works. The B120V titanium had the characteristic strength and was lightweight and resistance to high heat. While it possessed all these great characteristics, it was a beast to work with. The early milled metal was dumped because of the impurities that occurred in the production. The metal was hydrogen embrittled, and if dropped, it would shatter. Eventually, the CIA had to go "out of town" to the USSR (clandestinely) to obtain the initial batch of metal which was pure of hydrogen to start production. Later on, the CIA and Lockheed quietly told the Titanium Metal Corporation that the need for hydrogen pure titanium was an unconditional necessity and TMC had to reconfigure their process. It wasn't the only thing that had to be reconfigured to match the want list for the A-12.

OXCART

Project GUSTO, the design phase soon changed to *Project OXCART,* the final product. This was actually an "inside joke" considering the speed of the A-12. Never had anything so fast been named for something so slow. Both the pilots and the Lockheed staff felt that *OXCART* was a "weighty "nomenclature for such a fast plane. Later on in the program, Jack Weeks, an A-12 pilot, gave her a name equal to her stature: *CYGNUS* after the constellation of the Swan. Weeks even designed the rare *CYGNUS* patch for the rest of the *OXCART* drivers to wear on their low-level flight suits. *OXCART* was now on the CIA books. The rest would soon be Aviation and Reconnaissance history.

Skunk Works

In 1943 at the height of WWII, the Lockheed Advanced Development Projects Company came into being when Lockheed began work on the XP-80 fighter. The XP-80 was created in143 days, 37 days ahead of schedule. The success story of the XP-80 not only had to do with great production management, it had to do with an engineering principle adopted by Kelly Johnson. He decided that the best way to completion was to have all the work done "under one roof." This allowed creativity to pass among the rest of the designers. The designers could freely come together and discuss what was going on. It also allowed the designers to go onto the shop floor to see how their "drawings" were being bent into metal. Johnson worked along the same lines.

The *Skunk Works* actually began its magnificent career in a circus tent, analogous as this is to the way aircraft are sometimes born. When the project for the XP-80 came into being, the Lockheed hangars and facilities were running full bore with fighter/bomber production for the USAAF war effort. What better excuse could someone have for separating him or herself out of the fold? Kelly Johnson rented a circus tent, which would give him the needed security necessary for the new P-80 fighter. As an added precaution for security, Johnson set the tent up near enough to a rather rude smelling plastics factory. Much in the way that Groom Lake was picked for being next to a radioactive bombing range, it sure kept the traffic down and nosy people out of the way.

Lockheed's upper management decided that Johnson could keep his "circus tent" except that it now moved to Building 82 (an old bomber production hangar) in the Lockheed complex and he had to make sure that this new set up didn't take up too much of his official time and duties.

As the "new" *Skunk Works* moved into its new digs, it wasn't much to talk about as far as comfort was concerned. The space as small, tight, stuffed with different types of machines for production. The designers and engineers found themselves in quarters that were small, airless and close. Ben Rich, in his book *"Skunk Works"* describes a rather humorous situation when the hangar doors were opened which added to the eccentric flavor of the place:

> *"When the hangar doors were opened, birds would fly up the stairwell and swoop around the drawing boards and dive bomb the heads of the engineers, knocking themselves silly against the permanently sealed and blacked out windows, which Kelly insisted upon for security."*

This gives a good idea of the just what the place felt like and must of smelled like. As with the U-2 development, Johnson had the designers working back to back at desks where there was little or no privacy. There was no such thing as personal space. What this set up grew was not only brainstorming, but also good-natured humor, teasing and harassment.

This story tells exactly how the *"Skunk Works"* got its name. The *"Skonk-Works"* was actually a place in the Al Capp Cartoon, "Li'L Abner."

A character by the name of "Injun Joe" concocted a poisonous potion, which passed for moonshine. Into this potion, "kickapoo joy juice," anything dead would find its way in, including dead skunks and old shoes and anything else not tacked down. A Lockheed engineer, disgusted with the smell from the plastics factory next door, came to work one day wearing a gas mask. Irv Culver, a Lockheed designer saw this, commiserated with the gas-masked colleague and innocently answered the phone at the circus tent with a "Skonk Works" one famous day. The name went down in Aviation history. Culver too, almost went down in Aviation history since Kelly Johnson "fired" him when he got wind of the little joke. It has been noted that Johnson "fired" Culver and many others of the circus tent crowd just about twice a day anyway, so Culver didn't get too concerned about it. Little did anyone know that the circus tent would evolve into the greatest Black Projects hot-house in aviation history.

In 1973, the official Lockheed skunk *"SeyMore"* was added to the logo. Earlier in the history of this famous design and development section of Lockheed, you would find "Lockheed Advanced Development Company "stamped on drawings and documents. There was never TOP SECRET stamped on anything. This kept down the cost of the project because it kept down the cost of security.

The teams put together by Johnson embraced the problems of thermodynamics, propulsion, stability, control, strength and load issues. By consigning his engineers to a part of the project and keeping all in the same room, Johnson was able to control the developmental phases of the project and shrink the possibility of something getting out of the room. The responsibility for assuring that drawings were put away in the safe every night, was everyone's responsibility. If someone didn't adhere to procedure or forgot, they were very sure to hear about in the morning. Johnson had no patience for poor quality and he made sure that all his engineers understood that. Lockheed workers on this special project knew not to discuss anything about their work outside the office. That meant wives and other family members. There was never a blueprint or piece of paper that was marked "TOP SECRET". It also followed suit with Johnson's favorite saying, "Keep it simple, stupid." This is also known as the "KISS" principle. Skunk Works had become the quintessential black projects symbol, so much so that it is listed in the dictionary as such. Skunk Works gave birth to the idea of stealth on an aircraft, even as early as the A-12 and transcended down to the F-117 Night Hawk. There have been some pretenders to the throne of the Skunk Works, but none have ever taken its place among the annals of aviation history.

AREA 51

Area 51 is such a magical name. No name in the American vernacular inspires more excitement, more paranoia and more hysteria than the name Area 51. There has been so much in the news, tabloids and UFO world about Area 51 that you would think it was just as it was shown in the movie "Independence Day". The president in the movie knew nothing about it, only the

CIA had the knowledge of what was kept there and they weren't telling. It's called "Plausible Denial." Well, as wonderful as the film "Independence Day "was, it didn't expound on the miracles that were being performed at the infamous Area 51. However, it almost told the truth about "plausible denial" because very few in the Washington D.C. world knew anything about what went on out in the desert of Nevada's Lincoln County township. Miracles in aviation, the art of aerial reconnaissance and technology were kept hidden for decades. USAF and contractor husbands didn't tell wives what they did for a living. Wives knew better than to ask. Husbands disappeared for weeks at a time. Commercial jets, which were painted white and otherwise unmarked, left McCarran airport on schedule every Monday morning and came back on Friday nights, no questions asked. Road Runners were running rampant in the desert, except these Road Runners belonged to the 1129th Special Activities Squadron and they didn't say "meep-meep". All of the time, they said nothing at all about what they were doing out there in the Nevada dust. It was truly the stuff that sci-fi or spy novels were made of. However, the "real science fiction" that was happening in the quiet of the desert was years ahead of its time. Aircraft like the U-2 and the A-12 were being born and tasting the air for the first time. They were later to be followed by their dark sisters the F-117 Nighthawk and the B-2 Spirit. There were wonders being created there for the protection of the USA that was in the midst of a deadly Cold War. There is no way that this country could ever repay these silent warriors for what they did and continue to do and how they carried their sacred trust during the Cold War. The aficionados of the Area 51 "alien" brigade would do well to remember that the only aliens that were flying over the Nevada restricted airspace, were the pilots of Red Flag, flying those MiG 21s gotten by "mysterious" means meaning defectors from the USSR. The exotic shaped aircraft the Kelly Johnson and Ben Rich had created had nothing to do with little gray men. It had to do with "blue suiters" that were sheep-dipped into "civilian" pilots, master aircraft designers that were decades ahead of their time and programs that would protect the United States from an enemy's attack.

The legend of Area 51 began much earlier with the beginning of the U-2 program. Even as far back as the "Manhattan Project", the need to conduct projects in secrecy was always an issue. Great care was taken to make sure that no details of the new "project" got out. The Manhattan Project's far reaching security is responsible for the some of the familiar techniques used today such as compartmentalization. This was done to maintain secrecy at the highest levels, that included giving a project the ability to support itself independently away from the eyes of bureaucratic Congress. Since WWII, the CIA and the military services worked feverishly to hide the location of their secret projects. It cost plenty of taxpayer dollars to do that, but as always, the taxpayers along with members of Congress never knew until many years later, if at all.

As Area 51 grew in silence, the birth of the *Cygnus* was imminent. The *Dragon Lady* had moved on into the theater of operations. It was time for the OXCART to take up residence at the place that didn't exist. It was obvious to all working on the OXCART project that it would virtually impossible to test the new aircraft at the Burbank facility where she was being built. The public would have had a field day trying to figure out just what kind of strange aircraft was flying over their backyards. The Lockheed Burbank facility runway could not support the new aircraft. It was too short. This new aircraft would need a runway of at least 8,000 feet. The best possible scenario would be to find a place so out of the way that only the neighborhood avian wildlife would wonder what had taken over their skies. The new place would have to support the incoming aircraft, along with the rather large staff that had been assembled to support her and the weather had to be severe clear and dry. The other hope would be that this place would be near an accommodating Air Force base. In the search for the perfect location, ten Air Force bases were looked at. The bases were closed for budgetary reasons. The site for the OXCART program was not the first choice for the developing and testing of secret aircraft. However, none of them quite fit the criteria that Richard Bissell and Johnson had been looking for. There was one place that did fit the bill. The search for a place to hang a secret hat on, began back at the start of the U-2 project AQUATONE. The place where the U-2 was tested at Groom Lake, had an adjacent area that might just be the right spot. The amenities were not the best, but it had some accommodations for staff. There was some storage capacity but not enough for the new OXCART program and the runway was again too short.

Bissell and Johnson initially could not come to terms regarding the new location. Johnson was not happy with it. Yet, not having much of a choice, Johnson accepted the new spot. New construction started in September of 1960 to accommodate the OXCART program. The day the new construction started was also the day the start of a four-year construction and re-construction for expansion of Area 51 began. The actual redevelopment of the site was called "Project 51". As the old U-2 hangars were refurbished, even the airspace over the site was getting a new stature. It didn't take long for the airspace surrounding the area to expand. August 1, 1961, saw the FAA designate the air space over the Area as restricted. R4804N became the official off limits site for any aircraft roaming the Nevada skies. All airspace was restricted within 440 square miles of the Nellis Air Force range. As the politics surrounded the OXCART project, the area was "unveiling" itself to the eyes of many CIA people involved with the money/security end of the project.

By October 31, 1961, Lyman B. Kirkpatrick, who held the position of CIA Inspector General found himself visiting Area 51. In a September 26-28, 1961, visit to the "DPD Development projects division", Kirkpatrick listed 3 points that he felt should be noted:

1. "The AREA" in my opinion appears to be extremely vulnerable in present security provisions against unauthorized observation.
2. "Second Observation is that "Overall" (OXCART) project has now reached the stage where top management at the Area needs consolidation with clear and precisely defined authority"

3. "The final point on which I wish to comment at this time is the question of survivability of the program's hardware when and if it is employed in operations."

This was just the beginning of the Area 51 security, as we know it today. The USAF and the CIA came up with a joint cover story calling the newly acquired land *"A joint USAF and CIA radar test site"*. One of the biggest headaches on the plate was the runway length. Kelly Johnson was also concerned that runways needed to be smooth with no cracks that would cause undue stress on the A-12 airframe when landing and taking off. Vibration was a deep concern. Another big issue on the list of things to do was the location of where the support crews and pilots were going to live. The U-2 project had left behind some things, but more was needed.

One situation that came up during the initial reconstruction in 1960 was that the construction workers that came in to work at the Area, had quarters staked out in provided surplus trailers. Nevada had laws on construction sites that required the names of all personnel and companies from outside the state that resided in Nevada for more that forty eight hours had to sign in with state officials. It went without saying that given the nature of the project that could really compromise things beyond repair. However, the CIA's attorney general found that Government employees were not liable under this law. Giving all the contractors "appointments" as government consultants, who received no payment for their services, solved the problem. That allowed for no reports to be written and should anything be questioned they would fall back on the fact that they were government employees.

September 1960 saw construction start up with a vengeance. It continued at a frantic pace with double shifts until the middle of 1964. One of the major issues was the runway. The A-12 needed a runway of 8,500 feet. The existing tarmac runway left over from the U-2 program was only 5,000 feet and could not support the weight of the A-12. Between September 7th and November 15th over 25,000 yards of concrete were laid. There is an existing memo, which shows just how difficult it could be to do something like this. In a memo dated November 13, 1961, questions were being asked regarding the necessity of the further extension of runways.: The memo, written by James Cunningham, the Assistant Chief of Development Projects Division, stated that:

> *"I would agree that if in the last analysis we must increase the length of the bloody thing that we should do it sooner than later, I believe that to do it now might well be premature."*

Cunningham goes on to say that:

> *"at least in the testing of the J-75 version, and presumably even during a portion of the testing on the qualified engine, reduced vehicle loads will compensate for the increase in design weight."*

Cunningham goes on to suggest that if the flights were made in the night hours with ambient temperatures within reason, it would solve a multitude of problems. This didn't work in Kelly Johnson's mind, to say the least!

Apparently, there was an issue concerning a safety factor that would be in a maximum gross weight take off in high ambient temperatures. Cunningham made the point of saying that perhaps it would be that day that they would consider:

> *"sacrificing a portion of the lake bed in the manner (redact) suggested."*

The memo states:

> *"runway length is always a compromise including gross weight take off, thrust available, field elevation, ambient temperature and the like.* Cunningham suggested *"they keep a close watch on the gradual weight increase because if we do not, "one of these days v_2 will be out beyond the end of the runway and then we are in trouble."*

Cunningham states:

> *"You are also aware that Kelly will be sensitive about people telling him his head is up and locked on a matter of this sort".*
> *"I would suggest that we quietly ask—redact—to have-redact—give us a cost estimate on the order suggested by-redact—and that we do it quietly or we will hear about it and then we will be in for the usual blast from Kelly Johnson".*

It is obvious that while Kelly Johnson was considered first in the world of aircraft building, he was also considered a bit of an attitude problem, too. This memo showed some of the inner workings that went on during the OXCART program. This would not be the first time the CIA and Johnson bumped heads. It also would not be the first time that politics reared its ugly head.

There were no existing storage facilities for the 500,000 gallons of fuel that would be needed. Many things had been considered which included, pipelines, airlift, truck transport. Truck transport won out as an early solution. One additional good thing that came out of this was that eighteen miles of roadway, which led to the base, was re-surfaced. However, by early 1962, a new tank farm sprung up with a holding capacity of 1,320,000 gallons. In the meantime, while the new tank farm was being built, there were fuel deposits set around the country, California, Eielson AFB, Alaska, Thule AB, Greenland, Kadena AB, Okinawa and Adan, Turkey. Because of the JP-7 requirement for fuel used by the A-12, these tank farms were exclusive for the use of the A-12 and OXCART. Only a few technicians were placed at these different locations to make sure that the fuel was checked for integrity. Other requirements needed to be met regarding the flying paths of the A-12. The FAA was notified that certain of their ATC's (air traffic controllers) were cleared for the project so that there would be no mishaps when reporting that there was a high performance aircraft in the area.

One man, John "Hank" Meiredierk, whose career spanned not only the U-2 program but also the OXCART program, remembered what he found when he arrived at Area 51. Mostly it was Quonset huts and desert sand. Meiredierk said he was very anxious to find out just what OXCART was. While he had been given the job of Operations Director for OXCART, he always felt that Lockheed was looking over his shoulder as the prime contractor. Meiredierk commuted from Washington D.C. to Area 51 and had to attend all the meetings, but really had no power to interject anything into it, at least not at this junction. Colonel Meiredierk admits to having many fights with Colonel Holbury, who was the Area 51 commander. Meiredierk would not give in to Holbury's "outlandish" requests. Everyone else had to go through Meiredierk except when it came to money, security etc. Meiredierk had not flown the A-12, so he was not allowed to dictate tactics, however, he was given his shot to fly the YF-12 and made five touchdowns before landing. Meiredierk gained his golden spurs (a blackbird tradition for pilots) and hung them over the bar in his home with much pride. Meiredierk did monitor the contracting issues and spent many hours at meetings between Lockheed and the USAF and Pratt & Whitney. Meiredierk also remembers the great mess that they had at the Area. There were New York size steaks on Wednesday nights along with plenty of vegetables, along with the great mess; there was also a movie every week. Meiredierk recalled how if the movie wasn't any good, someone would pull the plug. As the projectionist for the night went to figure out what happened, someone would put the projector into reverse. The rest was Area 51 history.

Meiredierk's basic job was to let Headquarters know about the logistics and operational responsibilities for mission plans. He also told HQ bosses what was going on. In short, Meiredierk was the eyes and ears of the Washington overseers of OXCART. The A-12 was still having developmental problems. One of the things that would show up later on was that the A-12 couldn't get supersonic under it started to dive. Meiredierk saw it all; His impression of the A-12 was she was "a fantastic bird". As he observed in his position as "director", he felt the title was a misnomer because his job was to monitor and observe. Meiredierk said that there were plenty of capable people at the Area and he noted that the USAF was "very jealous of their position there." The USAF didn't want any part of their stature diluted. Meiredierk always felt that "they were doing a great job and there was no need to stir the pot". While the pilots for OXCART had been picked, Meiredierk did have a hand in picking the pilots for the SR-71 part of the program. Meiredierk was a one of a kind "Roadrunner" of great distinction. He was a Cold War hero, one of the ones you don't hear about. Meiredierk always carried a big stick and spoke softly. His OXCART/ Cold War-Roadrunner brothers remember him with great affection.

Housing was another issue, not only for the aircraft but also for the staff. Three surplus navy hangars, taken out of storage, were raised on the north side of the new base. The Navy supplied over 100 housing units to support offices and habitation. The older buildings that were left over, were being repaired. Water was needed, so a new well was under construction. This all took a lot of time; however, the basic services were ready as the first A-12 rolled out in August 1961. However, that was one hope that was not fulfilled. The A-12 was not ready.

The Birth of the Archangel

As Area 51 grew to support the new project, the A-12 was not going to be an easy birth. While everything was ready as far as the new facility to support the aircraft, the aircraft was having problems in the delivery room. The A-12, as she is called in the working manuals, was described as a "supersonic, long range, research airplane" which is sort of a tongue in cheek way of saying spying was her mission. The development of the A-12 had the prerequisite that many of the materials needed were produced from scratch. For the aircraft to function at the advertised altitude of 85,000 feet and Mach 3.2, with skin temperatures of 470 to 1,050 degrees Fahrenheit, her skin required a material that could support the heat created by her speed. Thermal expansion, extreme heat and contraction would cause unbearable stress on the airframe and skin. The material that could support all of this had to be titanium. As noted previously, titanium was going to be the crisis of the hour. There were issues regarding what type of hydraulic fluid was used. For instance, anything too temperature resistant would result in a fluid that would be almost solid. Many problems remained to be solved and the engines would not be the least of them.

The A-12's fuselage would be primarily titanium alloy and composite material. Composite material was used on the engine air inlet, rudders, upper and lower inserts to the nose section, nacelle chines, wing leading edges, elevons and tailcone. The inlet spikes incorporated titanium alloy in some portions of the aircraft, while others would be using a titanium alloy substructure with the exterior surfaces and some of the internal parts made of silicone-asbestos-reinforced plastic composite. One of the first major issues confronting the A-12 was the unforeseen issues for metal fabrication. Some of that had to do with the fact that the A-12 was the first aircraft to use a titanium alloy. Alloy is the operative word. Titanium was a remarkable metal; it could be made even more remarkable using the right alloy to support whatever the final outcome for the metal would be. The A-12 was 93% titanium. The A-12 used three types of titanium: A-A110AT (5Al 2.5Sn), B-120VCA (13V 11Cr 2Al) and C120AV (6Al 4V). The A-A110AT contained approximately 5% aluminum and 2.5% tin. B120VCA contained 13% Vanadium, 11% chromium and 3% Aluminum. The C120AV contained 6% aluminum and 4% Vanadium. Corrosion resistant steel was used on the A-12. The alloy was a high temperature application which was called A286. This was a heat treatable alloy that had 15% chromium, 26% nickel, 1% molybdenum and 2% titanium. It could withstand temperatures of 1200 degrees Fahrenheit.

There were two types of nickel alloys used: Rene 41' and Hastalloy"X". These were used in areas of the aircraft that were to sustain high temperatures, most especially around the engine nacelle ejectors. The Rene 41' is a nickel base metal that was alloyed to chromium, iron, molybdenum, cobalt, titanium and aluminum. Rene 41' withstood temperatures up to 1600 degrees Fahrenheit. Hastalloy"X "was a nickel base metal that was alloyed with chromium, iron and molybdenum. This could withstand temperatures of up to 2200 degrees Fahrenheit. The A-12 was made with silicone-asbestos laminates. This material was used in area that operated in 400 degrees to 750 degrees Fahrenheit temperature range. This material was mostly used in the wing and fuselage areas that were installed in the form of replaceable panels.

The A-12's titanium was allergic to many different materials and great care had to be taken to make sure that the aircraft was kept free of them. One of the more serious matters that could occur had to do with stress corrosion cracking. This problem was caused by inter-metallic reactions to certain materials: mercury, mercury amalgams, and cadmium. Should the aircraft metal become contaminated by these elements and then exposed to heat, the contaminated area would become subject to cracking because of the high temperatures and the stresses imposed while flying. Certain compounds in the halogen family like, chlorine, bromine, iodine, fluorine revert to acids when subject to heat. Materials containing any of the halogens listed above could not be used in contact with the titanium. The Teflon and Viton rubbers that were used as fuel tank sealants could be used because they were in a stabilized state, even though they contained fluorine. With the titanium strength came many warnings. It was not an easy metal to work with as the Skunk Works team found out. While titanium could be equal in strength to stainless steel, titanium was lighter, more corrosion resistant and had a high temperature tolerance. However, titanium had its manufacturing problems. The metal was lightweight, had strength, was corrosion resistant and had a high temperature tolerance; however, the manufacturing process was not up to grade. Titanium could be hardened up to 200,000 psi and had an aging process of up to 70 hours, which would bring it to full strength. With the right quality control applications, the aging process was brought down to 40 hours. However, a major problem occurred in the development process.

Titanium processing in the United States did not have the needed purity required. What this meant was that the U.S. produced titanium was hydrogen embrittled. Hydrogen entry into titanium processing can cause a loss of ductile or elastic strength and cause frailness, which encourages cracking known as HIC or hydrogen induced cracking. What all this means is, if a plate of hydrogen embrittled titanium is dropped, it would break into many pieces. This problem became the root of the A-12's construction process. All manufactured titanium delivered to the Lockheed facility for the A-12, via the *Titanium Metals Corporation* was trashed. The existing "heat treating pickling process" seemed to be the cause. That process too, was trashed.

The CIA was becoming desperate, seeing the amount of production time that was being lost. The CIA located an "outside" source until *Titanium Metals Corporation* could fix their problem. The "source" turned out to be none other than the Soviet Union! The Soviet titanium had a higher quality and the USSR also had the only 25,000-pound forging press that was needed to form the basic material. The CIA was able to procure the needed titanium from the Soviet Union under clandestine conditions. The Soviet Union was not cognizant that they were aiding and abetting the aircraft that might one day over fly them. By 1961, the Titanium Metals Corporation executives were informed of the high priority of the project and they soon fixed their problems. While the new titanium helped the building process along, it did not solve some of the other unique problems associated with titanium. Lockheed workers were finding that the titanium was reacting to just about anything it came in contact with. The most identifiable culprits were: cadmium, cadmium plated tools, halogens (chlorine, fluorine, bromine, iodine) lead from pencils, ink from some felt tip pens which would actually eat a hole in a sheet of titanium is under 12 hours. Other things were occurring right under Lockheed's nose. After a good deal of detective work, Lockheed found that some of the welds that were done during the summer months were disintegrating. Their reason for it had to do with the Burbank water supply. During the summer, Burbank water would develop more algae in it because of the heat and humidity. To control that, the municipal water supply would heavily chlorinate the water supply. That water unknowingly was used to wash the titanium plate down and it would eat away at the welds.

Something else was giving Lockheed and Kelly Johnson headaches, the titanium wing extrusions. OXCART deliveries were in peril. A CIA memo dated January 11, 1962, to the Deputy Director of Plans, in which Kelly Johnson had made a comment that his objective was to build five A-12's, one AF-12 during 1962. This would make the initial first flight of the A-12 later than agreed on. The reason for this was that Johnson felt that the tank scaling and nacelle construction would be a limiting aspect. Johnson did not want to run any more fuselage parts because of the very expensive hot forming process. The CIA was right in construing that this would delay the project even more.

Johnson felt that while the project required thousands of feet of extruded metal, which at the time was being processed for just about $19 a foot for a rolled mill product, he felt that there was a chance that it could be done more cheaply. In fact, after some research it was found that the price could be rolled back to $11 a foot. With the reduction in price came a compromise, it would take more time.

One of the other issues titanium brought with it, was the problem of machining and tooling. Drill bits were only holding up for just about 17 holes. Again, after difficult research into the basics of cutting tools, cutter fluids, guides and drill bits, a system was devised that maintained the drill bits for at least 150 holes. After all of this, the airframe would be the next hurdle to climb. It was going to take hand jigging or one by one assembly to keep the production line moving. All thirteen of the A-12s are built by hand. Should you choose to look at an A-12 at a museum or on static display, you will see something unique: they are basically hand built. The usual aircraft assembly line was not for the A-12.

With all the problems that titanium production brought with it, one thing held a distinction. It was the way that titanium processed heat. The hotter that the A-12 would get in flight helped the titanium airframe "recure" itself, which means as the A-12 flew to higher Mach speeds. The heat generated would cause the metal to make itself stronger the same way it was treated in initial metal processing.

The next step would be the large wing panels. There were two separate test panels made to study the thermal effects. Tests showed that when the panels heated to the temperatures that the aircraft would encounter, the panels warped. Notes from the first thermal test on the wing section, Johnson said, *"(It) crumpled up like an old dish rag."* Creating corrugations in the test wing, which controlled the shape and direction of the crumpling, solved the problem. As the titanium heated to Mach temperatures, the corrugations simply deepened and then returned to their original shape when cooled. This test did result in the redesign of the A-12 wing panels, which now incorporated chord wise (longitudinal) corrugations. Stand off clips, attached the panels to the frame, were also devised so that there would be no tearing or separation of the panels. This also guaranteed that there was some heat shielding between any adjacent components. There are some less evident problems which slowed down the production of the A-12. The A-12 carried within her miles of tubes and wiring. As usual with anything electrical, wires were color-coded. Johnson realized that mistakes were made and he decided to investigate. Johnson had color blindness tests run on the Lockheed employees. Amazingly, ten percent of the technicians that worked on the A-12 were colorblind! The Lockheed managers solved the problem by developing odd shaped terminals, which assured that the colorblind technicians would not insert the terminals inaccurately.

Wiring connectors and components had to withstand temperatures above 800 degrees F. along with structural flexing and vibrations and shock. In some cases, it was more than some materials could stand. In other cases, it had to do with carelessness of Lockheed employees. The CIA Office of Special Activities was concerned that the OXCART would not meet its schedule; Meetings with Kelly Johnson on August 3, 1965, were set to discuss the problems with the project. Johnson not only assigned more of his top supervisors to the project, but also decided to go to Area 51 and take charge of the development himself. Johnson's presence made a difference. Kelly's log shows this entry:

> *"I covered many items of a managerial material and design nature. I had meetings with vendors to improve their operations... changed supervisors and had daily talks with them going over in detail all problems on the aircraft...increased the supervision in the electrical group by 50%...I've tightened up the inspection procedures a great deal and made inspections stick. It appears that the problems are 1/3 due to bum engineering. The addition of so many systems to the A-12 has greatly complicated the problems but we did solve the overall problem."*

Johnson got onsite management back on schedule.

It was not just the wires, wing panels and drill bits that plagued the A-12 production. Something simply taken for granted by any normal aircraft development, like hydraulic fluid, was just another bump in the road for Kelly Johnson. Normal hydraulic fluid would not work for the A-12, due to the extraordinary heat conditions. The A-12 needed a hydraulic fluid that would operate at 600 degrees Fahrenheit. Johnson looked over to the XB-70 Valkyrie program for some help. As late as August 14, 1964 Johnson in his diary noted:

> *"Fred Ball of ASD and Ed Dawson of North American came here to discuss hydraulic problems on the B-70. I am amazed to find they built no hydraulic mockup whatsoever and they are into troubles that we solved in 1961. Incidentally, I showed Dawson a letter I had written to General Ascani in 1961, pointing out these problems."*

Johnson began contacting various manufacturers for a hydraulic fluid that would be compatible with the A-12. He was not having much success. One sample arrived at Lockheed in a canvas bag, a crystalline material that would work as a hydraulic fluid when heated to temperatures over 960 degrees. Since it was a solid, it was evident that this was not the answer.

The Pennsylvania State University was contacted for help. The scientists there designed a workable solution that merged some seven chemicals into a mix that would sustain stability at high as well as normal temperature. High temperature stress caused many other issues with components for the A-12. In place of the usual leather gaskets and rubber o-rings, stainless steel was used.

The fuel tank sealant was produced by Lockheed. The sealant when exposed to cold temperatures, however, would revert and turn into something similar to a watery putty. In essence, when the aircraft would be in flight and heated, the fuel tank components would seal via expansion. On the ground and cooled, the tanks would leak without mercy. The problem was never rectified, and extra fuel was simply factored into fueling and storage decisions.

As late as March 1962 found Kelly Johnson once again looking over the fence at the XB-70 Valkyrie project. In his logbook Johnson noted:

> *"March 12, 1962—it appears that our problem with Viton shows that the material planned for the B-70 is no good, either. Sent information and a can of our sealant to Wright Field for use by (General Fred) Ascani (B-70 program director) to help the B-70."*

When the issue of finding the right hydraulic fluid was finally accomplished, Kelly Johnson went over to the XB-70 hangar, once again. Johnson modified a pump that was designed for the XB-70 into a pump for A-12 use. It is so interesting to see the melding of technologies of these two aircraft, one on the white side of the apron and the other on the black side, both of them having such different missions and similar problems. Testing of the A-12's electrical systems opened up another bag of tricks for the Lockheed engineers to solve. High altitudes or vibration brought many of these problems on. One most troubling problem occurred with the transducers controlling the inlet spike. The problem was so severe that the Skunk Works developed a high temperature adaptation of Kevlar, which was wrapped with asbestos in the high heat areas.

With all of the initial issues that the OXCART program faced, it is a solid wonder she was built so well. When you consider that all of it was produced for the first time, the mind bending that had to have occurred to meet every one of the small crises that emerged is a part of an engineering legend to be sure.

This is an engine test for the A-12 Blackbird at Area 51. The aircraft is still in bare metal and has not been painted the signature black. (Lockheed)

Building the RCS (Radar Cross Section) model of the A-12 at the Lockheed Burbank Plant. (Lockheed)

Clarence "Kelly" Johnson, the genius behind the Lockheed, Blackbirds and many other amazing aircraft. (Lockheed)

The 100th flight of the A-12 #121 at Area 51 January 24, 1964. (Roadrunners Internationale Collection)

Jeannette Remak and Joseph Ventolo, Jr.

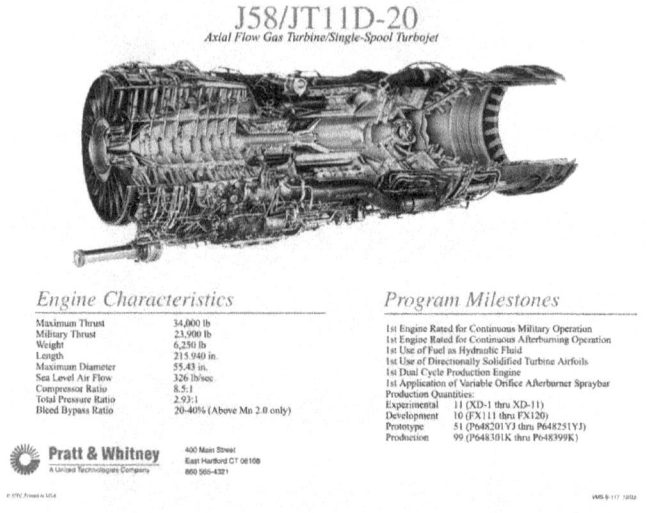

Breakdown of the Pratt and Whitney J-58 Engine which was the literal heart of the Blackbirds. (Pratt & Whitney)

A-12 #121 on first flight at Area 51 in a touch and go on the runway. (Lockheed)

Hidden carefully under a canvas constructed trailer the first A-12 is on the long, lonely road to her new home at Area 51 in Nevada. (Lockheed)

Only half of the A-12 is visible in this rare shot of the aircraft in their Area 51 Hangar. The reason for the half view could be because of the "White Room" used to remove the film pallets for processing. (Lockheed)

An early wind tunnel model for the A-12. (Lockheed)

In the Lockheed Burbank plant, they are creating the transport that will haul the A-12 out to the Area 51 complex. Behind the curtain on the left the YF-12 was being created out of sight of the A-12s that were on the floor. The USAF was particular that no one knew what they were getting. (Lockheed)

Black Lightning

Laying down the runway at Area 51 under very strict regulations so as to keep the vibrations of the A-12 to a minimum. (Roadrunners Internationale)

CIA pilot Frank Murray with his A-12 at the Area 51 base.
(Roadrunners Internationale Collection)

CIA pilot Dennis Sullivan with his A-12. He later became a Brigadier General. (Roadrunners Internationale Collection)

Tony LeVier Chief Test Pilot for Lockheed. (Lockheed)

CIA pilot Jack Weeks was lost over the Philippine Sea on June 4, 1968, in a routine engine check in the A-12. (Roadrunners Internationale Collection)

The first of the U-2s #001 at Groom Lake, Nevada. (Lockheed)

Evolution of A-12

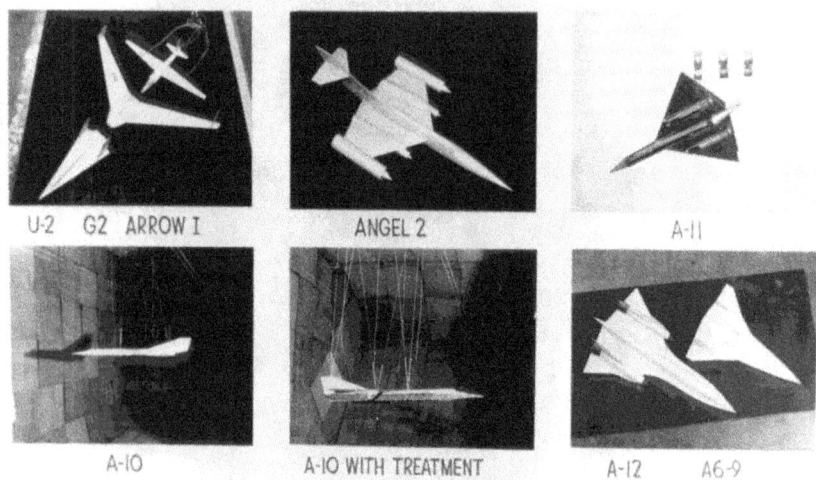

Compilation of the various phases of the A-12. (Lockheed)

Aerial view of the Lockheed plant in Burbank California circa 1960s. (Lockheed)

Article #121 taking off at Area 51. (Lockheed)

A-12 #121 refueling from a KC-135 tanker with an F-104 chase plane in attendance. (Lockheed)

Construction of Article# 122-the second test flight model for the A-12. (Lockheed)

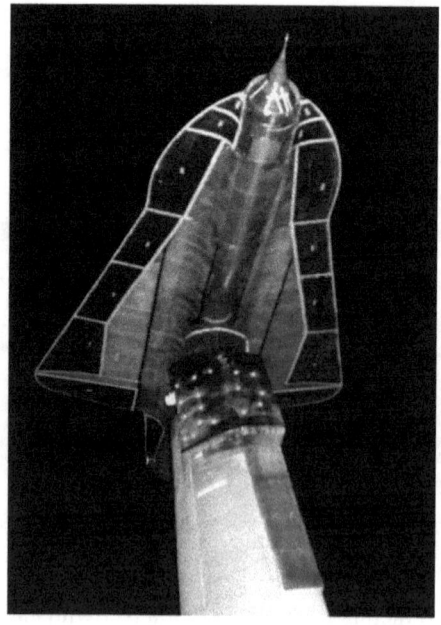

A very early model of the D-21 on the RCS pole at Area 51. (Lockheed)

A J-58 engine on the test stand at Pratt and Whitney. (Pratt and Whitney)

The trailers used to transport the A-12 secretly to Area 51. (Lockheed)

All of the A-12s and YF-12s lined up at Area 51. (Lockheed)

A-12 CIA Article #121- tail# 60-6924 in flight. (Lockheed)

A-12s cocooned after service at Palmdale plant. (Lockheed)

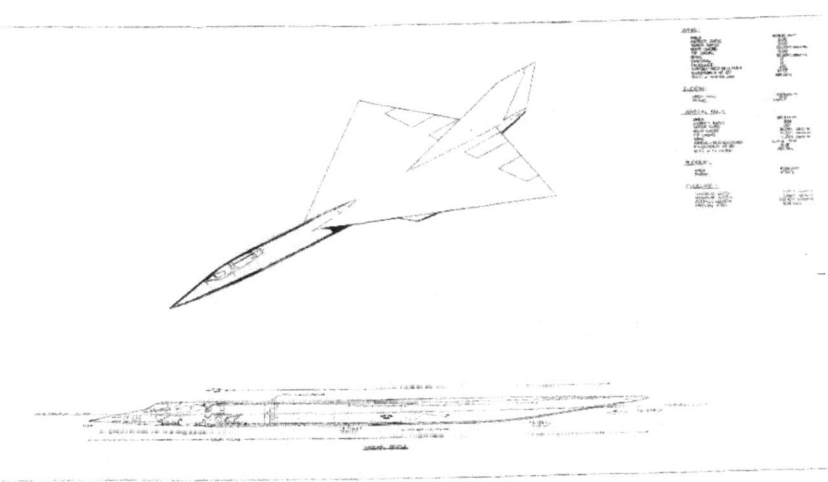

Line art for the A-11 with specs. (Lockheed)

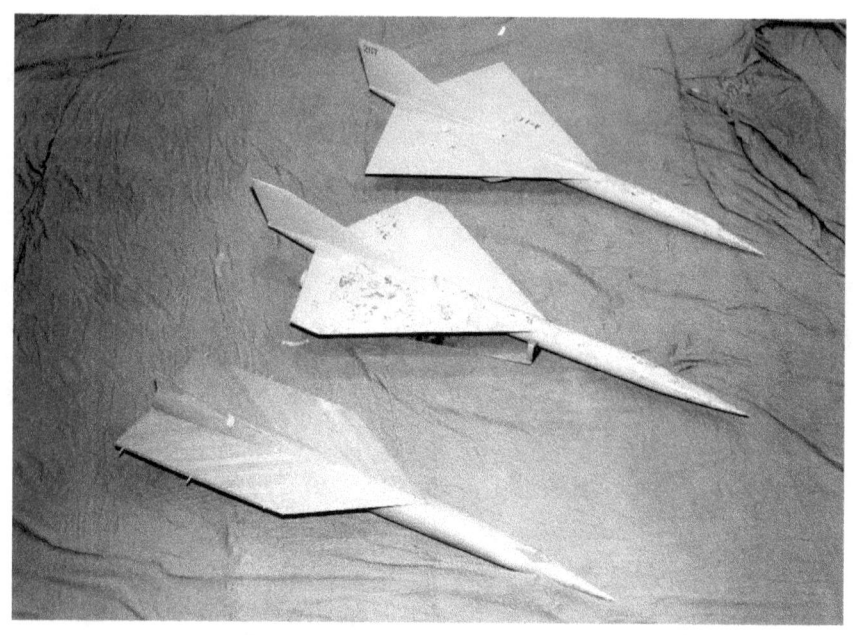

Wind tunnel models of the A-11. (Lockheed)

Bottom construction of chine area on the A-12. (Lockheed)

Cutting the wedge-shaped panels for the A-12. (Lockheed)

YF-12 #606934 in flight. Note the ventral fin in the lower aft fuselage, used for stabilization when launching the AIM 47 missile. (Lockheed)

Lining up the D-21 for a fit on the M-21 mother ship. (Lockheed)

D-21 drone of "TAGBOARD" Program. (Lockheed)

SR-71 first flight chased by an F-104 Starfighter. (USAF)

Kelly Johnson on his first and only ride in one of his Blackbirds the A-12 Trainer #606927 known as the "Titanium Goose". (Lockheed)

The Perkin-Elmer Type 1 camera used in the A-12. (Author Collection)

The Kodak Type II camera used for the A-12 Blackbird. (Author Collection)

Sunrise at Edwards AFB, California for the SR-71B # 956. (Lockheed)

The D-21 drones under the wings of a B-52 Mothership. This was for the "Captain Hook" program. (Lockheed)

The SR-71 being tanked up with liquid nitrogen as an inert filler for the JP-7 fuel. (USAF)

A-12 #606925 or CIA Article #122 on the RCS pole at Area 51. (Lockheed)

Loading the D-21 onto the Marquardt booster at Area 51 Hangar. (Lockheed/Author Collection)

The Construction floor at the Lockheed Burbank plant, just a hub of activity building Blackbirds. (Lockheed)

Jeannette Remak and Joseph Ventolo, Jr.

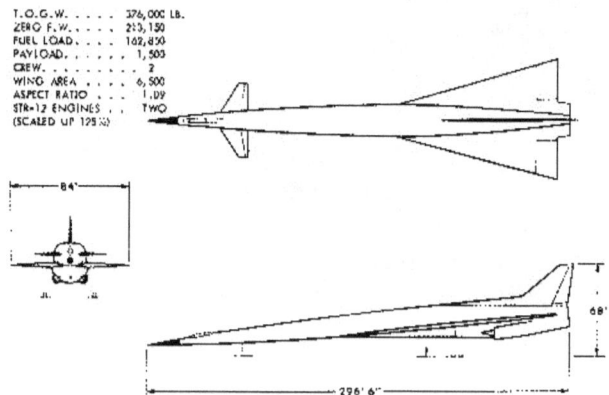

The Lockheed CL-400 planform with specs. The CL-400 was the start of what would be the A-12. (Lockheed)

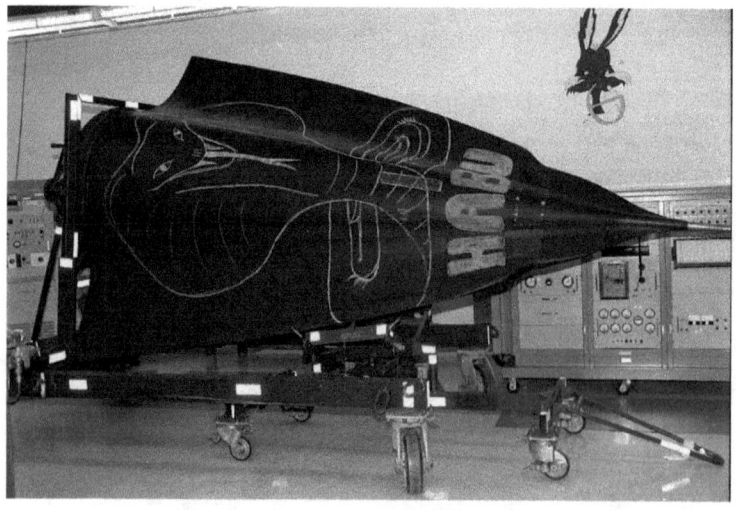

The SR-71 nose was interchangeable to allow for different packages and sensors. This "creation" of the HABU snake on the nose of this SR-71 is just perfect! (Author Collection)

SR-71 #972, which was the Lockheed test aircraft, you will note the Lockheed Skunk on her tail, is just airborne in full afterburner, with shock diamonds trailing behind those J-58 engines. (Lockheed)

The SR-71 in the early morning, cold hours being preflighted for a day's work for NASA at Edwards AFB, California. (NASA)

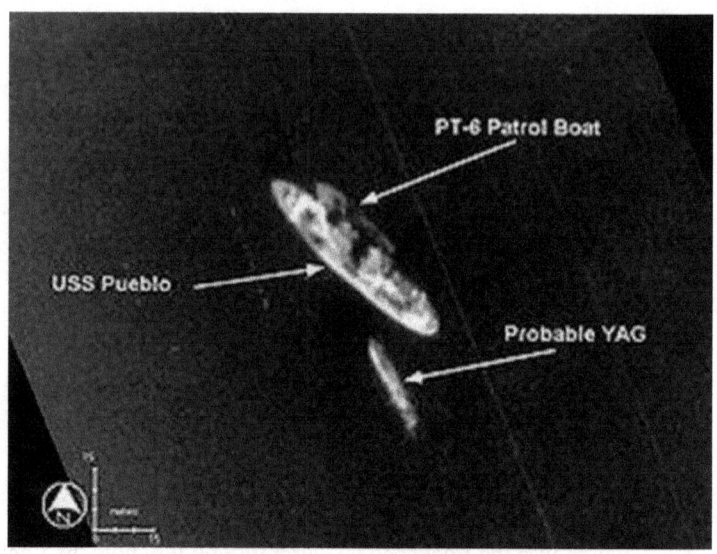

A rare image of the film taken by CIA pilot Jack Weeks of the USS PUEBLO in Wonson Harbor after her abduction by the North Koreans.
The mission flew on January 27, 1968. (CIA)

The HABU. A name given to the SR-71 after a snake that lives only in Okinawa. It only comes out and night and its bite is deadly. Detachment 1 -9th Strategic Reconnaissance Wing. (USAF)

A view from the SR-71 window 100,000 feet altitude. (Lockheed)

A very early view from Area 51 of the YF-12 in test bare metal. This was the first flight and landing with chute deployed. (Lockheed)

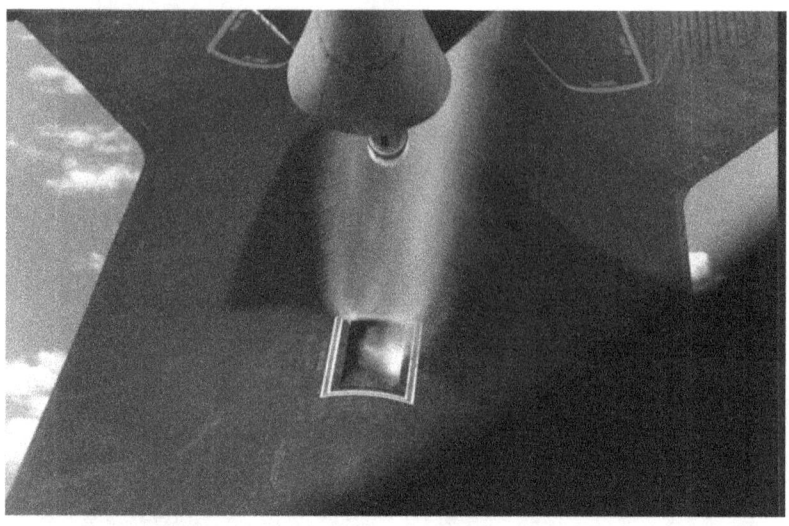

One of the best shots of a boom detaching from an SR-71. You can actually see the fuel spray as the boom pulls out. This photo taken by KC-135 tanker crewman Kevin Westling. (Kevin Westling)

A promo shot of the YF-12 with the AIM-47 Falcon missile. (Lockheed)

Black Lightning

Construction of A-12 #123 at the Lockheed Burbank Plant. (Lockheed)

This amazing photo was taken of the YF-12 606935 as she was making a final pass before landing at Wright-Patterson AFB in Dayton Ohio.
(National Museum of the USAF[tm])

Test Pilot Lou Schalk receiving congratulations from VIPS at Area 51 after the successful 'Maiden" flight of A-12 #121. (Lockheed)

Damage to the D-21 #503 after a failed test attempt. The drone is still mounted on the M-21 mother ship. (Lockheed)

Ben Rich the chief aerodynamicist of Lockheed was known for his work with Kelly Johnson. They were the quintessential team for Aviation and innovative ideas. (Lockheed)

SR-71 #959 in the BIG TAIL configuration. The BIG TAIL stinger was moveable and a 9-foot extension carrying sensors in the stinger. The test proved that performance wasn't hindered by the extension, but little was gained by the extension and sensors. The program was cut Oct. 29, 1976. (Lockheed)

A J-58 salute from the SR-71 at Edwards AFB. (Lockheed)

The remaining D-21s lined up and in spray latex at Davis Monthan AFB, Arizona. (USAF)

With the B-52 mothership above still carrying another D-21, the released D-21 launches on her Marquandt booster engine. (Lockheed)

Building an Enigma

Airframe of the A-12

To say that the A-12's airframe was exotic is an understatement. However, it really was a very conventional semi-monocoque (stressed skin) design, which was made up of longerons, stringers, frames and bulkheads. Most conventional aircraft designs allowed for the skin to act as the central load bearing member. When the load increased, the need for strength to weight ratio changes, hence, longerons or stringers were added to the structure to increase strength. This also allowed for the thickness of the wing to lessen.

However, with larger aircraft, thicker skins were used for better weight to strength ratio. The A-12 utilized A-286 steel which was corrosion resistant. A-286 was comprised of a heat treatable alloy that consisted of 15% chromium, 26% nickel, 1% molybdenum and 2% titanium.

Just like the XB-70, much of the success of the autoclave process was dependent on how well the titanium was kept from the influence of oils and other foreign materials, which would compromise its integrity. As with both aircraft, spot welding initially produced problems on both aircraft.

The unique nose section of the A-12 was pressurized. It held the VOR (VHF Omni Range), glide slope, UHF-DF antenna, the ADF (Automatic Direction Finder) loop, remote compass transmitter, periscope optics, air inlet computer, angle transducer and radio equipment. The other parts of the aircraft, like the air inlet spikes, rudders, upper and lower inserts in the nose section, fuselage, nacelle chines, wing leading and trailing edges, air inlet ducts to the outboard chines and elevons were made of composite material.

The rudders for the A-12 were on the engine nacelles. This was the first aircraft to use this configuration. The rudders were supported on stub fin pivots, made of steel. Each rudder extended some 75 inches above the stub fin. Electro hydraulic assemblies allowed the rudders to move divergently, 20 degrees either way, left or right. The rudders were inwardly canted, to reduce radar signature and served to offset asymmetric yaw in the event of a single engine failure. One of the first attempts at "stealthing" an aircraft began in the 1960's. The A-12 had a high RCS and Johnson was constantly trying to reduce this. One of the ways he succeeded was canting the rudders on the A-12, 15 degrees inward.

Not all A-12s were made alike. The 13 aircraft assigned to the program were numbered with "ARTICLE" numbers for the CIA end of the operation, #121 to #135. Titanium rudders were assigned to aircraft #121, 124, 127, 134, and 135. Other rudders made of high temperature, composite plastic material, were assigned to aircraft #122, 123, 125 and #133. The metal rudders were built and supported by a wing box section in the mid fuselage, leading edge. Trailing edges and tips were built into the central box section. The composite or plastic rudders had basic frames of titanium alloy, while the secondary members, including ribs, spars and exterior surface panels were made of bonded silicone asbestos and reinforced plastic materials.

The blended edges of the chines gave the A-12 the "U-shaped" concave look on the fuselage leading edge. This was a unique design, which made the A-12 look like an aerodynamically charged dart. The sharply pointed nose with the pitot-static and alpha beta mast blended into the forward tip of the nose section. If anyone has ever looked at an avian blackbird's beak, most especially the raven, the comparison of the nose section lines and the beak of a raven is uncanny.

The wing of the A-12 is a design never before seen. The wing itself is double-delta, fully cantilevered and very thin. The wing also incorporates both the inboard and outboard elevons. That basic structure does what both the ailerons and the elevators would do. The wing also does double duty as a fuel cell, between the leading edge and the elevons support beams. The fuel cell also travels from mid wing to mid wing span wise. By the mid span of each wing, the wing supports an engine nacelle. The upper wing panels above the fuel cell are removable. The external surface of the wing panels are corrugated and beaded which permit the skin and structure to expand and contract under temperature changes. This design was incorporated due to the first testing of the wing panels. The panels curled up like damp dishrags under heat. This allowed the panels to deepen and controlled the crumpling effect.

The May 1961 delivery date for the A-12 had slipped to August. One of the big issues had to do with the Pratt & Whitney engines. They were not ready. Kelly Johnson told the CIA:

> *"Schedules are in jeopardy on two fronts. One is the assembly of the wing and the other is in satisfactory development of the engine. Our evaluation shows that each of these programs is from three to four months behind the current schedule."*

Richard Bissell of the CIA was not pleased with this. His message to Johnson was this:

> *'I have learned of your expected additional delay in this first flight from 30 August to 1 December 1961. This news is extremely shocking on top of our previous slippage from May to August and my understanding as of our meeting 19 December that the titanium extrusion problems were essentially overcome. I trust this is the last of such disappointments short of a severe earthquake in Burbank".*

Bissell made the situation very clear to Johnson. No more delays would be tolerated. However, the problems still existed. A huge part of the problem had to do with the Pratt & Whitney J-58 engines and the weight, power and delivery date of the engines. With the dates for the first flight pushed back further and further, completion time for the engines were critical. Aircraft #121's finish date had slipped from December 22, 1961, to February 27, 1962. Johnson finally decided that the Pratt & Whitney J-75 engine would be substituted for flight test.

Until the J-58 could pick up some production speed and the J-75 already endemic to the U-2, production wouldn't be a problem. At least the A-12 could get to 50,000 ft. of altitude and Mach 1.6. With this decision made, the test programs were finalized. Things started to build up at the Area by the spring of 1962. Much of the support teams and material had arrived. Eight F-101's for training, two T-33's for proficiency flying, C-130 for cargo and a U-3A for the administrative crews travel, one helicopter for search and rescue and a Cessna 130 for any incoming subcontractor use. The F-104 Starfighter would be used as the A-12 chase plane. Other critical components, including the inertial navigation system, stability augmentation system, air induction system and pilot environment equipment, all developed for the program were working in normal flight test. The ARC 50 communication system for tanker rendezvous was also flight- tested successfully.

Tanker support facilities at overseas bases were under construction. Foreign object damage resulted in 20 J-58's engine removals and extensive aircraft nacelle modifications suspended. All Mach number extension flights between April 5 and May 17, 1963, had corrective measures taken and no more removals made. Duct roughness was most severe at Mach 2, and one of the more critical problems. Modifications were made to the flight test aircraft. In some cases, it reduced severity of roughness. Yet, complete identification of the sources of roughness were not known. Maintenance problems, involving fuel and hydraulic leaks, false fire warnings, malfunction of instruments and electrical systems had delayed the flight test program.

OXCART Vehicle RCS Reduction

Lockheed tried to reduce A-12 RCS (radar cross section) through application of certain materials used in fabrication process. (i.e. composites). Two specific projects, KEMPSTER and EMERALD were brought in to accomplish protection for the aircraft via electronic ion jammer systems. KEMPSTER and EMERALD were two in a number studies and projects that were underway in conjunction with the Office of Scientific Development.

This office along with other departments were looking into the development of a complex analysis of Soviet defensive systems to provide security.

KEMPSTER- A-B was an RCS (radar cross section) device that utilized different devices on A-12. KEMPSTER generated an electron cloud that could absorb radar frequencies. The equipment was held in the Q bay of the A-12. The ion guns created a stream of ionized particles that materialized from small holes in the chines which was just ahead of the air inlets. The concept was solid and had the A-12 remained in service and not been cancelled for the SR-71, all A-12s would have carried the system. In a restoration process for the A-12 #122, at the Intrepid Museum, the author found the small holes in the chine at station #715 on the aircraft denoting the place where KEMPSTER had been installed.

EMERALD This program was the development of device which would generate a seeded plasma electric arc for the purpose of absorption of radiation. EMERALD was not continued.

High speed flight and heat:

One of the main issues with high speed flight was heat build up. This is a problem the A-12 managed with the corrugated panel. This panel allowed for expansion and contraction of the skin. The panels were located above and below the fuel cells and between the leading edges and the elevon support beam ranging from midwing to midwing. The inner and outer wings are multispar construction with stiffened panels attaching to crosswise beams. The triangular (V) shaped sections made up the leading and trailing edge of the wing. Those wedge shaped sections were filled with composite plastic that absorbed and dispersed radar energy to inhibit the return of the radar signal. Composite plastic was made from asbestos silicone laminate and was the same as used in the chine and control surfaces. Aircraft #121 and 124 differed from the others in that the fillet panel's skin and hot section were made of A100AT titanium alloy instead of silicone asbestos. The asbestos components would eventually become an environmental issue during restoration later on long after the A-12's retired from service and were placed in museums.

Fuel system:

It was obvious from the onset of this concept that a new type of fuel had to be devised. The fuel would have to have a chemical lubricant that could meet the temperatures that the A-12 would dish out. Pratt & Whitney teamed up with Ashland, Shell and Monsanto Corporation to develop the new fluids. The A-12 needed adequate fuel to reach the unprecedented speeds and sustain long reconnaissance flights over a broad range of temperatures. Weight and the volume of the fuel had to be contained in a way that did not undermine the aircraft's ability aerodynamically or small radar cross-section. Kelly Johnson and his engineers designed the fuel system for the A-12 that consisted of 6 tanks and wing fuel cells that could hold 69,000 lbs. of fuel. The fuel was used in the heat sink system.

The titanium airframe would heat to more than 500 degrees F. Lockheed made exceptions for expansion. When the aircraft was standing, cold metal caused the expansion joints to be at their widest. These gaps were sealed with pliant sealant but the fuel acted as a very strong reducing agent that softened the sealant causing leaks. When the first load of fuel went into the A-12, 68 leaks developed in fuel tanks, causing shower of fuel all over the floor of the hanger. Lockheed had no choice but to strip the tanks, which was an agonizing job, and replace all the sealant. The process required the sealant to have 4 curing cycles, each at different temperatures over 30 to 54 hours. Engineers at Lockheed never found a sealant that remained elastic enough to expand and contract sufficiently. Since the tanks continued to leak, the aircraft was partially fueled to get airborne, and then would rendezvous with a tanker to top off with fuel and climb to operations altitude. As the aircraft flew and generated heat, the tanks expanded and sealed themselves. The problem of the leaking tanks was unsolvable and it was "characterized" ever after as "venting".

Fuel supply for the fuel feed system was controlled within the 6 integral tanks that adjoined each other with exception of the #4 and #5 tanks. These tanks were separated with a dry bay area that was used as a wheel well for the main landing gear. Sixteen electrically operated, submerged fuel pumps, supplied fuel to a left and right fuel manifold. The fuel tanks #1 and #4 each had 4 fuel booster pumps and tanks #2-3-5 have 2 pumps each. Two fuel booster pumps in tanks #1- 2- 3- 4 delivered fuel to the left fuel feed manifold and feed the left engine. Tanks #1 -4 -5 delivered fuel to the right engine. Float switches mounted in the fuel tank distributed fuel to control the aircraft's center of gravity. The fuel supply was carried in 6 integral tanks that were sealed and used most of the fuselage volume. They are numbered 1 thru 6. Tanks #1-2- 3 -4 were contained in the forward tanks (forward of the main landing gear) and tanks #5-6 were in the left fuselage section. In addition to the fuselage section, #4 -5 -6 extended to the outboard and into the wing area to wing station 72L and 72R. A major portion of the fuel supply system component is located inside the fuel tanks.

Fuel Specifications

The fuel created and used exclusively for the Blackbirds was originally designated SK-1 (PWA-523C). It was also known as JP- 7and Mil-T-38219. It was exclusively used with the A-12 and later the SR-71 and the YF-12. JP-7 was made up of hydrocarbons, alkenes, cyclobanes, alkybenzenes with flurocarbons added to increase the fuel supply and to feed the fuel system contained within the 6 tanks of the A-12. This fuel was similar to kerosene and was handled like regular JP 4-5. SK-1 fuel had the following characteristics at sea level: Fuel was mixed with Pratt & Whitney approved source of PS567A lubricity additive.

       Flashpoint: 150 degrees minimum
       Initial boil point: 375 degrees F. min.
       Freeze point; -40 degrees F.
       Luminometer: 100 min (brightness of flame)
       Viscosity: -30 degrees F: 15 c max
       Gravity degrees API: 47 to 53

Specific gravity: -767 to 793 60degrees/66 degrees F.

JP-7 was unusual in that it is not a distillate fuel, but created by blending stocks in order to have a very low <3% concentration of aromatic hydrocarbons and almost no sulfur oxygen or nitrogen impurities. It was specified MIL-Dtl-38219. JP- 7 had a low vapor pressure and high thermal oxidation stability. JP-7 operated in a wide range of temperatures from near freezing at high altitudes to high temperatures from the airframe and engine parts that cooled. Its volatility was low to make it flash resistant even at high temperatures, because of enormous amounts of heat generated in-flight. JP-7 was safer than regular jet fuel and could not be ignited by flames or sparks. When flying the A-12 at high speed, part of the fuel supply was used as a intermediate to absorb heat. This heat dissipation capability is required to keep the temperature with in operating limits for certain components such as the hydraulics system, air conditioning, engine accessories drive and engine oil. The heat sink system is dual in all respects. One system was plumbed to left engine fuel lines and one to the right. The fuel was routed to various heat exchangers and after providing cooling it was then returned to the engine for burning or to the fuel tanks for cooling. Each fuel heat sink system, one right and left, had a circulatory pump engine, remote gearbox, exchanger, and mixing valve.

Inlet System

The A-12's engine air inlet system was one the most difficult challenges of the aircraft's design. The air flow into the engines had to be closely controlled to provide the proper specific mass velocity and pressure to keep the engines functioning correctly. Correct airflow depended on the A-12's speed, altitude and acceleration at any particular moment. The inlet spike controls consisted of bypass door control and high Mach restart provision (shock expulsion system). The spike and emergency door (N2 nitrogen) system aft bypass door and convergent/divergent ejector system.

The air entered the engine through the inlet assembly and was routed through the duct to the engine compressor face. Boundary layer control was provided for the spike and inlet duct by the use of porous bleed section, at the point of maximum diameter of the inlet duct. The air inlet was designed to provide the engine with subsonic airflow during supersonic flight. It consisted of a spike and bypass door system for each engine. The spike itself traveled on tracks that were attached to a fixed center body, secured to the duct wall by four struts. The bypass door would open and close to stabilize the normal shock wave in the duct wall along a defined schedule. The aft bypass door was installed in the inlet duct at the engine face. These doors opened to unload excess air flow during certain flight conditions and were manually operated. The spike in the forward part of the nacelle was movable and allowed for the supersonic shock wave to be positioned in the arc of the inlet throat. Movable bypass doors matched the inlet airflow to the engine. This was controlled by an automatic system that positioned the spike and the forward bypass doors so that the inlet duct could maintain prime performance.

The automatic inlet control system (AICS) merged the Mach number with the pitch-yaw sensors, pitot static probe, alpha beta probe, angle transducer, air inlet computer, spike and the forward and aft bypass doors and hydraulic servos. These AICS components were supplemented by boundary layer bleed air bypass doors, hydraulic servos and the ejector in the nacelle aft section. The AICS operated in answer to inputs from the inlet duct and from a total pressure probe located on the duct outer skin. Any disruption in this delicate inlet control system could cause a sudden "unstart" a condition in which an engine instantly losses efficiency and stops producing useable thrust. It was a violent event for the aircraft and the pilot. Unfortunately, in the beginning the Skunk Works engineers often had problems getting the balance right and tried to keep unstarts to a minimum.

Heat Sink

When flying the A-12 at high speed, part of the fuel supply is used as a medium to absorb heat. This heat dissipation capability is required to keep temperatures within operating limits for certain components such as hydraulics system, air conditioning, heat exchangers, engine accessories drive and engine oil. Heat sink system is dual in all respects. One system is plumbed to left engine fuel lines and one to the right. The fuel was routed to various heat exchanges and after providing cooling, it is then returned to engine to be burned or to the fuel tanks for cooling. Each fuel heat sink system on right and left, has a circulatory pump engine, remote gear box, exchangers, mixing valve and temperature limiting (smart) valve. The solenoid heat sink crossed fuel plumbing and the director valve for both the left and right systems. These were installed in the fuel return lines of tanks. Most of the components of the system are located in the wing at lower fillet area, just outboard of main landing gear both right and left. Wheel wells both left and right systems are identical.

LIquid Nitrogen incrting of fuel tanks

The A-12 used a dual liquid nitrogen inerting system. Basic functions for inerting the fuel system would be to maintain a positive pressure (1.5 psi above ambient pressure) with inert nitro at all times in each fuel tank. Pressure removes all oxygen from the tanks preventing possibilities of mixing combustible gases with hot fuel vapor. Analysis of the aircraft showed that nitrogen inerting was good while on the ground, to keep fuel tanks pressurized when engines were not running. This helped to supply replacement volume for fuel. As the aircraft started to climb into ambient conditions of continually lesser pressure, a small amount or no liquid nitrogen would be needed.

Fuel tanks were continually balanced through relief valves in the tail cone, to keep tank differential pressure from ever exceeding 3.5 psi. As the aircraft leveled off, in order to hold adequate tank pressure, no liquid nitrogen was needed. As the aircraft descended for aerial refueling into ambient conditions of increasing pressure, the need for liquid nitrogen would be needed to keep the fuel tanks pressurized 1.5 psi above ambient conditions.

J-58 Engines

The A-12 was powered by two J-58 engines, one in each nacelle.

The J-58 was Pratt & Whitney model number JT-11D-20. This was an axial flow, gas turbine, with 9 stage, single shaft compressor, a can annular combustion chamber and a two stage reaction turbine with afterburners. A *start cart*, which contained two V-8 racing engines, was used to turn the engines over on ground start. There was no pressurized air involved with the start cart. It was used to turn the engines over by mechanical means only.

Due to the high flash point of the JP 7 fuel, triethylborane also known as TEB, had the unusual property of exploding whenever it came in contact with air. It was used to start the engine burn. The ignition system injected the TEB from 16 points in the combustion chamber. When the fuel combined with the TEB and air, it exploded to light the engines. The explosion procedure caused a green flash which later gave the blackbirds the nick name "Green Dragons". The use of the TEB also kept the engine cooling requirement to a minimum.

The Pratt & Whitney J-58 engine was initially designed for the Navy's *Vought F-8 Crusader*, which was cancelled in 1959. The first J-58 was produced in 1956. It was designed to be an afterburning, turbo jet engine at 26,000 lbs. thrust max. takeoff speed, with a dash speed of Mach 3 for a few seconds. That Mach 3 life of a few seconds was thought to be the closest to what was needed for the A-12 system.

The J-58 had stated its life as a conventional ram compressor engine. Afterburners and convergent / divergent exhaust nozzles, were added later. The engines could produce 45,000 lbs. of thrust. To move the A-12 to Mach 3 cruising speed, engineers changed the engine configuration. By-passed air was taken from the 4th stage of the high-pressure compressor and dumped into the afterburner. This produced an efficient ramjet effect, which made the Mach 3 cruising speed a possibility. Early in the development of the J-58, Pratt & Whitney found that its cycle didn't match the inlet or the required thrust at high Mach number operating conditions. Pratt & Whitney decided to build a bleed bypass cycle, that would match the inlet air flow. It corrected the air flow which could now be held constant at a given Mach number, regardless of throttle position. The new bleed bypass cycle also provided more than 20% additional thrust during high Mach operations.

The J-58 had its problems. To resolve these problems, engineers needed additional time in testing. This delayed the testing and the OXCART program, Kelly Johnson wrote in his log:

> *"After a sleepless night, I decided that we should have to try to fly with the J-75 engine, doing everything possible to raise the takeoff power, such as using water injection and higher takeoff temperatures and RPM's."*

Later on in the test program, the A-12 was flown with one J-58 and one J-75 engine. As soon as two J-58's became available, Johnson was finally able to explore what the A-12 could really do. The trainer #124 stayed with the J-75's throughout the program.

Developmental problems of the J-58

There were some monumental developmental problems with the J-58 engine, that were not foreseen by Pratt & Whitney's engineers. As with every new program, there are always issues, but this one almost left the A-12 OXCART in the dust. There were many unexpected problems in the development of such a unique engine. The extreme environmental issue of flight for the A-12 created severe cooling problems for the J-58. The electronics in the engine was kept cool by a fuel-controlled solenoid, which was later added along with a trim motor that was buried inside the engine. Early testing showed that the straight turbo jet cycle was not a good match for the inlet of the A-12. It didn't supply the required thrust in high Mach number operating conditions. To overcome this, Pratt & Whitney invented the bleed by-pass system which could match the inlet air flow required. Another advantage of the cycle was that above Mach 2, the corrected airflow was held constant at given Mach numbers, regardless of throttle positions. The bleed by-pass cycle also provided more than 20% additional thrust during high Mach operations.

Fabrications and materials was also another issue with the J-58. Pratt &Whitney had to form sheet metal from materials never before used in turbine blades. Pratt & Whitney had to learn how to weld it securely. Discs, shafts and other components were fabricated from high strength temperature resistant material to withstand temperatures encountered. Even lubrication pumps were a new development. Newly developed fuel was not only hot but had no lubricity. Small amounts of flurocarbons were added to allow engine pumps and servos to work.

Instrumentation for testing

All the engine testing was done with the IBM 710 (logic computer) and hand held calculators. Can you imagine creating the fastest plane in the world, and it still is at least as far as we know, with a hand held calculator and a logic computer the size of a small room. Today's laptop could have done the job in nth of the time, but I'm sure not with the same accuracy. There is something to be said for "hands on" work, much of it has been lost today due to the new CAD programs that allow designs to happen on the computer screen. However, while this is a cost cutting measure, how much of the intuitive hands on design has been eliminated from aircraft design today.

Engine problems

The J-58 engines wouldn't start much to Pratt & Whitney's horror. That could really bring the development rate of a program down quickly and it did. Engineers found that the small inlet model did not show that the inlet was depressed at starting the J-58. In fact, instead of air flowing out of the compressed 4th stage, through bleed ducts and into the afterburner, it flowed the WRONG WAY! As a temporary measure, Lockheed removed an inlet access panel for ground starts. They later added 2 inch blow in doors. Pratt & Whitney added an engine bleed to the nacelle. This fixed the ground start problem. The blow in door, ejector or convergent/divergent nozzle, was built into part of the engine. Lockheed and Pratt & Whitney thought it would save weight if it was part of the airframe. This worked well as the main wing spar structure had to go around the throat of the ejector. Pratt & Whitney would still be responsible for the nozzle performance and would build a remote gearbox. The reason for Pratt & Whitney was building the gearbox, was that the gearbox vendor had no experience with the materials that needed to be used, or how to manufacture the seals or bearings needed. In short, he had no experience with high temperature fabrication. There was another problem potentially related to the ejector. The aircraft used too much fuel going transonic. Measurements were taken and two more problems were found. The back end of the nacelle was going supersonic way before the aircraft did. The fairing of the aircraft transonic wind tunnel data was not accurate. While figuring out a solution—a pilot in a flight test decided to go transonic at a lower rate of attitude and higher KEAS (knots equivalent air speed). This actually solved the problem. Pratt & Whitney learned not to run the nacelle wind tunnel tests unless the model contained at least a simulation of adjusted aircraft surfaces.

Shifting Gear Box

The gearbox mounts on the engine had started to show heavy wear and tear, not to mention cracks. The drive shaft between the engine and the gearbox showed twisting and heavy spline wear. Pratt & Whitney decided that the location of the gearbox relative to the Mach number was unknown during high Mach flight. Pratt & Whitney resorted to a simple test of putting a stylus on the engine and mounted a scratch plate on the box. They found the gearbox had moved about 4 inches relative to the engine. That was much more than the shaft between the gearbox and engine could take. The problem's solution came by providing a new shaft, which contained a double, universal shaft.

The next problem to rear its ugly head, was the aircraft fuel system plumbing. Immediately ahead of the engine, it started to show fatigue and distortion. Measurements with a fast recorder showed a pressure spike at the engine fuel inlet was going off the scale. Over-pressuring was caused by feedback from the engine hydraulic system. This originally did not show in Lockheed and Pratt & Whitney's tests. Lockheed came up with a fix. They created a high temperature sponge named "football", which was installed in an accumulator ahead of the engines. This reduced the pressure spikes to tolerable levels.

Mounting related problems happened under certain conditions when there was downloading on the wing. At these conditions, the outer half of the nacelle would rotate in the engine and crush the engine plumbing and anything else in the way. Originally, the engine was mounted on a stiff rail, which was on top of the nacelle that had a stabilizer link from the top of the engine rear mount ring to the structure itself. The problem was solved by Pratt & Whitney when they redesigned the mount ring, so that a tangential link could be installed between engines and the outboard side of nacelle. This maintained finite distance between nacelle and engine. There was a minimum of electronics in the engine control system because the electronics would not survive the heat and fuel was too hot to provide cooling. Control adjustments had to be manual (pilot operated vernier trim) to make fine adjustments in EGT exhaust (exhaust gas temperatures) as conditions changed. The pilot was provided with a scale of EGT versus engine inlet temperatures to make required adjustments.

Atmospheric conditions were also encountered. This is a combination of the speed of the aircraft which resulted in changes too fast for pilot to handle. By the time pilot could read the engine inlet temperature and adjusted the air inlet, the temperature had changed. This problem caused inlet unstart conditions (highly reduced inlet flow). To fix the problem Pratt & Whitney proposed to reverse the aircraft EGT by adjusting the temperature signal and adding some additional gadgets to trim automatically. The digital EGT readout was retained in case of failure. This modification worked very well.

Trouble with Unstarts

One of the most confusing problems of high Mach flight was the inlet unstart. Unstarts were a violent buffeting of the aircraft due to the failure of the shock wave that was kicked out of the engine. This problem was solved when Lockheed found that the stability augmentation system slightly over compensated for sudden one-sided drag. Pilots believed that the "wrong" (either port or starboard) side of the aircraft had un-started. The pilot's corrective action only made the situation worse due to being unable to detect which side had unstarted. Oddly, the engine did not blow out. It just sat there and overheated because the inlet airflow was so reduced that the engine minimum flow of fuel was approximately twice that was required. The inlet would not restart until the pilot came down to a much lower altitude and Mach number.

Some of the major areas isolated on this problem were:

a. Manual trimming of the engine.

b. High inconsistent nacelle leakage at the approximately 40:1 pressure ratio.

c. Alpha signal (AOA) forms nose boom to inlet control subject to G loading.

There were considerable improvements to the situation with the fixes made below:

a. Improved sealing on the inlet and bypass doors.

b. Auto trimming for engine installed.

c. De-richment valve with unstart signal installed on engine to protect turbine.

d. Increased area inlet bypass door and addition of aft /bypass door and which e. bypassed inlet air direct to ejector.

f. Added "G" on inlet control.

g. Automated inlet restarts procedure on both inlets.

These improvements eliminated the inlet unstart as a problem. Another benefit was also derived by the ability to use aft inlet door in normal flight, instead of dumping all inlet bypass air overboard. As the air became heated, it passed over the engine to the ejector, instead of going overboard. Drag was substantially reduced. Pratt & Whitney had become obsessed with the problem of hot fuel and hot environment. The problematic issues of sometimes the fuel was cold when the environment was hot and just the opposite, needed to be solved. When this situation of cold fuel and hot environment appeared, the engine fuel control did not read well. To correct this Pratt & Whitney had to insulate the main engine control body from the environment and made all servos and parts respond only to fuel temperatures. Eventually a major design on the controls was a necessity.

Pratt & Whitney spent tons of time coordinating inlet issues. This meant the air conditioning turbine discharge was located 45 degrees on the opposite side. Lockheed built one inlet as a mirror image of the other. The 1200 degrees air conditioner turbine discharge turned out to be the reason that one engine always ran a little faster than the other. Hence, it was no longer a mystery to both companies' engineers. To simulate the stress that the J-58 would have to live through at maximum power (M3.0 @ 90,000 ft.), it was tested in the exhaust of a J75 engine. During the course of this severe type of testing, many of the J-58 problems were solved. Pratt & Whitney had delivered ten J-58 engines to Area 51. The first flight with two J58 engines on an A-12 was January 15, 1963.

Special issues on the J-58

One of the real issues with the A-12 and J-58 combo was that the higher the speed (between M2.4 and 2.6) caused the A-12 shock wave to interfere with the flow to the engine, and lessened engine performance. The solution to this problem was a long, aggravating series of experiments that concluded that the entire air inlet system had to be redesigned. This meant that the air inlet system, which controlled the amount of air admitted into the engine, was redesigned into a new cone shaped projection at the front, which we know as the spike. The spike was designed to move in and out as much as 3 feet in order to capture and contain the air shock produced by the aircraft's high speed penetrating shock wave, from blowing out the inside fire in the engine.

One of the most annoying of all the problems with the engine had to do with foreign object damage or FOD. Lockheed actually took to x-raying and shaking the nacelles to see if there was anything left inside. They also installed screens over various inlets and including workers wearing coveralls with no pockets. One other source of FOD was trash on the runways. The giant J-58 engines acted like huge vacuum cleaners that sucked up everything not tied down while flying down the runway for take off or landing. The spike in the forward part of the nacelle was movable and allowed for the supersonic shock wave to be positioned in the area of the inlet throat. Movable by -pass doors matched the inlet airflow to the engine. They were controlled by an automatic system that positioned the spike and the forward bypass door so that they inlet duct could maintain prime performance.

The automatic inlet control system (AICS) merged Mach number with pitch, your sensors pitot static probe alpha beta probe ,angle transducer, air inlet computer, spike and forward and aft by pass doors, hydraulic servos. These AICS components were supplemented by boundary layer bleeds and air bypass door hydraulic servos. These AICS components were supplemented by boundary layer bleeds and air bypass to the ejectors in the nacelle aft section. The AICS operated in answer to inputs from the inlet duct and from a total pressure probe located on the duct outer skin. Any description in this delicate inlet control system could cause a sudden unstart: a condition in which an engine instantly losses efficiency and stops producing useable thrust. It was a violent event to say the least.

Engine spike assembly

The engine spike assembly is a conical structure located on the center of each nacelle inlet sections. It controls the amount of air going into the engine. The assembly is mounted on longitudinal tracks located on the forward part of the inlet body center. Guides inside the spike lock into the center body and allow the spike to be moved in a forward and aft position. Spike positions were governed by engine air requirements. In subsonic flight, spike position was governed by engine air requirements. In subsonic flight, the spike moves forward in supersonic flight, in subsonic flight the spike moves aft.

Periscope

The periscope system on the A-12, is somewhat similar to the U-2. The U-2 however, has a dome so the pilot could look all around including behind the aircraft to see if he was leaving contrails. On the A-12, there was no dome because any protrusion would cause enormous drag and create additional heat. The BAIRD ATOMIC 6642-1 Periscope System allowed the pilot to see the ground below, which could not be seen from the cockpit. There were two types of fields available. Wide angle: allowed a view of about 85 degrees forward of the NADIR (the point on earth directly below the aircraft) and a narrow field of view that provided coverage of 47 degrees forward of the Nadir. This forward view moved with the aircraft's altitude and attitude. The periscope allowed a view above the aircraft, through the sun compass, and a navigational aid to supplement the other internal navigation systems. When the pilot used the sun compass, he could take a visual fix on the sun and determine the aircraft's true heading.

The periscope system also supported a film projector that projected the map and a data filmstrip onto the periscope's presentation screen. This 35mm filmstrip carried mission data, operational procedure checklists and terrain maps. There were 5 periscope controls and their functions are as follows:

Mirror select handle: 3 position control that was used to select the periscope sun compass or film projector.

Periscope handle: 2 position controls used to select wide or narrow field of view during periscope operation.

Sun compass: 3 position switches used to rotate the sun compass polarizer disc.

Prop rheostat: Used to control the image brightness on the presentation screen during projector ops.

Prom. FWD: rev switch. 3 position switch that controlled the map and data film direction of travel.

The periscope was made of cast and welded magnesium and weighed about 27 lbs. It had focal lens and mirrors. The terrain image was received through a quartz entrance window mounted flush with lower fuselage. The sun compass, of course had a separate viewing window.

Inertial Navigation

The A-12 inertial navigation was one of the most advanced of its time. Up to 16 checkpoints were input into the system, permitting the autopilot to control speed, altitude, true heading, command course, ground speed, distance and geographical position information. Up to 42 destination points with geographical coordinates could be stored before and during flight. At any given time, the altitude, attitude, true heading, ground speed, and position were displayed. Position information could be updated to correct for gyro drift by taking fixes with periscope system.

BIRD WATCHER

While the A-12 was made to travel fast and quiet, she would not travel completely alone. There was still some contact with the ground as she flew. Communication from the plane to the pilot and to the ground crew was essential for monitory system. The A-12 was equipped with a BIRDWATCHER unit located in the aircraft's "E" bay to provide vital information to the pilot and a ground monitor. The BIRDWATCHER unit, although not part of the high frequency (HF) communication system, used the HF transmittal. It monitored many aircraft functions along with equipment systems. If a system reached a preset limit, of if equipment actively was sensed, the BIRDWATCHER keyed the modulated the HF transmitter with a coded signal. The coded signal was a multiplexed sample of each of the monitored items. BIRDWATCHER would trigger 3 short, consecutive 1/2 second burst, each separated by five second of silence. During each 1/2 second burst, the condition of all items monitored along with the aircraft was transmitted back to base. When the BIRDWATCHER was in operation the pilot would hear 3 chirps which corresponded to the 1/2 second burst. BIRDWATCHER didn't key the HF transmitter again until another system limit was reached or it sensed other equipment activate. The receiver operator on the ground monitoring the system could see which system or piece of equipment had triggered to BIRDWATCHER, and could monitor all the systems. There were 40 channels, 32 of which monitored individual aircraft systems. If not for the BIRDWATCHER, no info at all would have been gathered about the accident with #129.

OXCART Avionics

SYSTEM IV: Was a wide band video ELINT receiver and recorder. It was manufactured by the Thompson Romo Woolridge (TRW) Company. There was an inventory of three in the OXCART program. It weighed 70 lbs. It had a frequency cover of 5 bands 50 to 600 MHZ—600 MHZ to 10 GHZ with a time generator. Bandwidth: 30KHZSensistivity: (-45dbm). System IV provided continuous recording within the frequency bands.

BLUE DOG: Was a missile guidance jammer receiver that stored and retransmitted SA-2 "L" band missile guidance commands which provided false commands to the missile during the terminal portion of the intercept. It was manufactured by Silvania USA. There were seven of the systems in OXCART inventory. It weighed approximately 400 lbs. including the chine box. It had the capability to provide false commands to 27 missiles simultaneously. The peak power output was 20,000 watts.

PIN REG: Was a threat warning system, which detected the presence of FANSONG radar tracing the aircraft and provided light indication to the pilot and provided automatic jammer turn on. It was manufactured by Westinghouse. The number of systems in inventory was eight. The weight of the system was 30 lbs. Its frequency range: 2.86Ghz to 3.26Ghz, 4.8 GHZ to 5.26 GHZ. It would sort PRF, scan rate, pulse, width, frequency. It had a sensitivity of (-40DBM).

BIG BLAST: Was a barrage noise jammer, which provided wide band noise jamming to deny range information to FAN SONG radar tracking. This system was turned on automatically by **PIN REG** or **BLUE DOG.** The system was manufactured by Applied Technology Corporation. There were six in the OXCART system. Weight came in at 600 lbs. including the chine box and **PIN REG**. The typical band width (flat to within 1 DMB) 200 Mz each band. Average and peak power output: "S" band: 200 watts "C" band 400 watts.

Configuration for the **OXCART EWS** (electronic warning system) package went something like this:

> **PIN REG:** passive warning system, **BLUE DOG:** active guidance jammer and either **MAD MOTH** as the deception jammer or **BIG BLAST** as the noise jammer. When the **BLUE DOG** and possibly the **BIG BLAST** systems were no longer available in the inventory of the OXCART, the next package would consist of **PIN REG**, System 13C MOD D, which was modified and the improved **MAD**

MOTH. Later configurations might have included EWS available for the SR-71

RED DOG: Was a passive missile indicator using missile guidance commands as indication. It also had optional active transmission of false commands to the missile. As BLUE DOG was not used in the OXCART, there would be sufficient space and weight for System 17/W.

FAN SONG RADAR: Could locate and position radar sites in range and azimuth (angles used to define the apparent position of an object in the sky, relative to a specific observation point) within vulnerable zone. It also provides reference signal for correlation with **RED DOG**. It was in inventory by January 1965 with 2 units in service.

S and C Band: Had the ability to deny target range from FAN SONG to force missile in to a 3 point guidance mode. It entered inventory January 1965 with 2 units in service.

Missile Launch Indicator Radar: This was used to detect missiles approximately 4 seconds after launch while the missile is still in the boost phase. It would identify with Doppler frequency shift. It entered inventory in January of 1965 with 2 units in service.

Equipment Schedules

The ARC-50 refueling rendezvous equipment arrived for OXCART on Oct 15, 1964. All A-12s were equipped.

The signal intercept package: Intercepts and records signals of interest to determine after a flight the extent of how it was tracked. This came into service Oct 1964. Four Units were available.

Landing Gear

The landing gear for the A-12 was the common tricycle type. Each main gear had three wheels on a common axle and multiple disc brake assemblies, while nose gear had two wheels. Retraction was hydraulically and electrically actuated and controlled through a gear control handle on the pilot's left side panel. A failsafe lock prevented accidental retraction and collapse while weight of the aircraft was on the gear. Both of the main gear retracted inboard, which put the wheel tire assembly folded into heat-insulated muffs. This was inside the main gear wheel wells in the fuselage. If the system failed, the pilot could operate the gear manually.

Cockpit

The A-12 cockpit featured a V shaped windshield and was closed and opened, via a clamshell type canopy hinged at the rear. The windshield and canopy carried dual glass assemblies. The outer panels were a single unit glass assembly separated from the laminated inner glass by air space. The configuration also included rain removal and deicing system along with defrosting and defogging systems. Controls in the cockpit, consisted of a conventional control stick and rudder, trim control and system indicators, with warning lights, circuit breakers and the usual realm of cockpit equipment. Pitch and roll were controlled dual cables with a closed loop system for each rudder. Pitch and roll proportioning was handling via mixer systems in the tail cone.

Automatic flight controls system (AFCS)

Automatic flight control systems, (AFCS) included a redundant three-axis stability augmentation system (SAS) both the autopilot and the air data computer (ADC) and a Mach trim tab subsystem. Associated with these systems were the inertial navigation system (INS) flight reference system (FRS) hydraulic servos and the patch trim actuator.

SAS also monitored the AC attitude and provided for control signals relating to the change in altitude for all 3 axis. In the "A" system used on #121 through #130 each axis of the Stability Augmentation System was provided with 2 active channels, A and B. On the "A PLUS" SAS aircraft #131 and up, three channels known as A B and M were active. The autopilot was made for operational performance at mach 3 and 90,000 ft. but it provided satisfactory operation of other conditions as well. The Autopilot was a 2 channel system with a single pitch and a single channel in roll. Both channels were used together but could be used alone.

CAMERAS

The A-12 was also the CIA's new eyes to see with, and the camera systems developed for OXCART were without a doubt some of the most sophisticated. Here, there was a contradiction in the aircraft's purpose, flying at the limits of speed and altitude over one's subject is hardly good for decent photographs. Several prominent experts in optics and photography contributed to the A-12's camera equipment. Dr. Edwin Land dedicated much time and effort just to the US Government, during WWII, in the Army's radiation labs and served later as a leader in the Air Force Advisory Panels. As head of the Technological Capabilities Panel, a group that investigated US Intelligence gathering capability, Land encouraged development of the high attitude reconnaissance aircraft CL-282 which became the U-2. Land would go on to develop the polarizing filter and the instant camera specifically the Polaroid land camera. James Baker perfected the concept for the large cameras, originally developed the U-2 program. Land and Dr. James Killian were also involved in the early conceptual investigations and later helped devise the concept that began the "CORONA PROJECT."

Another man involved with the A-12 camera systems and who aided in the development of the camera itself was Richard Perkins of the Perkin-Elmer Company. Perkin-Elmer had contributed to the designs improved camera, periscopes rangefinders, and bombsights, along with other optical apparatus for the Army Air Force during WWII. His business partner, Charles Elmer, developed some of the optics used in the A-12 camera. Perkin-Elmer is known for its contributions to many other achievements in optics, including other high altitude photo reconnaissance lenses and camera systems and the Hubble telescope.

For Perkin-Elmer constant redesign and modernization was part of the art of developing high altitude reconnaissance systems of cameras and lenses. Some of the concepts used in the A-12 actually came from Richard Perkin interest in astronomy. Perkin-Elmer designed and built a telescope and camera instrument that could photograph celestial object from altitudes about the bulk of the earth's atmosphere. Perkin-Elmer sent its telescopic instrument aloft under an unmanned helium balloon, to drift more than 15 miles high above Minnesota. in September of 1951. When the balloon landed in Iowa, 230 miles away, it was carrying some of the most distinct celestial photos ever made. The photos had no atmospheric impediment—no dust, no smog, haze or clouds.

When the newspapers got hold of the story they wrote:

> "Perkin-Elmer telescope takes photos at an altitude of 81,500 ft. the story also described how the photos were taken with a telescope, hung from a helium filled balloon in free flight and how it was pointed at objects of interest and then held steady long enough to avoid blurring. Perkin-Elmer had dealt with the problems of flying helium filled balloons at 80,000 ft. while maintaining an operational telescope and camera system in sub-zero temperature."

The A-12 carried several different photographic systems. The TYPE I camera built by Perkin-Elmer used a F4.0, 18 inch lens and a 6.6 wide 5,000 ft. supply of film. It could resolve 1140 lines per millimeter and provided a ground resolution of 12 inches. The film transport used a concentric supply and take up system to keep the weight of the film centralized, minimizing any shift in the aircraft's center of gravity. As the film was advanced, a rotating cube mirror replaced a prism for the scanner.

The Perkin-Elmer PE model called the TYPE I was a high ground resolution general stereo camera with F4.0 18 inch lens and used 6.6 inch film. This camera produced pairs of photos with a 71 mile swath and 30% overlap. It had a 5,000 foot roll film supply and cold resolve 140 lines per millimeter with ground resolution of 12 inches. The TYPE I covered a ground swath some 71 miles wide and produced images with a 30% stereo overlap. A thermal barrier between film and lenses was necessary because of the high heat encountered. Most lenses were designed to compensate for high temperatures approximately 98°F. The A-12 in flight temperatures, however could range from –60° to 550°F making an isothermal window mandatory. The TYPE I camera was sealed to the glass and a pump was used to create a vacuum between the camera base and the glass. As a side note, when the A-12 had completed a run, she was sealed in a special hanger in Area 51 in a virtual "clean room" environment because of the film processing requirements of the TYPE I system camera. When the program went operational with Black Shield and the aircraft were stationed in Okinawa, the film was removed and sent to Kodak in Rochester, New York for processing.

The A-12 photo shop hanger had doors that fit tightly around the aircraft, so that all dust could be kept out while film pallets were offloaded. Before entering the shop, technicians had to put on complete clean room gear and go through a high velocity air wash. This procedure was also followed when film was processed at the Okinawa shop where a new facility was built so film could be swapped out overnight. At the time of the OXCART program, there was actually five TYPE 1 cameras in inventory. By the time OCART was phased down, 2 TYPE I cameras of the "A" series were placed in storage.

Due to the complexity of the Perkin-Elmer Type I camera, a second contract was given to Eastman Kodak. The TYPE II camera consisted of two separate panoramic cameras that gave convergent overlapping stereo coverage–and advantage in photographing areas that were partially obscured by clouds. By using a "refractor lens" and two rolls of SO-132 film, the cameras was simple in style and maintenance. However, its ground resolution was not as good as that of Perkin-Elmer TYPE 1.

The TYPE II camera used a 21 inch lens and 8,400 ft. 8" wide film supply. It produced photographic pairs covering a 60 mile swath with a stereo overlap of about 30%. It could resolve 105 lines per millimeter and had a ground resolution of 17 inch. While the Type II camera was designed to run at very high temperatures, it had too many operational problems. The Type II was a given marginally longer focal length for high resolution and better stereo coverage, but to no avail. Another camera would have to be developed.

The TYPE III camera was a modified HYCON B camera similar to the on that flew with Francis Gary Powers U2 when he went down over Sverdlosk USSR. This 36 inch focal length camera (on display at the Smithsonian) was brought on line because the first two systems weren't giving much resolution as was expected. The problem with the Hycon cameras was that it really was not made for the high speeds attained by the A-12. It too suffered mainly because the camera's engineers were never really given the A-12-s specs. In order to protect the A-12 secrecy, HYCON was told it was designing a camera system for another aircraft—the XB-70A Valkyrie.

The Baker designed TYPE IV camera which became known as the "BIG HAMMER" was an advanced version of the Hycon B camera. It used a 48 inch F5.6 lens and 12,000 ft. of 9.5 inch wide film for extremely high resolution spotting. It could resolve 100 lines per millimeter and produced a ground resolution of 8 inches. The camera covered a 41mile swath of ground with 50 % of it ground stereo ground overlap. This camera was difficult for photo analysts, as they had to rotate two huge 6,000 ft. long rolls of film in opposite directions. The Photo Analysts however learned to do this because of the extensive experience with the Hycon B camera. In this camera, the image rotated as the oblique angle increased. This camera was the one deployed to Okinawa just before the entire OXCART program was cancelled. The TYPE IV camera did not require special conditions of extreme cleanliness for processing which made it more suitable for advance deployment. No long axis camera was ever used on the A-12 as their size created too many installation difficulties. The aerial film for this camera was Kodak type 3414 with an ASA film speed of 6. That was very slow film but it was necessary to achieve the high resolution required for the reconnaissance operation. Film in general, the slower the speed the greater the resolution. Because of slow film speed and the high speed attained by the aircraft, image stabilizers had to be built into each camera head. There were initially five "C" series cameras in the OXCART inventory. HYCON was also responsible for the more compact camera that was installed in the D21 drone. There were 2 of the Type IV camera in the Oxcart inventory. Both were test flown and were operational. There was a third camera that was scheduled for test flight validation in January of 1968. The first summation included test flights at Mach 3 and 80,000 ft. and twenty two operational missions.

"Scope Crown E" program was developed as a camera package evaluation route. The resolution targets at Phoenix Arizona and Area 51 were covered and the route also had an over water air refueling arc 450 nautical miles off the California coast. That route was flown first on June 1967. Later on in the A-12 history with the inception of Black Shield, the Type I camera was used for all 22 missions with results bordering on good to excellent. There was only one camera malfunction in 22 Black Shield missions. An important limiter on the camera's quality was the quartz window through which it was aimed. This window had to be manufactured so that there was no temperature unevenness throughout, and it needed to tolerate the high temperatures generated by Mach 3 flight. It took almost three years and about $2 million to find an effective method of manufacturing the window. Finally, the glass used on the Type IV cameras was sourced from West Germany after many failed attempts to manufacture glass of adequate quality in the US. This glass was fused to the metal frame by a process that used high frequency sound waves.

Equipped with its sophisticated cameras, the A-12 produced some of the finest aircraft reconnaissance photos ever taken. It could cover three times more area than the SR-71. The A-12 also performed marginally better, flying 2,000 to 3,000 ft. higher and with a speed that appealed M3.3 compared to SR-71 M3.1

A CIA report issued Feb 19, 1964, stated that camera systems 1A and 1B were being used in flight test status and were showing gradual improvement. The improvement apparently was due to retrofits that had been incorporated.

The TYPE IC camera system was to be delivered to Area 51 on Feb15, 1964. Two type II camera systems were also in flight test status, having demonstrated design goals within the air speed and altitude limits that were flown up to that date.

There were more than 50 photographic test flights flown but proof of the cameras utility at higher speeds and altitudes had to wait until Project Skylark was started when additional fixes for speed an altitude were incorporated.

A-12 camera comparison:

Type I: offered the best resolution but was very complex and less reliable.

Type II: Had a lower ground resolution than the Type I but high reliability.

Type III: Considered a back up system.

Type IV: had good resolution and didn't have excessive maintenance or processing requirements.

In a March 13, 1964, memo, there was an announcement of the OXCART camera systems:

Two camera summaries:

1. The 115A camera built by Perkin- Eastman was known as the Type I camera.

2. The 118A camera systems built by Hycon as known as the Type IV camera and also HR-333. The A 12 versus the SR-71 as a stable platform, the location of the A-12 camera is in the Q bay behind the pilot as compared to the other locations (chine bays, nose etc.) in

the SR71 contributed to platform stability since aerodynamics and environmental effects are considerably reduced. The overall effect of stability can be seen in the quality of the photos produces.

SLR: Side Looking Radar

The A-12 had the capacity to use side looking radar and achieved resolutions of 12-21 feet in non-operational testing, just prior to mothballing the entire fleet. The primary factor to recognize is that the A-12 had a single sensor capability. When the side looking radar was used conventional photography and infrared photography can not be employed during the same mission. While you can look at all that is described here about the A-12, you really can't put it together until you take a look at this magnificent aircraft.

Considering the time period and the materials, how she was put together and her enormous engines, it really is hard to believe that this was done in 1962 and not 2002. The A-12 was hand jigged, no assembly lines for this aircraft. The A-12 was limited to 13 aircraft, and hidden in the CIA's black halls for so long that even today, it's hard to grasp that she is still the fastest aircraft that we know of today and yet many don't know really anything about her and her history. So much so that much of her credit goes to her later sister the Sr-71.

Learning to Fly

Moving to Area 51

The A-12 Cygnus had been manufactured at Lockheed Skunk Works in Burbank California. Covert testing could only be carried out at Area 51, the remote location chosen earlier. Moving the newly built A-12 out to Area 51 site in secrecy promised to be a job. February 1962, Kelly Johnson and his CIA /USAF staff were devising a movement plan, while the Lockheed employees placed the A-12, in three pieces, into enclosed wide load trailer.

The plan was for a pickup truck, fitted with two poles that approximated the height and width of the trailer, would proceed down the road to the site, before the A-12 was placed on the road to travel. Whenever the poles hit something such as a road sign, the driver would stop, get out, handsaw the sign down, then re-bolt it back together, replacing it back in the spot he found it. When the real item came down the road, the trailer crew simply removed the sign and replaced it after they passed, with no threat to the trailer or anyone following behind.

There was only one incident occurring with the strange entourage to Area 51. A Greyhound bus traveling down the same road, was damaged slightly by the wide load trailer carrying the A-12. After a payoff of $3500, the bus driver signed an agreement not to talk about what happened. The secret was safe and the A-12 continued to her destination without further incident. There was much done to the roads for the plane's arrival; the roadways leading up to Area 51 were repaved to make the final stage of the trip easy. The aircraft arrived safely and silently just the way that Lockheed and the CIA wanted it. It was a quiet delivery for a most auspicious aircraft. The A-12 was re-assembled and now the "fun" would really start.

Test Flights

The A-12 unofficially began test flights on April 25, 1962, when test pilot, Lou Schalk took #121 on her first flight—less than 2 miles at 20-30 feet altitude. During the short hop, Schalk discovered that the control linkages were not correctly installed which is what caused the quirky first flight. #121's semi- maiden flight took place at Area 51 the following day. This flight lasted approximately 40 minutes during which some chine inserts were lost and were replaced. The landing gear was positioned down throughout the flight.

The first official flight of the A-12 #121, it's true inaugurals with Lou Schalk again as pilot, lasted 59 minutes and came several days later (April 30, 1962) in the presence of CIA and USAF observers. #121 took off at 170 kts, climbed 30,000 ft. and attained a top speed of 340 kts. The aircraft went supersonic during the second official flight on May 2, 1962. Four additional aircraft one of which was the two-seat trainer arrived at Area 51 in 1962. The J58 engines were still not ready and early test flights were done with the J75. The aircraft flew with the J58's as they arrived at the Area. In one instance, the A-12 flew with one J58 and one J75.

The first A-12 equipped with two J58's flew in January 15, 1963, as you can imagine, the time lapse in getting the J-58 engines created tension within the program. The first test flights had begun in earnest in 1963 and by July 20, 1963, the A-12 had flown to Mach 3. Before the year was over, nine A-12s were in the inventory and made 573 flights, for a total of 756 flight hours. November 22, 1963, dawned as a day of unspeakable horror for the United States. President John F. Kennedy was assassinated in Dallas, Texas. The A-12, in the quiet of the desert, had made its speed goal, hitting Mach 3.2 at 78,000 ft. By this time, Kelly Johnson wrote in his log: *"The time has come for the bird to leave the nest"*. It had been three years and seven months, since the contract had been signed to put OXCART on the boards. Kennedy's assassination had rocked the world, but out in the desert of Nevada, a U.S. aircraft found Mach 3.

Neighbors in distress and outing the "A-11"

Although the Area 51 base was indeed remote, there were a few people who lived in the desert. There were airliners that flew overhead and some private airplanes that also took the chance. A-12 test flights covered large areas, sometimes beyond the restricted range, and it was inevitable that people who, by and large, had no idea what they were watching, witnessed some of those flights. In one case, an Air Force officer, who was working an early morning shift, saw something strange in the sky. When he asked his control tower, *" Did you see that airplane?"* The tower responded, *"What airplane?"*

Only a couple of incidents disturbed the few "neighbors" that were living the area surrounding the A-12's Area 51 home. Though never confirmed, a team of mules was said to have tried their own version of flight, by jumping off a cliff after sonic booms. Much further afield, two people in West Virginia, apparently died when a chimney collapsed on them because of an A-12 sonic boom.

Some of these people no doubt, had their suspicions confirmed when the President publicly announced the existence of the Blackbird on February 29, 1964. Lyndon Johnson wanted to impress upon his Republican critics (and fend off a Republican attack at the polls), as well as show he too, had a strong hand to play in National Defense. The White House sent the press an announcement declaring the "Existence of the A-11". The president handled the matter, as to protect the secrecy of the A-12 as well as to cover Area 51 mystery by using the A-11 nomenclature. Well, that is just a possibility. The real reason the A-11 was used, had to do with paper work that had not caught up with the White House. Remember, A-11 was the "working title" Kelly Johnson had given the A-12 because he was in the process of developing the last of the A series, the A-12. Since this program was so deep, it is possible the change of name never reached the White House, which was a good thing. However, for the president, it was just another political ploy as far as Johnson was concerned. Johnson had found out about the OXCART program on Nov 25, 1963, just days after Kennedy was assassinated and he had taken the reins of the country. He decided to unmask as much as he could about the Blackbird, without jeopardizing too much of the OXCART mission.

When the Johnson Administration decided to tell the public about the existence of the so-called A-11, the parties who should have been informed, weren't. Since the information was released to allied countries as well, there was a mad dash to get the two Air Force's YF-12 aircraft, which were being disguised as the "A-11", flown from the Area to Edwards AFB in California. According to the press release, Edwards was the place that the "A-11" was being flight tested, and the administration wanted some airplanes for the press to look at.

The big press introduction did not go as well as the Johnson Administration had hoped, due to a technical oversight. Blackbirds develop lots of heat when they fly, both from air friction and through their exhaust. When these hot aircraft, fresh from flying, were pulled into the hangars at Edwards where they were to be shown to the press, it was only a matter of minutes before the sensors in the hangar ceiling detected the heat pouring out of the aircraft. This triggered the hangar's sprinkler system. The hangar was soon flooded, leaving the press and dignitaries running for cover. According to the reports, only one person was available who could turn off the sprinklers, however, because of the security rule protecting the aircraft, he wasn't allowed to go into the hangar and shut off the water. Eventually someone did turn the deluge off, but the press conference had to be held up for about an hour so the hangar floor could be cleaned up and the press could dry out. Despite this small oversight, the YF-12s were spectacular and the secrets of Area 51, were never compromised. Neither was the Johnson Administration's reputation.

The Johnson Administration was falling over itself to make sure that the allies and adversaries alike, knew just what was going on without really telling them the entire story. The statement that President Johnson made on February 24, 1964, read in part:

> *"The United States has successfully developed an advanced experimental jet aircraft, the A-11, which had been tested in sustained flight at more than 2,000 miles per hour,*

and at altitudes of 70,000 feet. The performance of the A-11 far exceeds that of any other aircraft in the world today. The development of the aircraft has been made possible by major advances in aircraft technology of great significance for both military and commercial applications. Several of the A-11 aircraft are now being flight-tested at Edwards Air Force Base in California. The existence of this program is being disclosed today to permit the orderly exploitation of this advanced technology in our military and commercial progress."

If they only knew the real truth of what was going on in the Nevada desert. But, that wouldn't happen for another forty years. The president had shown the country's hand, but not all of it. The *A-11*—not the A-12 had come into the light. The A-11 would be the aircraft that went down in the books politically and publicly, at least in 1964. At the end of 1964, A-12 pilots had made 1,160 flights equaling 1,616 hours, with one of those hours at speeds above Mach 3. Thirteen A-12's had been built and two were being used for testing while the remaining eleven had been assigned to detachments for operational use. By November 25, 1965, an A-12 had achieved a speed of Mach 3.29 at 90,000 ft. and had sustained Mach 3.2 for 74 minutes. The final validation for the A-12 and OXCART program was complete. The OXCART achieved its design goals and was going to fly at its expected altitudes and speed. In exactly 48 months after the ink dried on the contract. It was an amazing feat and that is the understatement.

TEST FLIGHT Losses

As with any other new aircraft the A-12's were subject to catastrophic failures and loss of pilot and aircraft. Out of the 13 aircraft built, five had been lost in accidents. The 42% attrition rate was high, but not unexpected, for the A-12 pushed the limits of aviation technology. A CIA document referring to those five losses pointed out that "not any of these accidents happened because of Mach three reach of the aircraft." There was nothing unusual about those accidents, and in hindsight, most of them were probably preventable. The following A-12s were lost:

May 24, 1963

Aircraft #123: Ken Collins was piloting the aircraft on a routine training flight out of Area 51. The test he was performing was an inertial navigation system proficiency flight test. *"I think I'm in trouble",* Collins called out before he ejected from the A-12. After safely descending to earth, Collins was picked up on the roadside by a passerby. The ejection had left Collins in Wendover, Utah. According the CIA records, the radar tracking the flight only picked up the F-101 chase plane on the screen. The radar never saw the A-12, and in an effort to keep the crash a secret, no one planned on mentioning the existence of the Blackbird. Yet, secrecy is never that simple. Many in the surrounding area noticed the accident. Art Kent, a reporter from Salt Lake City, Utah was industrious enough to get photos of the crash site before it was sanitized. He was later "convinced" by the USAF to "bring the photos in". Shortly after the photos were retrieved, General Boyd Hubbard of the USAF, one of the brass in charge of the investigation, put out the story that a "Wright-Patterson based F-105 that had flown out of Nellis Air Force Base had crashed." The security people had their cover story but they were still having fits over the photos that Kent had taken.

Answers needed to be found on what caused the crash, but secrecy was paramount. Kelly Johnson urged that the remaining wreckage at the site be dynamited, during the night to prevent any further photos being taken. While the USAF and the CIA were trying to get the area sealed, Ken Collins was being questioned on what happened. In his testimony, he said there were erratic airspeed indications, which caused him to descend into the clouds to maintain air speed, and then the aircraft became uncontrollable. Collins believed that the aircraft entered a flat spin, just as he saw the impact area. Collins ejected safely, and the aircraft burned when it hit the ground. On June 4,

1963, days after the accident in a CIA cable, Kelly Johnson had suggested that hypnosis and sodium pentothal (truth serum) be used on Collins to find out "precisely what happened" in the final moments of the flight. Johnson had used this method on the pilots that had bailed out of the F-104 early in the flight test program. The USAF agreed to go ahead with this plan. The rest of the fleet of A-12s was grounded until the investigation was completed. The only A-12 flights were test by aircraft #121 and #124 to find out more about the accident. The test flights and the truth serum did not produce any additional clues. It was later ascertained that a pitot tube had iced over due to entrapped moisture, and that had caused the erratic airspeed readings which led to the crash. Subsequently, there was a discussion of the use of "black boxes" on the A-12 to simplify investigations in the event of another accident, but it was never put into play.

July 9, 1964

Aircraft #133: The accident occurred during the landing approach at Area 51 when a malfunction of the flight control surface actuating system caused an uncontrollable roll. Pilot Bill Park had zoom climbed to 96,250 ft., which damaged the engines and caused the crash. Park ejected safely, even though he ejected from a height of 120 feet. He was blown sideways out of the aircraft. He was unhurt, as he landed on his parachute's first swing. No news of this accident ever got out.

January 5, 1967

Aircraft #125: This incident occurred during the aircraft descent about 85 miles from Area 51, when a fuel system gauging malfunction resulted in higher-than-actual readings of indicated fuel, which mean the pilot was already low on fuel while the gauge was telling him just the opposite and the pilot was short on fuel before he reached the home base. The pilot, Walter L. Ray was killed on impact with the ground due to a malfunction of the ejection seat, which failed to separate him from the seat after the ejection. Ray was an experienced test pilot with 358 hours in the A-12.

There was a major problem to keep the accident quiet and away from the press. Many precautions were taken to ensure that the A-12 wreckage would not be discovered. Instead, a story was leaked that it was an SR-71 that had crashed, and the USAF was following up on it. Of course, a few people in the press felt that something else was afoot, and went so far as to send a letter to the Chief of Staff of the USAF to tell him so. The Los Angeles Times aviation editor, Marvin Miles, suspected that there was more to this story than the USAF was telling. He threatened to publish his views on the accident.

The USAF's draft press release worried Kelly Johnson because it referred to the plane as an "SR-71" type aircraft. With Johnson' s input the parties reworded the description to read "an experimental model of the SR-71 model aircraft." In a March 1, 1967 memo, the CIA's Deputy of Operations Office of Special Activities, implied that "pilot factors" would or could be involved as the contributing cause of the accident." According to the memo, "a certain amount of overconfidence and/or mission urgency," might have been involved, since the pilot elected to fly the mission "as briefed" in spite of an inoperative autopilot, and continued the mission as "briefed", with less than full tanks after the second air refueling. With some indication that the fuel or fuel gauging problem existed, during the refueling process, (which was apparently indicated when the fuel quantity went below "BINGO" fuel during the second air refueling).

In essence, the memo said that the pilot went against regulations regarding the problems with the aircraft and flew without the issues being resolved.

The accident follows:

Ray took off from Area 51 at 11:59 A.M. for a routine test flight. The first aerial refueling, immediately after takeoff was normal, with the aircraft taking on 36,000 lbs. of fuel. After climbing and executing a Mach 3.1 cruise, Ray descended for his second aerial refueling. He took on another 61,000 lbs. of fuel, which was 4 to 5,000 pounds less than he was supposed to get, as the tanker had insufficient fuel. Ray was to compensate for this fuel shortage by executing a fuel-saving, reduced power climb on the next outbound leg. The idea worked fairly well and he was able to hold onto enough fuel on the outbound leg. Ray was able to manage the 800 to 1000 lbs. shortage below what he should have had, to complete the turn to go home to the Area. It was then that things started to turn bad. By 3:22P.M., near New Mexico, Ray reported that he was down to 7,500 lbs. and said, "I don't know where it's gone." At that point, Ray was supposed to have 13,000 lbs. of fuel in the A-12's tanks, but Ray felt he could still make it home. 3:52 P.M. found Ray declaring an emergency near Utah. By 3:56 P.M., Ray called in that he was 130 miles out and have 4,000 lbs. of fuel left. He was losing fuel excessively. Five minutes later, Ray reported that the low-pressure fuel lights were on. He was almost dry. Thirty seconds later, the next call from Ray said that he was flaming out. By 4:03 PM, on what should have been ten minutes from being safe on the ground at Area 51, Ray called in his last transmission stating that the engines had flamed out and he was ejecting from the aircraft.

 The ejection system on the A-12 was not what you would consider usual. After ejection, the pilot is still strapped in his seat. The seat releases a small drogue parachute, which helped to slow and stabilize the pilot and seat. After reaching a lower altitude, the seat releases the straps, and the pilot is propelled out of the seat by the tightening of the "butt straps". These were literally under the pilot's butt and forced him out of the seat. From there, the pilot's parachute opened automatically and he finished his descent safely. When Ray passed through 16,000 feet, the seat tried to work as designed, but something went very wrong. The butt snapper straps were trying to force Ray off the seat, but his parachute backpack was jammed under the seat's headrest. One of two things may have happened, Ray was a short man and to make sure he had a good fit in the seat, the seat's head-rest was modified and extended further down. The other possibility was that the screws in the seat were installed so that the screws protruded a bit.

 Why Ray couldn't get out from the ejection seat is not known. There was no reason for Ray to be unconscious. One possibility is that he might have made it partially out of the seat and that could have sent the entire frame spinning, causing disorientation. It could also have been the release mechanism was jammed by something. In what must have been a nightmare of a ride, Ray and the seat hit the side of a mountain peak at 600 feet and Ray was killed instantly. The seat, with Ray attached, bounced almost 100 yards down the mountain face and came to rest against a large cedar tree. Article #125 crashed almost the same time that Ray did, some distance away.

Thirty minutes after the crash, Nellis AFB sent out two T-33's and an F-101 aircraft along with two helicopters. By 5:30 PM, the T-33s were recalled and a C-130 was sent out in their place, to search for signs throughout the night. The next day, in what should have been a simple search, turned up empty until a U-2 was launched to photograph the entire area. By 3:06 P.M. the day after the crash, #125's wreckage was found. It was not until the next day around 2:00P.M. Saturday, that Ray's body was finally recovered.

In essence, according the CIA and USAF reports, the pilot was the problem. No thought was given to the fact that the aircraft may have malfunctioned. As it is even today, with commercial accidents, the pilot is always to blame. It is not a valid conclusion, if no conclusion was found. The statement concerning malfunctioning of equipment, was not proven. That is why they call it "test flight" and there is never anything routine about it!

December 28, 1967

Aircraft #126: This aircraft was involved with a test flight that was a performance check of the rendezvous beacon test with a KC-135 tanker. The weather for this flight was good. The pilot was Mele Vojvodich, a seasoned fighter pilot with years of Cold War reconnaissance flights under his belt. The aircraft was preflighted by the maintenance ground crew, and cleared for takeoff, with a gross weight of approximately 118,300 pounds, and a nominal 20.9% CG. The takeoff distance was approximately 6,800 feet and everything looked good. Ground witnesses said that the takeoff ground roll was a little long, but not enough to worry about.

Immediately after the main gear left the ground, things started to happen. The aircraft yawed to the left and became uncontrollable, with a series of violent yawing and pitching actions. Vojvodich attempted to regain control, but had no response from the stick or rudder. Faced with an uncontrollable plane, Vojvodich then ejected from the aircraft at approximately 150 to 200 feet, at the top of a maneuver. The aircraft went into a final pitch down before it crashed. The whole crash sequence took less than 30 seconds. The A-12 broke first on the left wing and then into various sections, covering an area about a mile long and 300 feet wide on the dry frozen lakebed. Vojvodich landed safely.

The primary cause of the accident was referred to as maintenance error. A flight line electrician connected the wiring harness for the yaw and pitch gyros of the stability augmentation system in reverse. CIA Director, John McCone, ordered an investigation to make sure that this was the result of negligence and not sabotage.

June 5, 1968

Aircraft #129: The loss of this aircraft and pilot Jack Weeks, over the Philippine Sea, occurred during a routine operational check flight and is discussed in detail in another chapter.

Other A-12 related Mishaps:

Aircraft #123: Not all the A-12 mishaps ended in the destruction of the aircraft or harm to the pilot. Aircraft #132 had a normal takeoff, in preparation for a training mission. Shortly after takeoff, the aircraft refueled taking on 44,000 lbs. of fuel. After refueling, the aircraft increased in airspeed from Mach 1.7 to Mach 2.9, with a short turn to the east leg of the mission. Minimum fuel was reached (34,000) pounds. At that point, the aircraft could not maintain Mach speed or altitude in a turn (30 degree bank at max. power). The fuel quantity was running low, due to excess fuel consumption, in the acceleration and the turn. The pilot was directed to Kirkland AFB, in New

Mexico, where #132 landed safely. A KC-135 tanker was launched from Beale AFB with 60,000 lbs. of fuel for the A-12 to Kirkland for an emergency ground refuel. The A-12 program managers could not say enough good things about the way Kirkland handled the situation. The aircraft received expert care, albeit in secrecy and was prepared for a flight back to her Area 51 home.

September 26, 1967

F-101 #56-0286: The F-101 flew chase on the A-12 #124 (trainer) on a refueling training mission. Refueling accomplished, the aircraft was on its way back to the Area. The time the aircraft flew back was almost twilight. While the A-12 was on approach to runway 32 (at approximately 8,500 ft.), the conversation between the F-101 pilot, James S. Simon Jr., and the A-12, indicated that Simon did not have visual contact with the A-12.

The pilot of the A-12 advised the chase plane, an F-101 Voodoo, that he was OK and that he didn't have any further need of the F-101. Witnesses on the ground saw the F-101, when the A-12 turned to its final approach. Asked where he was, the F-101 replied that he was "in trail and moving over to the right side." From the witnesses position, it seemed that the F-101 had lost some altitude in the turn, but regained it prior to rolling out on a parallel final. During the final approach, it appeared that the F-101 was approximately one mile off the A-12's right wing, and observing the approach of the A-12. Just about 3 miles out, the F-101 appeared slightly lower than the A-12 and initiated his go around at 500 feet above the ground at 190 knots. The A-12 pilot saw the fireball of the F-101 in the distance.

In the final CIA report of the accident, on October 6, 1967, it was shown that the F-101 flew 4,000 feet short and 2,000 feet to the right of the approach end of Runway 32. The primary cause of the accident was decided as pilot error. The pilot of the F-101 flew into the ground while flying a night chase mission. The impact occurred as the A-12 trainer passed the minimum altitude on the glide path. The pilot of the F-101 was killed and no attempt to eject was made.

Tankers:

The A-12 did not fly without support, and lots of it. The basic support for the OXCART program began back in 1959, when the first of the new KC-135A tankers were coming off the assembly line. Fifteen KC-135A tankers were assigned to Beale AFB in California. It was a typical SAC (Strategic Air Command) wing supporting B-52s as their refueling tankers. At that time, the coldest part of the Cold War had aircraft on nuclear alert, 24/7. This meant that pilots were on the flight line, sitting for hours, just waiting for the call that all of them never wanted to hear. In 1962, it almost happened with the Cuban missile crisis, but fortunately, it was stopped just before anything serious could happen.

Later in 1962, a small group of tanker crews and five KC-135As were stationed at Castle AFB, also in California. They were to be the original group that would service the new A-12. Five of the KC-135As were refitted to the Q model at the time, to meet the requirements of the A-12, along with operation training for the crews.

After some wrangling with the USAF, the Castle AFB operation and the CIA /USAF study, had concluded that the five aircraft were not going to be enough to support the OXCART mission. It was decided that the 903rd Squad from the 4126 Strategic Wing at Beale AFB, would be the only group that would support the A-12. The decision was made due to the air refueling tracks that were used for the A-12 test and training mission. It also had to do with the somewhat secluded location of the base. SAC decided to transfer five more aircraft from Castle AFB to Beale AFB and into the 903rd Tanker Squad. in 1963.

Another group of KC-135s were transferred to Beale AFB from a tanker group based at McCord AFB in Washington state, which brought the total number of tankers to thirty, in support of OXCART. These tankers were a modified to the newer Q standard. By 1963, the tanker crews were briefed as to what and who OXCART was. The tanker crews were assigned four crewmembers: aircraft pilot/copilot commander, navigator, and boom operator. A commander in this elite group that served the A-12, had to rights to remove any crew member that he felt was a security risk, for whatever reason he deemed reasonable. The group commander also had to right to approve or disapprove any new crewmember that SAC had transferred to the unique group, as they saw fit. This allowed for the 903rd's crewmembers to be top notch and melded together as a team.

The 903rd refueling squad flew sorties in support of the A-12, in both its test and pilot training phase, from Area 51. No tanker ever crossed over airspace or landed at Area 51. The odd thing was the 903rd Tanker Squad had one commander, an operations officer and administration staff. That meant the 903rd Tanker Squadron had three operations officers (pilots) and three staff which consisted or navigator, squadron navigation, tanker plans and program officer and a squadron-scheduling officer. However, considering the speed and the need for fuel for OXCART, it was easy to understand why there was need for intricate support.

A typical mission out of Beale AFB to support the A-12, was really a straightforward operation... all A-12 refueling missions were done in a restricted area. The air-restricted area was closed to normal military and civilian aircraft. This allowed the A-12 to climb out, descend and stay at lower altitude (under 45,000 ft.) while training to control, on the off chance that an A-12 might be sighted. There was a planned refueling track in the restricted area, to facilitate the A-12 descent corridor and ARCP (point for completing rendezvous), a start refuel and end refuel point, and an A-12 climb corridor after refueling. The KC-135Q arrived at the refueling sector about 30 minutes prior to the air refueling. The control center (ARCT) receiver was scheduled to arrive at the (ARCP) and wait for the A-12 to arrive. At a pre-determined range, the KC-135Q turned in from the A-12 and descended 1000 feet and accelerated for refueling with an air speed of 310 knots. The A-12 slowly closed on the lowered boom on the tanker, until it was close enough for the boom operator to insert the boom in the A-12's receiver receptacle.

Once the two aircraft were hooked together, the aerial ballet would begin and refueling would commence. As the A-12's weight increased, its stall speed increased. This necessitated a gradual increase in refueling speed as refueling progressed. To do this, the tanker left its throttle at maximum thrust.

As the tanker's weight decreased, the tanker's speed would increase, and if all worked correctly, a refueling would start at 310 knots. Speed would gradually increase so that the refueling would be 345 knots, which was the top speed for the KC-135Q. One thing to remember, there was an F-101 chase plane following the A-12 and most of the time, an air refueling was also done for the F-101 after the A-12 was finished. After the refueling was accomplished, the KC-135Q would go on to anything else it needed to complete and the A-12 would head off with a full belly.

Sept 6, 1963, tanker support facilities overseas were already under construction to be ready for the A-12 mission. This meant that Kadena and all the other facilities needed to support the A-12 at Okinawa and other refueling stops on the routes, were being made available to carry the JP-7 fuel that the A-12 used exclusively.

Patches –Symbols of the OXCART:

Symbols have distinguished friend from foe in warfare throughout recorded history. Military organizations employ heraldic emblems as a means of identification and for esprit de' corps. The emblems symbolize an organization's history, mission, or function. By the 13th century, official (that is, recorded) awareness of symbols began to appear on embroidered cloth over the knights' armor as well as on shields and became known as coats of arms. Later the term "coat of arms" became synonymous with the shield, its crest, and its scroll, bearing a name or motto.

A system of heraldic emblems evolved within the air arms of the allied and central powers during World War I, the first major conflict in which the newly-developed airplane became an instrument of war. On April 6, 1917, America declared war on Germany, and shortly thereafter, Brigadier General Benjamin D. Foulois became Chief of the Air Service, American Expeditionary Forces (AEF). A year later, on May 6, 1918, Foulois established the policy for insignia of aerial units, declaring that each squadron would have an official insignia painted on the middle of each side of the airplane fuselage. *"The squadron will design their own insignia during the period of organizational training. The design must be submitted to the Chief of Air Service, AEF, for approval. The design should be simple enough to be recognizable from a distance."*

As the Air Force grew so did its insignia, emblems and patches. Emblems and patches give a unit a unique identity, similar to that of a mascot for a sports team. The insignia has come to represent the unit, its members, its equipment, and its accomplishments.

Oxcart Patches

As most military units, groups, and organizations have done throughout history, participants in the OXCART program chose to signify their mission by the creation of symbols in the form of "sew-on" patches. These "patches" were emblematic of that mission, or its supporting unit. While some unit emblems might receive official heraldic recognition, many are less official, and represent the personality of the unit itself. In the case of formal military uniforms, however, very few unit patches were authorized by the higher officials in the service. However, some of the most creative patches find their way onto flight suits and work uniforms. Many patches also wound up as artwork painted somewhere on the aircraft or support equipment associated with the assigned unit or its aircraft. Often the theme of the artwork displayed on the patches or emblems was obscure to all but the unit's members. It mattered little that outsiders had no idea what the patches represent. The patches purpose was to instill pride and unity in the mission for the people who carried it out.

Program 665A, Recce-Strike

Program 665A was a "feeder" program conducted at Wright-Patterson Air Force Base in 1962-1963. The test program used a JKC-135 that had been fitted with consoles, and a large bulge on the side of the fuselage to house the sensors. The mission was intended to support the development of a Reconnaissance-Strike version of the XB-70, the short-lived RS-70. When it became evident that the XB-70 program would not proceed beyond two test aircraft, which were then in assembly, Program 665A and its personnel were diverted to the OXCART program with this, the systems and sensors that would be used by A-12 and the SR-71 would be tested. The JKC-135 was flown over the countryside at top speed, just a few hundred feet above the ground, to approximate the high speeds of the A-12 and SR-71. The original patch shown here came from Donn Byrnes, a member of Program 665A, and later, author of the book *Blackbird Rising*.

Road Runners "Beep Beep

This rare original patch was created to represent the 1129th Special Activities Squadron (1129th SAS), the unit established at Groom Dry Lake, Nevada, to operate the A-12 aircraft. The program was known as OXCART and was a CIA run operation, but was almost wholly dependent upon the maintenance support provided by the U.S. Air Force. The 1129th SAS adopted the Road Runner as a mascot. The Roadrunner is a clever, relatively large, quick, and shy bird, a ubiquitous resident of the Mohave Desert and environs. The Warner Brothers Road Runner versus Wile E. Coyote cartoons shown in theaters until the later part of the 20th century, and still seen on television in the 21st century, have popularized it.

Cygnus

CIA pilot Jack Weeks gave the nickname *Cygnus* (Swan) to the A-12 after seeing the airplane for the first time. To him, the A-12, in its original paint scheme of bare titanium and black on the leading and trailing edges, resembled a swan. The 12 original *Cygnus* patches were made when the A-12s deployed to Okinawa. This one belonged to CIA A-12 pilot, Dennis Sullivan.

*A-12 3+

This patch was made at the same time as the *Cygnus* patch. The patch's design was based on the Lockheed 3+ lapel pin given to anyone who went Mach III in the Blackbird. The Lockheed lapel pin portrayed the SR-71, with two canopies, but the A-12 pilots wanted a patch that showed their single seat aircraft. This is the only known patch design that accurately depicts the A-12. Only a couple of these ultra-rare patches exist. This one belonged to CIA A-12 pilot Frank Murray.

*Sullivan

Name tag belonging to A-12 pilot Dennis Sullivan. He wore it on the low-level flight suit he used on training flights in the two-seat A-12.

*1054 & 1055

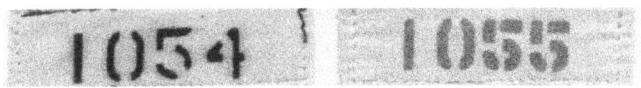

Some reports have claimed that CIA pilots carried no form of identification on operational missions. That was not true, at least in the case of A-12

pilots. Each received individual Personal Identification Numbers. The PIN numbers, were written or sewn into items the pilots wore. The sewn versions depicted here were affixed to the "Long John" underwear the pilots wore under their pressure suits. The number 1054 was the PIN of A-12 pilot Dennis Sullivan; 1055 was the PIN of A-12 pilot Frank Murray.

Vires Per Unitatem

This is the official squadron patch of the 903rd Air Refueling Squadron, the only squadron to refuel the A-12s. The 903rd was based at Beale AFB, CA. The Latin phrase means, "Strength through Unity."

*"Tally Ho" 903rd ARS

A very rare original made by members of the 903rd when they accompanied the A-12s to Okinawa for Operation Black Shield. According to 903rd

Navigator, Robert Q. Williams, the patch depicts "a pissed off Cygnus swooping down onto a KC-135Q."

*Voodoo One-O-Wonder

This original patch, belongs to A-12 pilot and 1129th SAS commander, Hugh "Slip" Slater. The patch represents to F-101 Voodoo fighters used at Area 51 to fly chase on the A-12s.

*1129th SAS "Beep Beep"

This is a reproduction of the second, and more rare version of the famous Roadrunners patch.

*"Walking HABU" or "Seasick Cygnus"

This rare, one-of-a-kind patch was reportedly made at Okinawa in 1968. Both the A-12 and the SR-71 were at Okinawa during that time, but it is thought that the patch's origin can be traced to OXCART. The patch is almost identical to the drawn portrayal of the A-12 on a poster celebrating the 500th flight of the A-12 trainer at Area 51 in October 1966. The poster depicted a space-suited cowboy riding on the back of an A-12, along with the date and the phrase, "This Dutchman is Ready to Roll." A-12 pilots used the call sign "Dutch." Hugh "Slip" Slater was the pilot of the 500th flight.

*4786th Test Sq. USAF – F-12 Test Force – NASA

This rare original patch from the joint NASA/Air Force Test Force, established at Edwards AFB, in December 1969. The test force was in charge of Category II or Developmental Testing for the YF-12, the only version of the Blackbird ever to carry weapons. This unique patch shows the YF-12

firing two missiles. One of the YF-12 crewmembers, Gary Heidlebaugh, designed the patch.

*NASA FRC USAF F-12 Test Force NASA

A rare second version of the missile-firing patch, FRC stands for Flight Research Center (now Dryden).

*1 May 65

The patch depicted here, commemorated the May 1, 1965, record-breaking flight of the YF-12. The patches were made in two versions, a large one with bottom scrolls for the flight/utility suits and the small one without scrolls for baseball caps. The patch shown is original.

Skylark, Silver Javelin, Black Shield

SKYLARK and SILVER JAVELIN

The Cuban Bay of Pigs disaster of the Kennedy Administration, resulted in the firing of Richard Bissell, one of the pillars of the OXCART project. The Cuban Missile Crisis saw the United States and Russia never closer to nuclear war. However, fortunately the crisis did pass, but that didn't mean that the United States was taking their eye off the ball. An idea was pushed forward to use the OXCART as the new "eye on the ball" over Cuba. No matter how hard this issue was pushed, however, by September 15,1966, the 303 Committee said no to the idea of sending OXCART to Cuba. The 303 Committee was an interdepartmental committee, which reviewed and authorized covert operations for the United States. This was established under NSC5412/C act, in December 28,1955. It was known as the *Special Group* or *5412 Committee* until the *National Security Action Memo No. 303* of June 2, 1964, then changed the name to the 303 Committee.

In 1964 - 1968, the committee consisted of the Assistant to the President for National Security Affairs, Deputy Secretary of Defense, Deputy Under Secretary of State for Political Affairs, and the Director of the CIA. The 303 Committee, true to its political form, was afraid it would "disturb the existing calm previously in that area of our foreign relations." While the operations were still a big no, proficiency training remained the main order of business. This did lead to the improvement of mission plans and flight tactics for the A-12 and that allowed the detachment to reduce time required before deployment to Okinawa from 21 to 15 days. The OXCART program just kept breaking records out in the desert, while looking to get into some game.

"SCOPE LOGIC" better known as "UPWIND"

May 1967, found the CIA forwarding detailed requests to the 303 Committee to use OXCART to collect intelligence on the new Soviet missile system. As early as 1962, the intelligence community was concerned about the new missile site that appeared near TALLINN, Estonia and spread along the northwestern quadrant of the Soviet Union. There were attempts to photograph the site but the cloud cover in the area frustrated the CIA. Because of the lack of accurate information on the new missile site, there were many views about its real job. The views ranged from the CIA idea that the installation contained the long-range surface to air missiles designed to counter strategic bombers. The USAF felt that the TALLINN site represented deployed antiballistic missile systems. Of course, the photo interpreters said that the needed to have the resolution on the photos of 12 inches to 18 inches in order to determine the missile size, antenna patterns and the way the radars were laid out for the system. The ELINT analysts also needed the information about the TALLINN radar. There was no collection site near enough that could monitor TALLINN output when the radar was being used.

The Soviets never used their radars in tracking or lock on modes to prevent the CIA and USAF from getting any information like performance characteristics. Since there was no conclusion to the problem of the purpose of the TALLINN radar, the Office of Special activities tried to come up with a mission that would expose TALLINN by the use of high altitude photography. That meant in short, OXCART. Only the OXCART cameras, along with the U2 ELINT collection equipment were sent to do the job. This new project was known as "SCOPE LOGIC", which was the unclassified name. The classified name was known as "UPWIND". As the project was written, it would involve launching an A-12 from a classified area, thus sending her over to the Baltic Sea and then meet with the U-2, also flying from a classified area in support of the A-12.

The A-12 would fly north of Norway and then turn south along the Soviet Finland border. Just before reaching Leningrad, the A-12's pilot would have to head west-southwest down the Baltic Sea, on the coast of Estonia, Latvia and Lithuania, then Poland and Germany before heading west to return to the undisclosed landing site. It was planned that the entire flight would take something like 8 hours and 38 minutes and would cover 11,000 nautical miles with 4 aerial refueling planned. The OXCART would not violate any Soviet airspace but it would appear on Soviet radar network operations to be headed in an over flight in the vicinity of Leningrad. It was hoped that this maneuver would bring the Soviet air defense TALLINN radar on line. In essence, this whole procedure was done so that the OXCART could light up the TALLINN radar. The maneuver continues with the OXCART making a dash to the Baltic Sea with its Type I camera filming the entire southern coast. If the CIA was correct in the idea that the TALLINN was designed to counter high altitude aircraft at long range, then the OXCART would be in jeopardy during the dash down the Baltic Sea. However, the CIA's weapons experts felt that the A-12's speed along with its collection of ECM equipment would keep OXCART safe from the Soviet SAMs. Both the CIA and the DOD (Department of Defense) were in support of the mission, but the Secretary of State Dean Rusk opposed it and the 303 Committee never sent it on to President Johnson for review. So went the OXCART's chance to do what she was built for, to fly over the Soviet Union.

SKYLARK

Due to the tension with the USSR, Castro's close ties with Khrushchev, and the fact that Cuba was 90 miles off the U.S. coast of Florida; the CIA was flying U-2 surveillance flights over the island, just in case Castro and Khrushchev had some plans. In 1962, the CIA continued to monitor Cuba with periodic U-2 over flights. Those missions were how the United States found out that there was SAM missile sites in Cuba, but it did not show the surface-to-surface missile construction as of yet. As the summer progressed, military strategists came to believe that the SAM site pattern was similar to the layout the Soviets had used at home to defend nuclear missile installations. On October 14, 1962, U-2 reconnaissance revealed clear evidence of long-range missiles with nuclear capability, being moving on trucks in Cuba, showing sites that had been set up. President Kennedy promptly mobilized U.S. forces and placed a naval blockade around the island, facing the prospect of a full-scale nuclear war. By October 28, 1962, Kennedy got the Soviets to blink after Khrushchev had sent a letter demanding that the U.S. not invade Cuba, and he would dismantle the sites and remove the missiles. At that time, however, no one knew that our Jupiter missiles in Turkey were part of the deal to halt the standoff.

There was little question following the Cuban Missile Crisis, that the United States would continue to monitor activities in Cuba closely. The problem was that the U-2, which had served the United States well for many years, was becoming increasingly vulnerable as surface to air missiles and radar defenses became more advanced and widespread. The A-12 was an obvious and intended replacement but at the time, everything about it was virtually untried and brand new. This led to the development of *Project Skylark*, an opportunity to test the plane's operational limits and abilities through possible flights over Cuba.

Politicians in the U.S. were looking for new ways to keep an eye on Fidel Castro without getting airplanes shot down, and the A-12 was looking more and more like the answer. Yet, to upgrade the aircraft and get authorization to fly it over Cuba, the politicians would have to win the support of some key military officials, namely the Secretary of Defense, Robert McNamara and much of the Air Force brass. Less than two years after the missile crisis, the National Security Council, (NSC) was once again evaluating how it could continue the necessary reconnaissance, without sacrificing aircraft and men. In a May 1964 meeting that included Secretary of State Dean Rusk, Secretary of Defense Robert McNamara, and the NSC, the discussion on using the U-2 and electronic countermeasures (ECM) over Cuba was once again on the table. McNamara felt that an ECM equipped U-2 would not compromise implementation of McNamara's SIOP (single integrated operation plan). Many experts disagreed, however, contending that using ECM over Cuba would greatly endanger U.S. bombers if it was ever needed for an attack. Should a bomber go down, the ECM would be picked over for all the radar information that the enemy could discover. These experts also doubted that ECM protection would only be good for the first aircraft over, and would not be sufficient to support the U-2 on a regular mission, as the Cubans would quickly learn to counter the tactic. The estimated chance of a U-2 to evade a shoot down, after the first flight, dropped to 10%, assuming the Cubans were determined to get the plane out of its airspace.

General Maxwell Taylor, former advisor to President Kennedy and chairman of the Joint Chiefs of Staff during the Cuban Missile crisis, was also present at the meeting. He too believed that the ECM would not affect the SIOP condition, however, at the time at least 14 nations had operational Soviet SAM installations. He felt that using the U-2 in this way would be a red flag to those other nations. Such a plan, in Taylor's opinion, translated into "showing your colors", and eliminated the element of surprise. Yet, that was precisely what the United States sought to maintain—the secrecy of its reconnaissance operations.

Officials at the NSC meeting decided to decrease the use of unmanned drones. Up to that time, drones were not used for high-level reconnaissance, because they had limited operational capacity and numerous problems. There were enough drones, such as the *AQM Fire Bees* to carry out reconnaissance for at least for 90 days. After that, only 75% of the reconnaissance equipment requirement was met, assuming none of them were shot down. These figures required the drones to fly at altitudes as high as 54,000 to 59,000 feet. CIA director John McCone, added his concerns about the drones and their reliability. Only two drones that could fly at 50,000 feet were operational at the time, and only the U-2s could cover a 30 mile wide track across the island, while the drones could cover 325 linear miles, with a loss of track accuracy that could add up to nearly a 18 mile swath.

McNamara agreed with McCone, but McNamara was heavily influenced by the costs of drones (about $480,000), as opposed to $1,500,000 for a U-2. McGeorge Bundy who was the National Security Advisor, asked if McNamara had a plan for getting Castro to use up all his weapons. McNamara said yes. Using non-photographic drones, the United States could possibly get Castro to try to shoot them down or send up a MiG 21 to do it.

The discussion turned to other contingences: if enough drones were shot down, what kind of response would the United States have to make? Perhaps balloons were a viable platform and cheaper than drones? The discussion ranged on, concerning the use of drones *versus* U-2s *versus* other technologies and their implications. None of the proposals promised both secrecy and success. Secretary Rusk asked about the status of the A-12. CIA Director McCone had to reply that the plane was not yet ready for deployment. The "A-12" was flying successfully, but had not attained the speed for which it was designed, and it was still vulnerable to flameout and had other operational difficulties. Several more months would be need before it could be operational.

Elaborating, McCone explained that early versions of the A-12, had to come down to 35,000 feet to relight the engines after a flameout. A way around the problems was found. Each of the 13 aircraft were modified to include the new equipment that supported relighting the engines without descending. McCone continued with: everybody involved with the aircraft felt it would be dangerous to use it over Cuba without more testing. Kelly Johnson made a statement that he would not be comfortable with the A-12, flying in that condition referring to the relighting of the engines. McNamara, at first, agreed that the A-12 not be used. As the meeting wore on, and the government's top defense officials raised and dismissed the reconnaissance alternatives, the discussion shifted back to the A-12. There was one question, could OXCART be speeded up? What could be done, in all out effort, to get OXCART ready? McCone answered that the problems were being worked out as they arose; he promised to keep the pressure on, but he didn't feel that a crash program would be necessary. The rest of the powerbrokers were not convinced. They had discussed virtually every alternative to the A-12 but none was acceptable. They decided that the A-12 was the answer to their reconnaissance needs and the CIA and Lockheed were to get the A-12 ready as fast as possible. The program became "Operation SKYLARK".

An accident in July of 1964 indicated, as CIA Director McCone had agreed, that the plane was not yet ready to fly missions. Lockheed test pilot, Bill Park, had to eject from his A-12 when an outboard elevon servo had hung up. The accident did not deter the sponsors of SKYLARK. In a memo dated August 22, 1964, acting CIA Director, Marshall C. Carter, told the A-12 development team that the plan was to be ready for a Cuban mission no later than the week of November 5, 1963. The memo also laid down the flight characteristics needed for such a mission: Mach 2.8 with altitude capability of 80,000 feet and a range of 2,500 nautical miles or better. It would include four OXCART aircraft. Carter went on to state that Operation SKYLARK was to have the highest priority, unhampered in any way by contractors, commanders, or any other entity that would have a direct effect on the completion of the program's objectives. There were no holds barred, SKYLARK would have everything and anything it needed.

At the time SKYLARK program was worked on, the longest sustained A-12 flight with two J-58 engines was 4:25 hours. The trainer aircraft, CIA Article number 124, held the longest sustained A-12 flight record with two J-75 engines, 5:25 hours. The top speed the trainer reached was Mach 3.27 and the maximum altitude attained was 85,000 feet. On December 11, 1964, an unidentified A-12 flew sustained flight at 45 minutes, above Mach 3 at 81,000 feet, the longest sustained flight to date that closely approximated design conditions. Using wind tunnel tests, the A-12 engineers were able to improve aircraft inlet recovery and distortion to specifications requirements to maximize range and engine life. Yet major problems remained with fuel consumption during the climb to altitude: the fuel was insufficient to meet the specified cruise range.

Quality assurance was also a critical issue in the SKYLARK project. Engineers developed troubleshooting routines to minimize downtime caused by a variety of malfunctions including false cockpit instrument readings, fuel tank leaks, hydraulic leaks, and pressure fluctuations in the brake system. Even the J-58 engines were subject to intense scrutiny, although they were performing well in the test flights. Compressor disc durability problems, which involved excessive growth after repetitive cycles to Mach 3.2, were showing up on ground tests as early as 1964. A change involving a new strengthened compressor disc, was put into effect. Meanwhile, the flight speeds were restricted to Mach 2.8, which limited the maximum temperature and the steep thermal gradient imposed on the disc by rapid descents from a hot to cold environment. Because of all the connective measures taken in 1964, however, the eighteen flight engines, plus all the new production engines, acquired new discs and were not restricted in any way.

Other problems were showing up in the race to support SKYLARK. Engine nozzles and actuator pipes failed twice in flight. This prompted the investigation, which showed vibration and system instability problems. Those issues were addressed at the Nevada, Area 51 test site, and a search began for the cause of the vibration. The A-12's camera systems included five Perkin-Elmer and Hycon camera systems. The Hycon system proved to be working at optimum levels in flight test which were always more grueling than the mission flights. About 105 payload flights were made, with photography being secondary only to pilot training and aircraft checkout. No thermal gradients or turbulence problems were found at Mach 2.90 and pressure attitudes of 80,000 ft.

Because of the risks and demands involved, pilot comfort was another concern. Project workers developed a new parachute pack, lighter and 1-1/2 inches thinner than the previous version. This pack along with better seating, would allow the pilot more mobility on long missions that were in the planning stage. Much of the inertial navigation (INS) and the ARC-50 aircraft communications system were revamped. Detachment pilots helped conduct continuous ARC-50 test, ranging from 500 nautical miles down to 1 nautical mile, and the automatic direction finder (ADF) tests from 200 nautical miles to contact point. There was also a priority effort to produce a flight test program that would determine the actual operational range of the A-12. One idea was a long flight route that included only one 180-degree turn allowing the aircraft to fly in a straight line for sustained distance and time. The CIA told Lockheed in a memo that plans for extensive modifications programs to recover a major portion of the anticipated range degradation, were being held in abeyance until the long range flight tests were completed.

The Director of the CIA issued another status report as a first "briefing". The SKYLARK project was divided into two phases. Phase I increasing the A-12's flight capability from Mach 2.9 to Mach 3.5, would begin on March 1, 1965. Phase II, beginning on the same date, had a package called "Supermarket" that included new electronic countermeasures and a three refueling mission capability. The CIA report included a test mission summary. Since the first flight of the A-12 on April 26, 1962, 1,234 flights were made, totaling 1,745 hours; the 13 aircraft in residence at Area 51 did all of the flights. Of the totals, 794 flights accumulated 104 hours using Pratt & Whitney J-58 engines. The maximum altitude was 85,000 feet. Seven aircraft, including #124 (the two place trainer), were assigned to the detachment and were flown by operational pilots. Four of the seven aircraft were primary SKYLARK aircraft and included #125, #127, #128 and #132. Four were assigned to flight test, while two #129 and #131, were assigned to the detachment as operational aircraft, after the modification had been installed. By January 27, 1965, #129 had completed the first in a series of long range, high-speed flights.

SILVER JAVELIN

The A-12's maximum range project was known as SILVER JAVELIN. The total flight time was 1:15 hours above Mach 3.1, with total range based on final flight data, of 2,580 nautical miles at a cruising speed of 75,000 feet and 80,000 ft. This was the longest sustained flight bordering design conditions. Before #129 took the second SILVER JAVELIN flight in early March 1965. Lockheed engineers made a number of modifications to the plane, including additions to the air inlet duct seals to improve inlet efficacy, and strengthening the rudder actuator linkage, and rescheduling the fuel management system to keep the aircraft balanced and reduce drag.

There was little flying done while the modifications of Phase II SKYLARK were put in place. Yet, at no time, no less than five operational aircraft were available for service. The modifications established for the A-12 aircraft #'s125, 126, 127, 128, 130, 131, and 132 were ambitious but not out of reach. The CIA wanted the planes to have a 450-knot equivalent air speed (KEAS) climbing capacity. To accomplish this, and further fit the plane for extreme service, the CIA's modification plans included:

    a. Modifying the air data computer, which was the limited to 400 KEAS maximum.

    b. Increasing the fuselage station 715 joint strength, because of increased bending moment, primarily due to the installation of addition ECM gear and boxes. Basically, this meant the installation of **KEMPSTER** and ***EMERALD*** ECM system, which was only installed on #122 tested, and approved. However, the program was cancelled.

    c. Placement of the ARC-50 in the nose of the aircraft. Providing for a heavier payload capacity, plus some allowances for growth and safety margins: this was only used in the #132 aircraft.

    d. Increasing capacity for liquid nitrogen to a level sufficient for a three refueling mission.

    e. An SR03 compass to replace the MA-1 and the MD-1 compasses, which did not function well at high speeds TACAN (tactical air navigation) for system operational suitability.

    f. A Wilcox IFF, (identification friend foe), which smaller than the IFF that was in use, as required for the Lockheed inlet control modifications and ECM chine bay provisions.

    g. Conversion to the Lockheed inlet controls system for aircraft 125, 126, 127, 128 and 132. All aircraft had increased nitrogen capacity.

Note: the ECM packages that were installed: This also included the schedule for SUPERMARKET, which incorporated the new ECM package:

- A. **RED DOG #2:** Ready to ship
- B. **BLUE DOG #1:** March 1 1965 –Sept 1965
- C. **BIG BLAST/PIN REG** (Passive warning system): July 1, 1965
- D. **FAT FOX:** August 15, 1965

SUPERMARKET was actually a major modification program, which had to be accomplished, in order to carry out the special ECM packages made for the A-12, and incorporate the Lockheed inlet control system which provided capability for three aerial refueling missions. The present estimate, at the time that was given, was that overall mission reliability for theA-12 was 23%. This estimate was based on the flight results of the detachment aircraft as they were then configured. Profiling the reliability estimate for the China contingency planning, PINWHEEL was estimated that the overall reliability would be increased to 30% for the time period starting July 1, 1965. This also went along with a special ELINT measurements program, that was begun to assure the vulnerability studies that would be based on actual measurements of soviet threat radars. The OXCART would not be able to covertly penetrate the radar net undetected. SUPERMARKET was the development package of ECM systems carried out and produced a variety of threat warnings and jammers that were available.

J58 Development under Skylark;

Total J58 test hours:	16,914	
JT11D-20 engine ground test hours:	13,976	
Engine ground test hours above:	M2.4	435
Engine ground test hours above:	M3.3	400
Engine flight test hours at or above:	M3.2	29
Total engine flight test hours including AF-12 R-12 and A-12: 2,377		

SKYLARK continued to improve the A-12 aircraft. All of the work was done at the Area 51 facility, in hopes of pushing the A-12 to Mach 3.5-realm and goal of the Phase II modifications.

Phase II accomplished a new inlet system, auto forward bypass, J-cams and duct seals. Designers also improved the composite panels and used the Blackbird's signature black paint for the first time. Up to now, the aircraft were at first silver and then black on the leading edges only. There was improved nitrogen conservation, rudder improvements to support the 450 KEAS climb, film and map destruction capability and the first incorporation of "Birdwatcher" (electronic means of tracking the aircraft in flight on a separate frequency).

The Phase II summary of the aircraft performance shows that the A-12 achieved Mach 2.9, with a range of 1700 nautical miles, from tanker to tanker hookup, with an altitude of 76,000 feet in test. The projected performance for the A-12, after the Phase II mods were completed, was flight speed of Mach 3.05, with a range of 2500 nautical miles and altitude of 76,000 ft. The minimum reliability before the Phase II modifications for the A-12 was just 23%. While SKYLARK was preparing the A-12 for Cuban over flights, there was still deep concern for the A-12s ECM problems, and fear that those problems were being resolved too slowly. The A-12 might be able to overly Cuba, but it would have to do it without ECM protection. The CIA decided to try another approach—to develop some electron guns that could be added to the front of the aircraft to project an ion cloud ahead of the aircraft and reduce its radar cross section (RCS). This antiradar project was known as KEMPSTER. Unfortunately, KEMPSTER did not produce the hoped for success, and there were serious questions about how much added drag the electron guns might create. The CIA would have to wait for SKYLARK to come to fruition.

Ultimately, the SKYLARK modifications did move the A-12 toward the optimum performance the CIA and Lockheed had sought. The CIA began to qualify pilots and ground crews on a series of training flights that simulated missions over Cuba. A small detachment of five pilots, would be used for the mission. The goal was to get the maximum design of the aircraft to operate at Mach 2.8 and 80,000 ft. In order to meet the deadline, camera performance would need to be validated, and pilots qualified at Mach 2.8, and coordinated with supporting elements.

Only one ECM package would be ready by November, and a senior intra-governmental group of the President's Scientific Advisory Group, studied the problem of operating over Cuba with no ECM. After considerable modification to the aircraft, the detachment simulated SKYLARK. With 2 weeks notice the OXCART detachment could accomplish a Cuban flight, but with fewer planes and pilots than planned. The Detachment concentrated on working SKYLARK into sustained capability with five pilots and aircraft. The main job on this was to determine the aircraft's range, fuel consumption, be able to attain repeatable, reliable operation, finish pilot training, and prepare the SKYLARK mission and coordination routes with NORAD, CAD, and FAA which was all done without hindering the OXCART main mission. In March 19,1965, CIA Director McCone discussed with McNamara and Cyrus Vance, Assistant Secretary of Defense, the hazards to the U-2 and drone reconnaissance in Communist China. The memo consisted of this:

> *"It was further agreed that we should proceed immediately with all preparatory steps necessary to operate OXCART over communist china flying out of Okinawa, it was agreed that we should proceed with all construction and related arrangements. However, this decision did not authorize the deployment of the OXCART over Communist China nor does the decision to fly OXCART over Okinawa and over China.*
>
> *The decision would authorize all prepatory steps and expenditures of such funds as might be involved. No decision had been taken to fly the OXCART operationally over Communist China. This decision can only be made by the President."*

Four days later, Brigadier General Jack Ledford (Director of the Office of Special Activities), briefed Cyrus Vance, Secretary of State, on operations for the Far East. The project was known as **BLACK SHIELD.** It called for OXCART to operate out of Kadena in Okinawa, Japan. The training missions continued for nearly three months after SKYLARK and demonstrated that the OXCART A-12s were, indeed, capable of collecting photographic, reconnaissance information. Due to the delicate nature of the negotiations surrounding the crisis, the A-12s were not used over Cuba. Instead, U-2s continued to photograph Castro's installations as before, without encountering serious hostile actions. While the CIA proposed over flights on Cuba which would have tested the ECM in hostile environments. On September 15, 1966, the 303 Committee said no to the idea on sending the OXCART over Cuba feeling it "would disturb the existing calm previously in that area of our foreign affairs."

SKYLARK brought significant achievements to the A-12 and OXCART program. The plane never got the chance to use it over Cuba or the Soviet Union, but there were other trouble spots on the globe just ripe for airborne reconnaissance.

The modus for the OXCART program was to collect tactical intelligence rather than strategic information. This caused nervousness in Washington D.C. about the possible undetected introduction of SAMS to North Vietnam. President Johnson asked for a proposal on the issue. The CIA felt that OXCART should be used for just that purpose, but the Department of State and the DOD were still examining the proposal for political risk. By June of 1965, the United States was paying increasing attention to China's intensified defensive capabilities which were becoming apparent. The CIA decided that it was time to reassess the use of the U2 and the Ryan Fire-bee drones, the mainstays of the intelligence gathering section. The agency was already modifying the A-12s for better survivability and reliability. It was time to decide whether to use OXCART to support further reconnaissance in China, as it was obvious that the U2 was not going to be able to do the job. It still is amazing to realize that the most formidable reconnaissance aircraft the world had ever seen, had been built and yet the U.S. was still hedging as to when and if to use it because of the fear of a possible disaster, like a plane going down in denied territory or the possibility of being discovered. The point here is that the aircraft was untouchable because of her speed and altitude. That is what the entire OXCART program was built on and yet political entities in the U.S. didn't know how to field the OXCART program for fear of upsetting not some denied territory country, but the State Department!

On June 11, 1965, CIA director William Raborn sent a letter to Deputy Secretary of Defense, Cyrus Vance, discussing the plans to deploy the OXCART to Kadena Air Base in Okinawa, since it was the only viable site for this type of early operation. The project would involve as other A-12 efforts before it, unprogrammed funding. In short, no one but a handful of officials would know anything about it.

Under the basic provisions of an earlier CIA/USAF agreement on OXCART dated February 18, 1961, and with the National Reconnaissance Office (NRO) funding the arrangement, project planning moved forward.

In 1965, the United States began sending troops to Southeast Asia and South Vietnam, moves that created greater need for dependable reconnaissance. Defense Secretary McNamara, at the time, wanted to know if it would be possible to substitute the A-12, as the U2 which was becoming much more vulnerable to the SAM sites already growing in Vietnam jungles. The new CIA director William Raborn said that the A-12 could operate in an area, as soon as final operational readiness test were passed. The A-12 had no problem doing that.

President Lyndon Johnson decided to uphold the 303 Committee's decision. The CIA then proposed that the A-12 should overfly Cuba to test it out. The 303 Committee disagreed with that proposal, feeling that it might upset the already fragile peace. The State Department and the Defense members of the 303 Committee, decided to re-look at the requirement and political risks involved. While they were engaged in deliberations, the DCI Richard Helms, submitted to 303 Committee another formal proposed to deploy OXCART. Helms raised the matter to Johnson and at Tuesday Lunch on May 16th and received the president approval finally. Walt Rostow, later that day formerly conveyed the President's decision and **Black Shield** deployment plan was put into action.

OPERATION CAROUSEL:

Deployment to Southeast Asia.

Operation CAROUSEL began on May 11, 1967, with the first airlift of crews to Kadena AFB. By May 22^{nd,} the first A-12 #131, flew non stop to Kadena in 6 hours and 6 minutes. May 24th brought the 2nd A-12 #127. 127 left Area 51 and flew to Kadena in 5 hrs and 55 minutes. May 26th had the third aircraft #129 leaving Area 51 and on a normal flight until problems with inertial navigation and communication systems forced the flight down at Wake Island in the North Pacific Ocean. A pre-positioned emergency response team secured the aircraft without incident, and when fixed, the aircraft flew to Kadena the next day. Arrangements were made to brief the ambassador in the Philippines, Formosa, Thailand, South Vietnam, Japan and the high commissioner of Okinawa. The Prime Ministers of Japan and Thailand were advised of the situation as was the Defense Minister of China, Chief of the Air Force in Thailand. All reactions were favorable. There is a small anecdote about the first A-12 landing in secrecy at Kadena, or so it was thought. Apparently, someone got a photo and on the front page of the Okinawa newspaper was a photo of the aircraft. So much for secrecy of the operation! On May 29, 1967, the unit in Kadena was ready to fly and operational mission under the command of Colonel Hugh "Slip" Slater with 260 personnel had deployed to the **Black Shield** facility at the Okinawa base. **Black Shield** had begun.

By May 31, 1967 the first of the **Black Shield** missions was under way. This mission included one pass over North Vietnam and another over the DMZ (demilitarized zone). The A-12 flew at Mach 3.1 and 80,000 feet, for a total of 3 hours and 39 minutes. It photographed 70 of 190 suspected sites and 9 other priorities. The mission did not detect and radar signals bouncing off. Basically, that meant the mission went undetected by both the Chinese and the North Vietnamese. From June 19 through August 21, 1967, 7 more missions under **Black Shield** were flown, with 14 more from August 31 through December 16th. On the December 16th mission, there was one latch on by the Chinese Fan Song guidance radar, but it was not successful.

OXCART's efforts and results in Vietnam were truly stunning since it was the first time that non satellite reconnaissance at high speed and altitude could be maintained with out the worry of being shot down. Flying over enemy territory that included China, was just about what the A-12 was born and bred to do. In total, there were 22 **Black Shield** missions all flown and untouched by enemy hands. The photographs and the good quality of them provided the exact sort of information that the military and the CIA wanted. The Blackbirds' camera snapped pictures of the airfields, military hardware and military and industrial infrastructure.

On October 28, 29, and 30 1967, **Black Shield** flew missions that covered 55% of North Vietnam including Hanoi, Hai Phong, Pingshiany, and the Dong Dang area. The flights surveyed all of the six major airfields of North Vietnam, and more than half of the SAM 2 missile sites. The flights also covered 75% of the railroad network, and 42 priority bridges. These flights surveyed for bomb-damage assessment and to search for surface-to-surface missiles. Missions **6732** and **6734** of October 28 and 30th involved two passes over the North Vietnam panhandle. The **6732** mission passed along the Chinese border. Mission 6733, on October 29, also flew along the border, and the combined reconnaissance from all three missions yielded no evidence of surface-to-surface missiles. These missions combined, photographed more than 260 SA-2 sites in North Vietnam, which included two new ones. The SAMS that were plaguing U.S. pilots at every turn, and the more that could be discovered in their hiding places, the better.

Black Shield was also giving good assessments of the damage from carpet-bombing that the B52's were dropping daily in North Vietnam. That damage, however, was short lived. The photo taken showed that just as soon as the damage was inflicted by the B-52s, the North Vietnamese were patching it up. At the Phu Lac airfield, all the bomb craters on the runway were repaired, and the runway was made serviceable in short order. At Hai

Phong/Kien An airfield, all the bomb craters were repaired. The photos from the October 29th mission showed the continuous construction of the Yen Bai airfield in the northwestern part of North Vietnam. The Chinese engineers who were helping the North Vietnamese were working fast.

The photographs also revealed that the carpet bombing along the lines of MiGs left on these airfields, had not done nearly as much damage as had been expected. At the Phuc Yen airfield, 10 aircraft could be seen, all MiGs 15 or Mig17s. Two were destroyed. At Hanoi/Gia Lan airfield, one MiG 15/17 was seen. There were two derelict MiGs 15/17s and two dummy MiGs 21s noted at Ho Lac airfield. On the October 28th mission, the lifeline for the North Vietnamese, their most important bridges, were seen to be destroyed or unserviceable. This carried through all the way to Hai Phong. The A-12 mission over North Vietnam also came home with other information. The volume of North Vietnamese shipping seemed unchanged, The October 28th mission revealed that bridges were quickly being repaired and railroad shipments were moving along. The photos also showed flatcars carrying 42 objects that were never identified, and construction of a rail to road shipment point near Ho-Kou, China, just across the border from Lo Cai, North Vietnam. The U.S. military believed the construction of this installation could portend an increase in supply shipments via northwestern North Vietnam. The Chinese engineers had been busy developing the road network and logistics facility so the border area for at least two years. Perhaps one of the most telling "business a usual" reports that came back from the October 28th mission concerned a Hanoi thermal power plant, damaged in a raid on August 21, 1967. The generator hall roof showed a penetration, and a possible internal detonation. About 35 civilian structures surrounding the plant was destroyed, and about 40 damaged. Although there was no evidence that the plant was again in use, as there was no smoke from the stack, the plant was reopened.

While the **Black Shield** cameras picked up these details, the pilot had a few concerns of his own. In flight, the pilot could see vapor trails and witnessed three missile detonations, while his A-12 was at 84,000 ft. The post flight inspection of the aircraft found that a piece of shrapnel had penetrated the lower right wing fillet area and lodged against the support structure of the wing tank. The piece was only a scrap of shrapnel and not part of the SAM warhead. This was the only time an A-12 had ever been touched by enemy fire. During the **Black Shield** stay in Okinawa, four more missions were flown during the first three months of 1968, the period during which the **Black Shield** mission flew its last flight over North Vietnam and its first and second over North Korea.

BLACK SHIELD MISSIONS OVER NORTH VIETNAM:

BX-001

May 31,1967: Flown at Mach 3, 1 and 80,000 ft. for 3:45 hours, the mission searched the Lao Cao area for SAM missile sites. Dien Bien Phu was searched and no dam installation was found. Hanoi had at least four occupied, revealed central guidance areas. There were four possible missiles and a guidance radar site. The Hai Phong SAM support facility consisted of one drive through building; five destroyed or dismantled buildings, and two support buildings. No missiles or missile related activities were found. Another Hanoi SAM site was found occupied with launchers and missiles and one position was unoccupied. The guidance area contained probable Fan Song radar and at least two vans in the area. This was the first of the **Black Shield** missions. The photo take was considered good.

BX003

June 1967: Flown at Mach 3.1 and 81, 00 for 4:30 hours. This mission covered a total of 97 SAM sites. On the 97 sites, 4 were newly identified (2 occupied and 2 unoccupied.), and the 12 were identified only (activity status was unknown). Of the seven major airfields covered, five provided Order of Battle (change of military posture.) information and two were identification only. Additionally, a large area of unidentified rail service activity was shown

8 miles south of Thai Nyguyen. It was analyzed for possible missile associations. Further analysis suggested it was unrelated. The photo take quality was good.

BX6705

June 20, 1967: Flown at Mach 3.1 and 82,000 ft. for a total of 5:30 hours. This mission produced imagery of a total of 133 SAM-2 sites that were identified. Of the 132, there were 2 new sites (both occupied) and 15 were identified only. Of the seven major airfields that were photographed, four provided Order of Battle information. The Viet-Tri Railroad yards appeared to be unserviceable. The yard had been subjected to air strikes and had numerous bomb craters. At least 20 pieces of rolling stock (seven derailed and overturned) were observed in the yard. Imagery was considered excellent.

BX6706

June 30, 1967: Flown at Mach 3.1 and 81,000 ft. for 5:00 hours. The mission produced imagery showing 109 SA-2 Sam sites that were identified. Of the 109 sites, 3 were newly identified with 1 being occupied, and 10 were for identification only. The photo take was considered good.

BX 6708

July 13, 1967: Flown at Mach 3.15 and 82,100 ft. for 3:40 hours. The mission was flown against targets in the north central area of North Vietnam. No SAM sites were noted. The photo take on these missions was considered good.

BX6709

July 19, 1967: Flown at Mach 3.17 and 82,000 ft. for a total of 4:58 hours. This mission was flown against central and south areas of North Vietnam. There were a total of 166 surface-to-surface missile sites located, including 4 new sites. Twelve of the sites were occupied and 5 of the 9 priority surface-to-surface missile target sites were covered. The photo take was considered good.

BX6710

July 20, 1967: Flown at Mach 3.1.6 and 82,000 ft. for 4:55 hours. This mission was flown against northeast area of North Vietnam. 80 SAM sites were identified, 20 of which were not covered in BX6709, 5 SAM sites were occupied and 2 seemed to be new. 7 of the 9 priority surface-to-surface missiles targets were covered. BX6709 and BX6710 missions were the first two to be flown consecutively. Once again, the photo take was good despite haze.

BX6716

August 21, 1967: Flown at Mach 3.2 and 82,000 ft. for 3:55 hours. Photo take was good to excellent. No other details were given for this flight.

BX6718

August 31, 1967: Flown at Mach 3.2 and 81,000 ft. for 5:12 hours. The photo take was good until the camera malfunctioned.

BX6722

September 16, 1967: Flown at Mach 3.5 and 80,000 ft. for 4:01 hours. The photo take was good.

BX6723

September 17.1967: Flown at Mach 3,16 and 81,000 ft. for 4:00 hrs. This mission observed a total of 126 SAM-2 sites. Of the 126 observed, 19 were occupied, 89 unoccupied and 15 were identification only. Hanoi and Hai Phong were imaged. Seven additional complexes, three major ports, and three railroad yards were included. From the photos taken over China, it was shown that the Ping-Hsiang, Hanoi railroad segment was covered and serviceable from Ping-Hsiang China to Dong Dang, North Vietnam with no unusual activity or rolling stock observed. At Hanoi SAM site A15.2, which had a Fan Song radar system, a transporter with possible missiles was found on a road west of the site. Sited was one transporter that was canvas covered loaded with three missiles, one Fan song radar, on Spoon Rest radar, five van trucks and two other trucks. The photography was excellent.

BX6725

October 4. 1967: Flown at Mach 3,14 and 81,000 ft. for 4:09 hours. This mission covered a total of 146 SAM-2 sites in North Vietnam. 18 were occupied, 116 unoccupied, and 12 were identification only. Hai Phong was over flown along with Hanoi. Photographed were 3 Shanghao PTF torpedo boats (observed for the first time) along with other military craft, along the banks of the Red River and the Canals des rapidses, in defense of the complex. This mission also over flew China to look at the Chia- Lai - Shih airfield, Hai-Kou airfield, Hsin Hsing Naval facility and Yai-cheng radar site. The photo take was excellent.

BX6727

October 6, 1967: Flown at Mach 3.29 and 81.000 ft. for 2:20 hours. The photo take was good. This mission was terminated, however, due to a faulty pressure gauge.

BX6728

October 15, 1967: Flown at Mach 3.39 and 81.000 ft. for 3:41 hours. This mission was flown with the express purpose of having Black Shield coverage of the DMZ and the panhandle area of North Vietnam, the flight located some nine MiG 21s stationed at the Puck Yen airfield in North Vietnam. Photo take was good.

BX6729

October 19.1967: Flown at Mach 3.21 and 81,000 ft. for 4:01 hours and photography was good.

BX6732

Flown at Mach 3,15 and 83,500 feet for 3:49 hours. On this mission, a total of 120 SAM-2 sites were identified in North Vietnam. Of the 120 sites, 14 were occupied, 90 unoccupied, 16 were identification only. An SAM-2 missile was observed in flight for the first time on 8x photography. The missile was apparently fired from the Hanoi SAM site AD1-2, which was imaged subsequent to launch. There was no incident to the aircraft. There was an occupied air warning radar facility, which was newly, identified south-southeast of Pei-Li China. There were 7 major North Vietnam airfields observed. The major port facilities of Hai Phong, Cam Pha, and Hon Gai were imaged. There was a Poltava large hatch freighter observed at anchor with a deck cargo of large cylindrical storage tanks, including 6 trucks. An Atlantic-class ocean-going salvage tug was observed for the first time in North Vietnam. Photography quality was good.

BX6733

October 29, 1967: Flown at Mach 3.23 and 82.000 ft. for 3:56 hours, Photographic quality was good. This is no more information for this flight.

BX6734

October 30, 1967: Flown at Mach 3:20 and 85,000 ft. for 3:44 hours. Photo take was good. BX6734 also found itself under fire from SAM missiles. At least 6 to 9 missiles were fired at the A-12. The System IV analysis on the A-12 indicated that the EWS performed as designed, in jamming a multi signal environment. The pilot first reported missile was rotating rather fast about the vertical axis, just about 100-200 yards to the right of the cockpit. The SAM-2 MOD I missile was judged to be out of control and no longer answering to any guidance information. The SAM exploded behind the A-12 and a piece of shrapnel hit the right aft fillet of the aircraft, lodging in the support structure by the #5 fuel tank. The pilot explains the incident:

> "These missiles were in a steep climb through the aircraft altitude of approximately 83,500 ft., then they made a sharp push to a moderate angle, leveled at my altitude and guided toward the stern of my aircraft to detonation. The missiles varied lightly in azimuth compared to my line of flight in their climb but all corrected in azimuth to an accurate dead stern position during the push over and dive phase. (missile altitude) estimated 90,000 ft. is probably quite close but could vary a few feet either way. It was not possible to view the entire contrail until down track a few miles due to the narrow angle view in the rear periscope." The pilot was referring the three missiles in the encounter.

BX6737

December 8.1967: Flown at Mach 3.20 and 82.500 ft. for 3:59 hours. Photography was good. No other information on this flight was available

BX6738

December 10.1967 Flown at Mach 3.17 and 81.000 ft. for 3:51 hours. Photography was good. No other information on this flight was available

BX6729

December 15, 1967: Flown at Mach 3.20 and 86.000 ft. for 4:09 hours. Photography was good. No other information on this flight was available

BX6740

December 16, 1967: Flown at Mach 3:20 and 86,200 ft. for 3:56 hours. The missions covered a total of 107 SAM-2 SAM sites in North Vietnam. Two sites were occupied with 1 newly identified, 79 were unoccupied and 26 were identification only. 7 major airfields were covered including the Hoa Lac airfield which had been subjected to an air strike. One runway was serviceable and about 7,000 ft. runway was under construction. Air Field facilities included five covered aircraft hangers with roof damage or destroyed at the northwest end and 5 uncovered aircraft revetments at the southeast end. There were two damaged MiG 15 and MiG 17 aircraft and two delta wing dummy decoys. The photo take on this mission was good.

All missions were flown by the A-12 and used the Type I camera. The altitudes and Mach numbers represent the maximum attained during that flight.

OXCART and the *Pueblo* Incident

All Americans who followed the news of the capture of the "research" quasi-Navy ship, USS *Pueblo* by the North Koreans on January 23, 1968, were truly moved and horrified by their plight. American soldiers were fighting for freedom from communism in South East Asia. The U.S. was deep into the Vietnam War. There was concern among the Communists in the region about the war spreading, especially with the large number of American troops stationed in South Korea. The North Koreans, via the Soviets, were very itchy about this situation, they were looking for a piece of meat for their propaganda, and they fell upon the USS *Pueblo*.

The *Pueblo*, during its first mission as an AGER class vessel, had all the problems that could possibly come to a light cargo ship converted by the Navy into a new AGER-2 (Auxiliary General Environmental Research 2) class, outfitted for surveillance. No one in the Navy really seemed to know what an AGER-2 class ship was or was not, nor even what its true mission was. Due to its position in the reconnaissance world, it was "Of the Navy" but not "in the Navy". The classified segment of the mission meant that the *Pueblo* was only a "broker", much like the CIA and the A-12, with the USAF's support of the project, men and supplies. All of the reconnaissance effort carried over to the *Pueblo*, over which the ship's commander had no real control or even knowledge of what was going on in that little room on his ship. It was a definite conflict of interest and a source of internal strife.

Although the *Pueblo* was supposedly on a mission to map the sea bottom, she was caught spying on Wonsan Harbor, North Korea. North Korean patrol boats captured the *Pueblo* while she was technically in international waters, killing one and taking 82 crew members captive. In those terror filled hours after the boarding, Washington was trying to discern through diplomatic means what was happening so many miles away. At the same time, it was clear that U.S. intelligence would need to examine the situation directly. The crews' lives were at stake, and there was no time for second-guessing. It was necessary to find out immediately what was going on and if there ever was a case for real time reconnaissance, this was it.

In the normal battle plan, the USAF was supposed to back up the Navy. There was a specific protocol for the *Pueblo* mission. When the *Pueblo* went on a mission, it was supposed to have "critical support". The Fifth Air Force was on "strip alert" in the event that something happened. The Commander, Naval Forces (CNF) in Japan, whose request was forwarded to CINCPAC (Commander in Chief -Pacific), would then authorize the alert aircraft to launch, this is the only manner in which it could summon help. In this incident, however, the Air Force was too distant to provide helpful intervention. The nearest aircraft carrier was the USS Enterprise, which was 450 miles away, she wasn't able to launch a flight quickly enough to prevent *Pueblo*'s takeover by the North Koreans.

The *Pueblo* had set sail from Sasebo, just off Japan on January 11, 1968. With a crew of 83—6 officers, 2 civilians, and 75 enlisted men—the ship was to patrol the eastern coast of Korea, north of the northern boundary in the Sea of Japan. It wasn't a particularly dangerous mission—at least that was what Capt. Charles M. Cassel, Assistant Chief of Staff of Operations for (CINCPACFLT) (Commander in Chief, Pacific fleet) thought and told *Pueblo* Commander Lloyd Bucher. As a matter of fact, USS Banner, sister to *Pueblo*, had performed the *same* mission a few months before with no incident at all. However, a strip alert was ordered for the Banner. *Pueblo*, however, would have to go it alone.

Pueblo had been instructed to remain at least 13 miles off the shores of North Korea at all times. The crew would maintain radio silence unless the *Pueblo* came under surveillance by passing ships. *Pueblo* was to remain at least 500 yards from any commercial ship and to keep her .50mm guns under wraps, unless she came under attack. The small blessing of the .50mm caliber guns came after the Israeli Six Day war, during which Israel attacked the USS Liberty on June 8, 1967. The incident justified the arming of all AGERs. The *Pueblo* was untouched from the time it left Sasebo, until January 22, just 11 days later. On January 21, at 1500 hours, *Pueblo* encountered two fishing boats; one had approached closing to 100 yards, only to withdraw and later return to close at 30 yards. The fishing boat then departed. Seeing no reason to break silence, *Pueblo* did not report the incident to CINCFLT until approximately 10:30 hours on January 23rd. The fishing boat encounters turned out to be the beginning of the end for *Pueblo*. An hour later, the North Koreans were challenging the ship.

By noon, January 23, *Pueblo* reported it was challenged again, this time by a North Korean submarine chaser. The chaser sent this message: 'Heave to or I will fire". *Pueblo* quickly reported its position off the Korean coast at a range of over 12 miles. *Pueblo* also replied with the international flag signal: "I am in international waters". *Pueblo* reported this information by radio to command center in Japan some 52 minutes after the encounter. The word was sent to CINCPAC, who in turn notified CINCPACFLT. The Pacific fleet Commander notified the USS Enterprise and her sister ships, Truxton and the USS Highbe, a Destroyer. But, it was too late. By 12:10 hours, the North Koreans sub chaser had radioed in, *"The name of the target is GER1-2. I judge it to be a reconnaissance ship. It is American guys". It does appear that there are weapons and it is hydrographic mapping by 1300 hours".* Three patrol boats joined the sub chaser and there were two MiG aircraft in the air overhead. The sub chaser was backing toward *Pueblo*, clearly intending to board the ship. *Pueblo* turned away and signaled her intention to leave. That was at approximately 13:15 hours. By 13:27 hours, the sub chaser ordered the patrol boats out of the way because it was intending to fire or *Pueblo*. *Pueblo* relayed a message CINCPACFLT with an SOS. The captain's message reported, *"We are being boarded, initiating emergency destruction of classified equipment. Request help SOS."*

By 13:45 hours, *Pueblo* was being fired on, had three wounded, and the crew couldn't uncover their .50 mm guns. *Pueblo* was boarded at 14:32 hours, at which time the ship made its last call for help. There was no one to help her, but soon U.S. intelligence would find her from distant skies.

CIA director Richard Helms notified the **Black Shield** forces at Okinawa to be ready for takeoff at 21:00 hours on Jan 25th (which would have been January 26 according to the difference in time from Washington to Okinawa) The memo from the White House read: *".... returning 4 1/2 hours later. The film would be offloaded and sent to a classified location (which turned out to be the 67th Reconnaissance Squad stationed at Yokota, Japan) for processing. No later than 04:30 EST January 27th"* which meant there was no room for error. Helms also indicated that there would be no additional resources or support beyond that normally used on a Black Shield mission over North Vietnam.' CYGNUS and her pilot were going out alone, as usual. However, this time there would be no spare aircraft on the runway in case something happened. The reason for this was due to the flight being so highly classified.

The total time over denied territory would be 17 minutes. The photographic resolution would be 1 to 3.5 feet.

**A note to this story before we proceed: Many historians and authors have given credit to Frank Murray, another renowned CIA pilot for this Flight. In 2007, this author found in a declassified CIA report, the flight log of Jack Weeks. In that log and in other material that this author had declassified via the CIA under special FOIA provision, this author located the proof that Jack Weeks did indeed make the first flight over North Korea. We must add that Frank Murray also made a flight over North Korea, BX 6853, much of which is still classified today, due to the intelligence found on that flight, two weeks later in February 1968.

CIA pilot Jack Weeks flew BX 6847, with Article #131. The planned takeoff time was 10:110 Z (Zulu), the actual time of takeoff was 01:11Z the time planned enroute was 4+01 hours, the actual time it took was 4+00Z. Weeks landed back at Okinawa by 05:11Z. Now all this may have sounded simple, but it wasn't. Week's takeoff was normal and the first aerial refueling was completed, leaving #131 with 7,500 lbs. of fuel. Weeks was on his way. All was preceding normally, except that as the flight went on, Weeks had a problem over Hangnam: his right inlet failed to retract all the way and an unstart in the right inlet made its nasty appearance. Weeks had been in straight and level flight at Mach 3.19 and had started a right turn heading southwest. Weeks operated the inlet manually and had a bad spike actuation. Weeks had exited denied territory at something over 80,000 ft., for the last time over Hangnam. This was a tough route to fly with both the climb and cruise temperatures being way above normal. For Weeks to make his first two passes both altitude and speeds he had to up trim the engines to 820 degrees "F" for a total of twenty minutes. This lined #131 up for an extensive engine inspection later on. According to the cable from General Paul Bacalis: *"Jack had to use some skill and cunning to make this mission good and he did."* Weeks left the first air refueling with 67,500 lbs., and the 2nd aerial refueling with 67,800 lbs. and landed back at Kadena with just under 13,000 lbs. A flash message was sent to John Parangosky, a Chief on the OXCART program. It was a bit later through the photography that Weeks had taken, that the *PUEBLO* had been sighted in Wonsan harbor. This was in addition to the reason for the mission which was to provide intelligence to the U.S. 8th Army as to further insurgency by the North Korean. None was sighted, but at least we all knew that the *Pueblo* was sitting in the frozen Wonsan harbor and had not been dismantled. Not much could not be said for the crew of the *Pueblo*, who were being systematically tortured by the North Koreans, and later released in much worse shape than could ever be believed, some 18 months later by the ruthless North Koreans.

Aircraft #129

Operation **Black Shield** had been a great success for the A-12, and the plane provided excellent reconnaissance of the *Pueblo* incident. After the rapid Skylark developments, which never produced a reconnaissance mission over Cuba, the missions over North Vietnam and North Korea seemed to prove that the A-12 was the definitive reconnaissance plane. In June 1968, however, during a routine flight to check out a new engine, CIA pilot Jack Weeks went missing.

Weeks left on a mission from Kadena AFB on Okinawa on June 4, 1968. The mission was a check flight to test a starboard engine that was just installed in aircraft #129. Initially, Weeks was supposed to fly the Route #3 training route, but due to Typhoon Kim, he was delayed and his route was changed to Route #7. Having been initially set up to leave at 1300 hours, he was now pushed back to 1400 hours. The new route was safer, having been flown earlier that morning, and thus providing more current weather updates. On a previous flight, a problem had been reported (a "squawk") about a late shift of internal bleeds during the acceleration part of the flight. A normal shift would have taken place at 150 to 190 degrees CIT (compressor inlet temperature) with a corresponding speed of Mach 2.2 to 2.3. There was another minor squawk involving pitch A and yaw M status lights that came on once, but reset perfectly. There was also some brake chatter at low-speed taxi, but nothing noted here could have caused the loss of the aircraft. The problems could not be duplicated and were not entered on the AFTO 781A form used to document maintenance issues.

The starboard engine installed for this flight (Engine 208) had been flown previously in other A-12s. The engine was flown in aircraft #122, from which it was removed on June 12, 1963, for excessive oil consumption, at 3 1/2 gallons per hour. Presumably, Engine 208 was fixed, as it later flew in aircraft #131, where it accumulated 2025 hours since its last overhaul. Once again, it was removed, this time for slow start problems. A new fuel control and fuel pump was installed. The engine was successfully run on a test stand, and cleared for flight on April 26, 1968. Engine 208 was installed in aircraft #129, on June 3, for its flight the next day. Her ground crew preflighted aircraft #129 normally. The Birdwatcher signal that gave the "all clear" was received without incident, and the flight was let go with no problems. Jack Weeks took off in #129 and rendezvoused with a tanker about 20 minutes later for a routine refueling. The tanker transmitted the required signal for the offload, and completed the 34,000 pound fuel transfer to the aircraft. At the time of the tanker disconnect, #129 had been airborne about 29 minutes.

The last anyone saw of Jack Weeks and #129 was after the A-12 disconnected from the tanker and climbed away. The flight was normal for all of 42 minutes, the time the first of the Birdwatcher responses were received. At 0542Z, Birdwatcher channel 54 received a signal that the starboard engine EGT (exhaust gas temperature) was in excess of 860 degrees. This was followed 22 seconds later by the Birdwatcher channel 7 indicating starboard engine fuel flow was less than 7,500 pounds per hour with a repeat of the channel 54 message of the engine overheat. Eight seconds later, Birdwatcher channel 3 was receiving indications that the aircraft was below 70,000 feet; the channels 54 and 7 indications were also repeated. After this, no further contact with Jack Weeks or #129 was ever received. The accident report was based on limited information, since Weeks and #129 were never recovered.

However, the engine's log back on the ground showed that there had been eight unstarts. The EGT reached 860 degrees in 3 to 5 seconds after the instantaneous compressor inlet pressure dropped to about 5 psi. Fuel flow dropped to 5,000 pounds per hour at approximately the same time as the 860 degree temperature was reached. This meant that channels 7 and 54 would respond when the right engine fuel flow was below 7,500 pounds per hour. This was the first indication on Birdwatcher that the pilot had retarded the throttle in response to the engine overtemp.

The accident board concluded that during the 22 seconds from the starboard engine going above 860 degrees to the engine dropping below 7,500 pounds per hour fuel flow, the pilot was using engine trim in an attempt to control the overheated engine. The board also suggested that the engine derich came into play, resulting in 900 pounds per hour fuel flow being bypassed from engine main fuel control. This would have been a further aid in controlling the problem of overheat. It appeared that this solved the issue for 22 seconds at least.

There was some possibility that the pilot was not aware of the overtemp and didn't take any corrective action. The board ruled this out, however, because the engine derich light would have come on, assuming the Derich switch was armed. The light on the EGT would have been on, and the Birdwatcher tone would have come through the pilot's headset. Birdwatcher channel 3, linked to the plane's altitude, was a critical warning system and was calibrated specifically for #129. This would show that there was a descent and was activated at 68,500 feet. Since there is an overall time lag in the system, the channel 3 signal would remain inactive until reaching 71,200 feet during ascent.

The Birdwatcher signals indicated in sequence:

0542:182, excessive right engine temp
0542:402, low fuel flow right engine
0542:482, altitude at or below 68,500 feet.

The Birdwatcher system was unique to the A-12 and provided the only clues to this mystery. The only other evidence was in the maintenance records of the engine that was swapped out to #129, which indicated no failure trend that could have initiated the accident. They mentioned only the write-up for slow starting that had caused the engine to be removed from aircraft #131 in April. Records on the #129's last 10 flights were also inspected, and there were no discrepancies that could shed light on the cause of the accident. The loss of A-12 #129 and its pilot Jack Weeks, remains a mystery. If not for the Birdwatcher system, there would have been no clues at all.

The loss of skilled pilot Jack Weeks and #129 was a sad moment in an otherwise triumphant period for the A-12. Together, the events over China, North Vietnam, and North Korea highlight the complexity and risk this plane embodied. At its best, the A-12 was a nearly unstoppable reconnaissance tool, flying at the limits of speed and altitude for manned aircraft. Yet rocketing through the sky at supersonic speed as the quarry of enemy radar and weaponry is inherently dangerous work. Most who accepted the risk were rewarded with experiences few can imagine, and fewer still will ever share. But, a few brave and talented men, paid the highest price for their courageous service.

BX6853

Flown by CIA pilot Frank Murray, on Feb 19, 1968, in Article #127, covered much the same territory as Weeks. 65 of the 75-programmed targets were covered. One SSM target was covered, 11 SAM sites were found, 8 of them occupied. There were an additional 88 bonus targets. This mission got good coverage of the southern two-fifths of North Korea. Snow and aerial haze covered the mountainous region, which made interpretation difficult. The total INS time as 4+06 hours. However, Murray took off six minutes early due to a B52/KC-135 tanker time conflicts. One of the items that was titled an "Outstanding Action" required: an alert briefing for the next North Korea Mission, that would be flown to determine the location of USSR fleet in the

Sea of Japan. A mention was made to adjust the EWS (Electronic Warning System) and camera turn on, to gain maximum intelligence.

BX6856

Flown March 13, 1968, by Mele Vojvodich. It was the next to last flight for the **OXCART/Black Shield** program. The flight went over North Vietnam, covering portions of Laos, Cambodia and the South Vietnamese and Cambodian border. The mission was designed to obtain coverage of the high interest areas around the DMZ and Khe Sanh. Chi-Con radars tracked the flight for at least 13 minutes at a distance of 436 nautical miles. The flight's EWS suite carried Type I camera, PIN REG, BIRDWATCHER, BIG BLAST, BLUE DOG II and System VI.

BX6858

The last flight flown by the OXCART A-12 on May 8, 1968, with pilot Ronald "Jack" Layton. It would be the last mission the OXCART and **Black Shield** Program would ever fly. The flight went out over North Korea and photographed two-fifths of southern North Korea. The flight lasted for 3:30 hours. The aircraft EWS suite carried: Type I camera, B/W film, PIN REG, Blue Dog II, MAD MOTH and System VI. After this flight, the program drew to a brilliant close. It would soon be time to return to Area 51.

In the CIA documents that have been released, there was a lot of material focusing on China, basically contingency plans. There was an ECM package called "PINWHEEL" that was used to overfly China. There were many political problems dealing with the over flight of a nation like China. The politicos in Washington D.C., felt that the Chinese would quickly acquire knowledge of the operation. It was also felt that the mission aircraft would be detected by Chinese radar, as that had already happened over North Korea and North Vietnam. Only by the virtue of speed and altitude could the A-12 outrun anything the Chinese could possibly throw at it. After the Chinese had identified the A-12 as a new reconnaissance aircraft, it was a sure bet that

Chinese aggression on the island of Okinawa would put two and two together, and realize that the flights were coming out of there. The Chinese would of course, try to knock down an A-12. Of course, the eventuality of that was negligible and any recourse against the U.S. was very small. However, the situation could be quite different if an A-12 happened to go down in Chinese mainland. This type of incident would really bring down the house and there would be a major political and propaganda campaign launched, especially if the downed pilot were picked up alive. To show the dramatization of the plan: Peiping (now Beijing) would hope to persuade the world body and Chinese public of the strength of China and the riskiness of the U.S. over flight policy. They would use resources they had to mobilize public opinion in Japan and Okinawa against the U.S. control of the Okinawa Island and against the existence of the U.S. bases in Japan itself. However, whether or not it was even flown is a question in itself.

On June 7, 1968 Article #131 left Kadena for the flight home to Nevada. The flight diverted to Wake Island because of a fuel leak. Pilot Ken Collins brought the first of the A-12s home. The next flight home on June 9, 1968 brought Article #127 back the Area 51 in 5 hours and 29 minutes. The last flight back was #131 flown by Frank Murray. #131 was ferried from Kadena to Area 51 and back to Palmdale CA. From there, came the ceremony that was again done quietly and away from eyes other than those who were "in the know". The wives of the pilots would see what their husbands were risking their lives in for the very first time. Kelly Johnson stated that the first two aircrafts #122 and 134 which were to be stored in late August 1968, were handled in a small hangar at the USAF Palmdale (building #211). Johnson stated that partitioning and the sprinkler system would be done by the time that aircraft arrived. Remaining aircraft were stored at main hangar at Palmdale and that had to be made ready. The first two aircrafts arrived in September. This was to be all inclusive costs on a one time basis. Col. Geary, project manager, felt the quote was reasonable. It was stated that there would be no "pickling" (canned storage) of the J-58 engines and they would be kept inside the aircraft. #134 would be trucked in requiring more expenditure to place it at Palmdale. #122 was flown in and only needed minimum care. By

September 16, 1968, #122 was flown in for the last time and the National Reconnaissance Office then took over the aircraft. The NRO worked with the USAF on the disposition of the aircraft after then turning it over to them for museum display. This was a silent end to a magnificent program. Could it be any other way?

Issinglass:

The CIA did have hope for a successor to the A-12. **Issinglass** was the next project on the boards as a possible replacement. The CIA planned for an air launched, rocket powered, high-speed manned vehicle project for 1965-68. Some of the basic technologies later used in the space shuttle and reusable launch vehicles were used here. The program studied several technologies that would be used in later Space Shuttle and SSTO programs, including light-weight structure thermal protection systems and diffusion bonded titanium. A large-scale test vehicle was built and tested to prove these concepts. The initial concept was designed by General Dynamics, based on work done by the B-58 Hustler, FISH and KINGFISH programs of 1958-60. This new design would be used with modern avionics and hydraulics systems developed for the F-111 and were capable of air breathing mach 4-5 cruise for 30 minutes at 30 km altitude.

The next General Dynamics / McDonnell aircraft project in 1965 was designated **Project Rheinberry**. This was a rocket-powered aircraft launched by the B-52 and flying at near orbital speeds, having the advantages in comparison to satellites to justify the high development and operating risk and cost.

Project **ISSINGLASS** was designed by General Dynamics and utilized the Convair FISH proposal and the F-111 Aardvark. In order to create an aircraft of Mach 4-5 at 100,000 ft., General Dynamics completed the feasibility study in 1964 and the OSA (Office of Scientific Activities) took no further action because the aircraft would still be vulnerable to existing Soviet countermeasures. In 1965, a McDonnell Design came under consideration. **Project Rheinberry** (parts of it came from **ISSINGLASS**, as well as **OXCART**) ended in the summer of 1968. CIA did not choose to venture into any other advanced successors to the A-12.

Cygnus Heads Home

After all the lives, trials, tribulations, expense, it took only one short mission for **OXCART** to be put out of the way. It wasn't because the A-12 had outgrown its usefulness, or pilot training was at a miss. No, it was because of politics. This is said in anger and rightfully so. Waste of this magnitude is always something to be irate about. The A-12 had not outlived her mission, her mission had been pulled out from under her by the bean counters and petty jealousies that ran rampart in Washington D.C. When you consider the entire program lasted 10 years (1957-1968) and there were only a total of 29 flown missions from Okinawa, there was something wrong with these figures. The **OXCART** surely had more life in her than that. It wasn't until Frank Murray flew the last A-12 home in article #131, that the wives finally got a good look at what their husbands were doing. As Sharlene Weeks, widow of Jack Weeks recalled, the airplane was the most beautiful thing she ever saw. Mrs. Weeks was moved to tears as she watched Frank fly past for that one final time with the A-12. The wives and husbands gathered at Area 51, one last time so that the pilots could receive the CIA Intelligence Medal of Valor. Sharlene Weeks received her husband, Jack Week's award. The CIA also awarded the Legion of Merit to the **OXCART** Detachment Commander and his deputy. The USAF Outstanding Unit awarded was given to the **OXCART** Detachment members of the 1129th Special Activities Squadron. And that was that, the part was over. Ten years of aeronautical history and a majestic aircraft that to this day looks like something out of the movie "Star Wars" were cocooned in a hanger along with the years of paperwork which the CIA nicely tucked away. There was something wrong with this entire picture. What was wrong had to do with budgets, resentment and plain stupidity.

As early as September 29, 1966, Deputy Secretary of Defense, Paul Nitze, proposed at an executive committee meeting that **OXCART** be phased out of inventory. He was ready to discuss the status of the **SR-71**, which was already in advanced tests. In Nitze's mind and many others, two supersonic spy planes was a redundancy the U.S. did not need and could not afford. However, they didn't understand the significant differences each system had to offer and that was evident.

Dr. Alexander Flax, Director of the National Reconnaissance Office (NRO), had circulated papers showing that the **SR-71** was in a satisfactory condition and could take over the North Vietnam reconnaissance flights as early as December 1, 1967. The Joint Chiefs of Staff concurred that the **SR-71** was ready to go operational. At least one attendee, Dr. Donald F. Hornig, special assistant to the president (Lyndon Johnson) for science and technology, disagreed. By Dr. Hornig's calculations—based on the equipment lists, statistical factors, and performance curves—the **SR-71** was two to four times more vulnerable than the A-12. He had looked at other factors too, including the aircraft's operational techniques and impact, ECM systems and capabilities, present enemy activity, and perceived future operations. He concluded that the committee should not be too quick to deploy the **SR-71**.

Dr. Flax pointed out that if there were no economic restraints, he would prefer to retain the entire force. Yet money, as always, was on the table, and Dr. Flax felt that there was a need for a firm decision. If no decision were made, keeping both programs going would cost around $32 million. The question of putting A-12s in storage and later retrieving them was also raised. It would cost $300,000 to $500,000 to reactivate each aircraft if they were put away and subsequently brought to flight status again. This cost was based on reactivation being done within the first year. The financial plan in place at the time would fund the A-12 and allow continued operation at Area 51 only through December 1966. Any longer would require additional funds.

Shutting down Oxcart would be appropriate. Even Dr. Flax suggested that the delay would give a higher degree of confidence that the **SR-71** would be able to carry out the job in the face of North Vietnamese defense improvements. He thought the **SR-71** should be delayed for three months and the deployment should be scheduled for February of 1968.

This meeting set the stage for closing down the **OXCART** program; it would merely be a matter of when it would be convenient. The **SR-71** was coming online. The A-12 was still the fastest aircraft, carried the best ECM, and was already a proven item. Yet, those details did not matter. Twelve single-seat planes and one two-seat trainer were constructed. The program had accumulated 3,727 hours of flight time, during which there had been 2,189 flights. The two-seat trainer, added another 1,067 hours in 614 flights. There had been 13 A-12s; 5 were lost in accidents, leaving 8 that remained. No A-12 had been lost to any enemy; it was the politicians who would ultimately bring the A-12 down. Bowing to the pressure of politicians, on December 29, 1966, the CIA and the Pentagon decided to close the **OXCART** program as of December 31 of the following year.

Today, we know the **SR-71** wasn't able to obtain operational ready status at the expected time, and **OXCART** had to be extended twice. The first decision to extend **OXCART** occurred October 23, 1967, extending the program through March 31, 1968. Subsequently, on December 29, 1967, **OXCART** was extended again through June 30, 1968, allowing a one-month overlap with the **SR-71** for photographic coverage of Southeast Asia. The **SR-71** finally assumed primary responsibility of the mission on, March 15, 1968, with the A-12 remaining for the 30 days to transition. The **OXCART** was on readiness through June 30, 1968.

Even in its final days, the A-12 continued to show its remarkable capability. On December 21, 1966, Lockheed test pilot, Bill Park, made an extraordinary demonstration flight. Parks flew the A-12 an incredible 10,198 statute miles in just six hours. The A-12 left her Area 51 home and flew over Yellowstone National Park, then east to Bismarck, North Dakota, then on to Duluth, Minnesota. Parks turned south and flew over Atlanta, Georgia, on his way to Tampa, Florida. He turned northwest and flew to Portland, Oregon, and back south, home to Nevada. He then turned east, passed Denver, Colorado, and out to St. Louis, Missouri. Finally, Parks turned the A-12 around at Knoxville, Tennessee, passed Memphis, and headed back to Area 51.

To this day, any other aircraft cannot touch this flight. There were no serious problems with sonic booms, except that a few residents of a town just 30 miles from Area 51 were "boomed" while the A-12 was gaining altitude. The lack of complaints about broken windows and rattled nerves surely must have pleased Secretary of Defense McNamara, as that was one of his reasons for opposing the SST. At its high altitudes, the A-12 produced no more than a menacing rumble on the ground below. No one could see the plane, so no one could pinpoint the source of the sound.

NICE GIRL

On November 3, 1967, perhaps in a final effort to insert reason into the U.S. reconnaissance program, an A-12 and **SR-71** were flown against each other in a reconnaissance fly-off. The code name was **Nice Girl**. The two aircraft flew over the Mississippi Valley, approximately one hour apart. The results of the test were inconclusive, which suggests that the fly-off was a tossup. So, was the A-12 retirement a matter of politics or a matter of funding? Or was it simply a lot easier to bring the **SR-71** out into the public eye, and ease the USAF's bad feelings by giving it something to show off, instead of keeping the Blackbirds quietly hidden, as demanded by the CIA?

USAF versus CIA versus Politics

In any case, neither of these demonstrations changed the minds of the people in charge. The A-12 was available, but the political will was not. The USAF had been supporting the A-12 since the inception of **OXCART**, and USAF pilots were not flying it—CIA pilots were, albeit they were former Air Force pilots. The A-12 was being serviced on the ground—and refueled in the air—by the USAF, but the USAF was not getting the glory of performing the missions. The USAF was not comfortable as the support team for a black project headed by the CIA.

Due to their overlapping capabilities, the purchase of the **SR-71s** by the Air Force effectively brought the A-12 off the flight line. As always, there was another political gain to be made. The purchase of the **SR-71s** gave the Air Force the lead in aerial reconnaissance once again. The Bureau of the Budget for years been deeply concerned over the fact that the A-12 and the two-seat Air Force trainer and the **SR-71**, were overkill. Yet the A-12 had a couple of things going for it that the **SR-71** did not: The A-12 was faster and had a one-man crew, and it could carry a larger, more sophisticated photographic and "spying" system. The A-12 was operated by a civilian force and could be deployed quickly and with a minimum of logistics. But, the aircraft's acquisition by the Air Force meant only retirement for the A-12. The Air Force wanted to show the world that the **SR-71** was the consummate USAF aircraft for reconnaissance, which next to the A-12, it was not.

However, that was not the end of the **OXCART**. Two other circumstances once again called on the CYGNUS. In 1973, a CIA/USAF paper was produced that would reactivate the **OXCART**. It was felt that it was *"technologically and logistically feasible"* to reactivate and operate up to 5 A-12 aircraft given approximately 15 months. The cost did not consider the Side Looking Radar (SLR) or the infrared systems. The A-12 carried sensors with mission single sensor ability:

PIN REG: (Passive Warning System) and 13C MODD was a jammer system that was put back into action. They even had a planning factor set up: The A-12 would use the Type I camera. Each aircraft would sustain a flying hour program of 15 hours per man. Initial logistics support would be from the stored 590 packages (these were support materials put away when the A12s were stored) CONUS leasing would be at Lockheed Palmdale plant.

Three operational A-12s would operate from a deployed location.

Reactivation cost and time schedule account for the aircraft and sub systems with necessary modifications to update, and the replacement of cannibalized parts and sub systems were all lined up. Annual operating cost estimates were developed based on FY1967 A-12 program. The program first reduced in consideration of fleet size and limited flight-testing. Modifications and system imprint then increased by 35% inflationary factor, to express the cost terms of FY1974 dollars.

There was even a breakdown of the A-12 System Status: The estimated 60% commonality factor between the A-12 and the SR fleet and lesser commonality between A-12 and the U-2 have had an impact on stored A-12 assets. The ARN 50 and the 612T communications equipment were removed from the airframe. Airframe bench stock, tool cribs, toolboxes, ILS mockup, life support systems and 44AGE were transferred to the **SENIOR**

YEAR/SENIOR CROWN program, the new project name for the **SR-71**, 15 of 40 of the A-12 J58 engines used for the trainer, were turned over to the U-2.

BLUE DOG (L band guidance jammed) and MAD MOTH repeater jammer) EWS systems were no longer available. BLUE DOG was not used. While the system 13C MOD D jammer would replace MAD MOTH.

This all turned out to be a beautiful pipe dream. While it looked to be a good practical plan, it never went anywhere. It was nice to think that it could have happened. The next interesting piece of hope for the A12 was a possible sale to another country. In light of today's current mid-east situation, it's a very good thing that this didn't occur, even though Kelly Johnson was pushing for it to happen.

With the demise of **OXCART** and the aircraft in storage, the hope of revitalization wasn't looking good. Kelly Johnson had another plan of action regarding his awesome creation. Lockheed, in 1973, had a good relationship with Iran. The nation at this time was till on good terms with the United States, and the Shah was still in power, Lockheed and the U.S. government had sold the Iranian nation 62- C-130 Hercules aircraft. On the hope that the close working relationship that the State Department had with the Iranian government, Kelly Johnson wrote a letter to James Schlesinger, the Secretary of Defense, in November 30, 1973. Johnson noted that he had a series of long discussions with the Shah and his staff regarding the defense of Iran. Johnson recognized Iran's need for better surveillance abilities. Johnson felt that this was just the spot for the cocooned A-12s to be sold. It would be a complement to the Iranian F-14's –F-15s. Johnson asked the Secretary of Defense for an approval of a plan to offer the A-12s, modified of course, to Iran. Johnson pointed out that the "substantial benefits" of this plan to both the U.S. and Iran. Johnson went on to say that there was no national requirement for the A-12 and no longer should it be held for an asset. Johnson noted that he knew the technology (aerodynamics, engines, etc.) would have to be approved, of course, but he was hoping that the matter could be concluded within a week. Fortunately for the United States, the deal was not to happen. One can only think of the issues that *could* have been brought to bear on the United States, had this request been passed. The Shah of Iran was deposed and left Iran during the revolution in November of 1979.

Black Birds of Another Design

YF-12A AND M-21

Resourcefulness is a key attribute when defending one's-self or one's country. Military and intelligence planners are always looking to get the most from a good piece of equipment, or a good idea. The A-12 was both, and therefore a natural base for derivative aircraft. Inspired by the aircraft 's tremendous speed and range, Lockheed and government officials discussed a number of variations on the design, but most of them, including a fighter, reconnaissance bomber, and interceptor, never got out of the discussion stages. But a few others did, including the YF-12A interceptor and the M-21 reconnaissance drone /mother ship. Of course, the A-12 was the basis for its own successor, the SR-71.

YF-12A History

In November 1979, a dinner was given in honor of the retirement of YF-12A 60-6935, to the U.S. Air Force Museum at Wright-Patterson AFB. Kelly Johnson was the after-dinner speaker. He started out his speech saying, "The YF-12 was built as a follow-on to the airplane we built for the CIA." Many of the 400 to 500 attending, which included members of the general public, almost fell off their chairs. Never had any of them heard Kelly Johnson actually give out the name of the customer! The A-12 was no longer just for "need to know" executives; it was for everyone to know. Or, at least, Kelly Johnson thought everyone should know.

The YF-12A was a good idea for a high-speed interceptor. Since the North American F-108 Rapier, which had been designed as a companion interceptor for the XB-70 Valkyrie, was never developed, and with most other fighters capable of only a Mach 2 dash speed, the Mach 3 YF-12A seemed to offer a valuable service.

President Kennedy had asked why the A-12 couldn't be turned into the F-12. At the time, he had the B-70 on his plate, and neither he nor Defense Secretary McNamara wanted it. Developing an A-12-based fighter would be a good reason to cancel the B-70, once and for all. Yet, it didn't work out quite like that.

The YF-12A, which could have evolved into the F-12, was an aircraft capable of continuous Mach 3 flight, something that other fighters could not match. The YF-12A would be able to sustain high speed at very high altitude, and being made of titanium, wouldn't have the problem with heat that other conventional fighters would. It also had an added attraction: the heat of high-speed flight would anneal the titanium, actually strengthening the YF-12A on every flight, while the aluminum aircraft would be weakened under the same conditions. Lockheed, which had been working with titanium alloys since 1949, pretty well understood that fact.

Lockheed also understood that it would have to come up with armament for this advanced, manned interceptor. The radar-guided GAR-9 (later redesignated AIM-47 by the USAF) Super Falcon air-to-air missile was a good candidate. The GAR-9 was a liquid-fueled, nuclear-tipped missile, manufactured by the Hughes Company; it could fly up to Mach 6 with a range of approximately 115 miles. The missile weighed 815 pounds and was 13 feet long, with a diameter of 13 inches and a span of 33 inches. The missiles were mounted on launchers, with one to a bay, and were carried in the YF-12's three internal bays.

The missiles were ejected by pyrotechnic charges in a downward direction. The launch speeds ranged from Mach 2.19 to 3.2 at altitudes of 65,000 to 76,000 feet. The missile was originally intended for the never-built F-108 Rapier. The Skunk Works also figured out that the YF-12 could carry four 400-pound bombs in a rotary rack located in the same Q bay that originally housed the surveillance cameras. The bomber concept was called the RB-12. A single Polaris missile was an alternative weapon. Depending on which weapons were used, the #1 fuel tank could be shortened to accommodate the armament. No external changes to the fuselage would be made, except for the bomb bay door.

By October of 1960, the Skunk Works had received a $1 million USAF contract to develop the YF-12A into an interceptor that Lockheed called the AF-12. Lockheed believed a fleet of 90 to 100 AF-12s could protect the United States and North America against any Soviet bomber threat. The AF-12, to be developed under a project known as KEDLOCK, was a modified A-12 with the AN/ASG-18 fire control system (another item initially developed for the F-108 Rapier), and three GAR-9 missiles for air-to-air strikes on attacking bombers.

The AN/ASG-18, developed by Hughes, was the first long range, pulse-Doppler radar of its kind. A second seat was added to the aircraft, in the deeper forward fuselage, for a radar officer. The pilot's seat was raised for better visibility. This new "bulged" canopy gave the AF-12 a distinctive look. To decrease the distortion of radar signals, the chines on the extreme nose were removed and the radome lengthened. These modified chines accommodated a pair of infrared search and track sensors that were similar to ones used on the F-102's aft fuselage.

Wind tunnel tests conducted in June 1961 showed directional instability at high Mach numbers, attributed to the removal of the chines from the AF-12's nose area, to allow for the radome. To compensate, Lockheed engineers added ventral fins under each engine nacelle, and later added a retractable ventral fin to the rear center fuselage.

Testing was extensive. Millions of data test points were used to develop the internal compression inlets. The main idea was to get the inlet away from the wind and the fuselage effects, within the limits of the shock patterns developed by the fuselage nose, and thus minimize drag.

The USAF would eventually order two AF-12s, and would negotiate with the CIA to use the seventh, eighth, and ninth A-12 airframes to help the project along. True to Lockheed philosophy, the AF-12 was built literally "around the corner" from the A-12. Walls were put up at the Burbank facility to shield the A-12 from the AF-12. By late 1963, the first AF-12s were already in assembly. Since the CIA didn't want the USAF looking over its shoulder, somebody suggested the flight tests be done somewhere other than Area 51. That idea was vetoed, and flight tests were done there, after all.

Once again, the trucks and the trailers were hauled out, and the first AF-12 was trucked to Area 51 to begin flight test in July, 1963. Flight-testing proceeded. During a flight on April 16, 1964, the YF-12A conducted the first ejection test of the XAIM-47 (GAR-9) missile. Fortunately, the missile was not powered, or it would have flown right through the cockpit of the YF-12A with disastrous results.

Test pilot Jim Eastman made a Mach 3.23 flight with the first YF-12A on January 9, 1965, and held that speed for over five minutes. Later XAIM-47 flight-testing proved to be more successful. On March 18, 1965, a XAIM-47 hit a distant drone with a closure rate approaching 2,000 miles per hour.

In May 1965, the USAF issued a contract for $500,000 so engineers could start development on F-12B, which was supposed to be the operational version of the YF-12A. In November 1965, the USAF released an additional $500,000 for the program. One of the differences between the YF-12A and the F-12B were small chines at the nose of the F-12B to give it more stability and eliminate the need for ventral fins fitted to the YF-12A.

A project called *Coldwall* was part of YF-12A development. *Coldwall* consisted of a stainless steel cylinder, cooled with liquid nitrogen. The cylinder was covered with an insulating material. When the aircraft reached cruise speed, the insulating cover was blown off, so the effects of the sudden change from very cold to very hot temperatures could be observed. The test was analogous to what happens to a space vehicle upon reentry.

Another experiment was the *"Shaker Vane,"* tried on aircraft 60-6935. Because the YF-12A had a step about two-thirds of the way down the nose bulkhead, there was room for this installation. It was part of the NASA tests, and it consisted of a cross shaft with paddles, and the hydraulics to rotate the assembly around the centerline at various rates, almost 10 degrees at 30 cycles per second. The purpose of the device was to excite the airframe at various amplitudes and frequencies and measure the results. Later on, a follow-up test was run to eliminate elevon trim, but this was never approved or funded. It would have reduced elevon drag, but was never brought to fruition.

Flight-testing continued, and by September 1965, the USAF had fired a XAIM-47 from an YF-12A at Mach 3.2 at 75,000 feet missing the target by only 7 feet. In another firing test in April 1966, pilot Jim Eastman launched an unarmed XAIM-47 against a QB-47 drone flying below the YF-12A. The missile went through the drone's horizontal stabilizer. If the missile was armed, the QB-47 would have been destroyed. Flight successes notwithstanding, time and money were running out for the YF-12A. On January 5, 1967, the USAF formally canceled the YF-12A and ordered the F-12B program shut down altogether. By Christmas of 1967, Lockheed had reassigned or laid off the workers on that program.

All was not lost, however. NASA decided that it would take the YF-12A as a new high-speed test bed. Having completed tests with the XB-70 Valkyrie, it was looking to go further with the YF-12A. The USAF was reluctant to lend out the SR-71, but decided to let NASA use the YF-12As.

NASA's plan was to explore flight loads with the different effects on aerodynamics that came from heating at supersonic speeds. The two aircraft assigned were S/N 60-6935 and S/N 60-6936. The aircraft #936 was just about to enter the program when a failure in the fuel line in the right nacelle caused a blockage and a fire, and the aircraft crashed. NASA was hoping for a third aircraft after the demise of 60-6936.

There is an interesting side note to this crash. When 60-6936 crashed on January 24, 1971, it was taking part in an exercise that was joint NASA and ADC test. The aircraft left Edwards AFB to go to a local intercept training area, and from that point to an aerial refueling, and a return to the training area at Edwards. On the first leg of the flight, the YF-12 completed the intercept training with two F-4s, and then rendezvoused with a KC-135 near Beatty, Nevada. The second leg found the YF-12 preceding to an intercept with a F-106 near Fresno, California. It then followed a racetrack pattern to another intercept point, with the F-4 at Bicycle Lake and then back to Fresno for a planned intercept with a B-57. The B-57 was canceled because the YF-12s radar was inoperative. The YF-12 then turned back to Edwards and entered the traffic pattern. Shortly after entering the pattern, the YF-12s right engine caught fire, and the crew ejected. Howard Plunkett was working in a top-secret test position and assigned to TAC (Tactical Air Command) between 1969-1973. Plunkett was on the F-4's maintenance staff. He saw a top-secret message about the F-4 test being terminated due to the crash of the YF-12. Due to its speed and altitude, YF-12 #60-6936 was being used in the position of a MiG-25 FOXBAT. The USAF was trying to determine if it was possible for the F-4, flying in an arc profile, to launch a Sparrow missile and hit a speeding, highflying FOXBAT. The only aircraft that could do it was the YF-12 because it could duplicate the MiG 25's profile.

The reason the memo was top secret was not because of the YF-12, but the demise of the air defense test program and what it implied. This test was part of a larger program to determine if U.S. air defense aircraft could shoot down a missile to stop a FOXBAT that was in attack on the U.S. The test was trying to determine, if there was an aircraft that might work against the MiG-25. Without the YF-12, the test program was canceled, and the conclusion was, the U.S. could not be sure that it could stop a high altitude attack from Soviet fighter.

Propulsion was another system to be tested, and about a month after the #60-6936 disaster, the USAF let NASA have the use of SR-71, s/n 64-17951. The SR-71 was still a well-kept secret, so the aircraft's identity was changed. It became YF-12C and carried bogus tail number 937, which had already been used on an A-12. The "937's" first flight was May 24, 1972. Aircraft 60-6935 flew at least 53 times, until NASA decided to ground the aircraft and use it for high-temperature load evaluation. YF-12A S/N 60-6935 did not fly again until well into 1973.

During the propulsion tests, the YF-12C generated data showing a strong vortex that came from the fuselage chines, and went into the engine inlets. After the end of the NASA programs, the YF-12C was returned to the USAF, along with the YF-12As. The YF-l2As were then headed for storage with the A-12s.

Much was learned with the A-12, although some feel much was lost, because the USAF decided not to fund the bomber version of the aircraft. The USAF lost an opportunity for high speed, long range, and low radar cross-section (RCS)—everything it wanted in a nuclear bomber. It was what the USAF was looking for in the B-70, yet, when it had it all in the YF-12A, it didn't use it. Officials who wanted a stealth bomber would have to wait for the B-2 much later in the 1980s.

YF-12A S/N 60-6935 was retired to the U.S. Air Force Museum at Wright-Patterson AFB on November 7, 1979. Its development proves the soundness and versatility of Kelly Johnson's design for a super-high-speed, high-altitude aircraft.

YF-12A Description

The Lockheed YF-12A was based on the A-12. It is a two-place, supersonic, long-range interceptor, powered by two Pratt & Whitney J-58 afterburning engines. The low-aspect-ratio wing incorporates an integral empennage that includes one rudder mounted on each of the two midspan nacelles, a fixed ventral fin under each nacelle, a retractable ventral fin under the aft end of the fuselage, and two pairs of elevons to perform the elevator-aileron function. Distinctive functional chines, running along the fuselage sides and truncated at the nose, extend aft to merge with the wing inboard leading edges.

The YF-12A airframe is different from that of the A-12. The YF-12A fuselage is of an all-metal, semi-monocoque construction, in which titanium alloy is the principal structural material. Dielectric (not able to conduct electric current and useful as insulation) material is used for antenna covers. Design parameters provide for pressurization of the crew stations and certain fuselage areas.

Internal arrangements provide for a left forward GAR-9 missile bay, and for two aft missile bays. The right forward bay houses fire control system components and the mission-traffic control equipment. The nose section contains radar antenna transmitter and receiver components of the fire control system. Infrared seeker heads are located in the left and right forward chine leading edges.

A portion of the fuselage interior was allocated for the landing gear and drag chute, but the major portion of the fuselage is occupied by six fuel tanks.

In the upper fuselage area, aft of the cockpit, a separate bay houses the inertial navigation system (INS), air conditioning, and other miscellaneous equipment. The wing is designed as an integral fuel cell between the leading edge beam and the beam supporting movable wing surfaces, and extending from wing station to wing station. Each wing is divided near mid fuselage between the nacelles. Longitudinal beams, in the upper and lower exterior wing surfaces, accommodate differential, temperature-caused expansion and contraction. The wing sections are multispar construction, utilizing stiffened skin panels to form box-beams.

Flight Controls and Automatic Flight Control System

The thin, cantilevered, and highly tapered wings incorporate inboard and outboard control surfaces, which perform the combined functions of ailerons and elevators. The elevons are hinged at the upper wing surface, and are positioned by hydraulic rams (6 to each inboard 11 and 14 to each outboard elevon). A full-moving rudder is mounted on a fixed stub section on top of each nacelle, and a retractable ventral fin is mounted under the aft end of the fuselage. Rudders and elevons are controlled by conventional stick and rudder pedals, which, through cable and mechanical linkage systems, control the metering of dual hydraulic system pressures for actuation of control surfaces. A three-axis Stability Augmentation System (SAS) is provided to supplement the natural dynamic and static stability of the free aircraft. SAS is part of the aircraft basic control system and is used under all flight conditions. A two-channel (roll and pitch axis) autopilot is provided, primarily for maintaining "hold modes," including altitude hold, Mach hold, and attitude hold, and heading hold. A Mach trim subsystem provides conventional trim characteristics during acceleration-deceleration flight, and an auto trim is provided for the pitch axis when the autopilot is engaged. Manual trim is provided in all three axes through electrically controlled, motor-driven trim actuators, which act on the primary control input linkages. Trim tabs are not provided. An Air

Data Computer (ADC) accepts pitot pressures and provides outputs to components of the AFCS and Internal Navigation system. The YF-12A has the same J-58 engines as the A-12.

Communications and Navigation

Mission control systems provide onboard facilities necessary to support precise operational utilization of the total weapon system. Interphone equipment remits communication between crewmembers during flight, and between members of the ground during ground operations. The interphone equipment also serves as a communications mode selector. HF and UHF transceivers provide for external voice communications and, in Aircraft 936, a two-way data link system is available. Selective identification capabilities are provided by the IFF transponder, which affords preset modes I, II, and III controlled by the fire control officer in the aft cockpit.

Tactical Air Navigation (TACAN) equipment provided bearing and distance data, which were displayed in both crew stations, and the ILS system contributes localizer and glide slope data, which are displayed to the pilot. The INS provides geographic positions and heading data, which were displayed in both crew stations, and attitude data, which are displayed only to the pilot. The compass system and the vertical gyro provide back-up heading and attitude data. Direct integration was afforded between the navigation and fire control subsystems.

Fire Control System

The ASG-18 fire control subsystem performs intercept and identification missions. Its primary mission profile includes the search for, detection of, and destruction of high-performance airborne targets operating at maximum altitudes. The kill task was accomplished by delivering GAR-9 missiles against the selected targets.

Three GAR-9 missiles were carried in individual missile bays located inside the lower fuselage. Doors enclose the missile bays, and air conditioning was provided to maintain proper thermal environment within the bays. The fire control officer selects and monitors the missile employment mode from the armament control panel in the aft cockpit.

Cockpit and Equipment

Conventional USAF flight instrumentation were installed, supplemented by an attack display and indicators for true heading with TACAN fix. A warning light panel permits the pilot to monitor systems functioning, and appropriate displays facilitate surveillance of engine performance, fuel supply, and the operational condition of electrical and hydraulic equipment. Each cockpit is equipped with an SR-1 rocket-powered seat, designed to eject upward. The seat accommodates fully pressure-suited personnel and incorporates life support and survival equipment, including normal and emergency oxygen supply, backpack parachute, and seat pack survival kit. Seat restraints included a lap-type safety belt, shoulder harness, knee guards, and leg retention cables that protect personnel during ejection.

Separate aft-hinged canopy installations cover the two-crew stations. Both canopies were constructed of metal and fitted with laminated glass panels. The forward canopy and integral V-shaped windshield are fitted with outer panels of monolithic glass, separated from inner panels by an air space.

The canopies were operated independently from inside the cockpits, and external receptacles are provided for locking and unlocking the canopies and for emergency canopy-only jettison. Canopy-only jettison was selected by crewmembers from inside the individual cockpits.

Environmental Control

Cockpits, missile equipment, and electronic bays were cooled by two separate air cycle refrigerators, which refrigerate engine bleed-air extracted from the compressor sections of both engines. Primary cooling utilized both ram-air and fuel as heat sinks.

A separate refrigerant package rejected heat from the electronic equipment liquid cooling systems. The radar antenna, receiver transmitter, infrared heads, and power supply were cooled by a liquid circulating system, and an ethylene glycol circulating system provides coolant for the missiles. Appropriate ground cart coolant liquid connections were included for fire control systems ground testing. Cockpit and bay air conditioning ground connections were also provided.

Cockpit pressurization begins at 26,100 feet. Cockpit altitudes remain isobaric (having constant or equal pressure) at all higher altitudes and cockpit differential pressure increased with airplane attitude, reaching a "normal" maximum of 5 psi when the aircraft arrived at maximum design cruising altitude. Cabin test fittings were incorporated to permit ground testing. Provisions were included for pressurizing canopy seals and for cabin pressure dump. The electronic bay was pressurized at 47,000 feet by equipment essentially similar to that which pressurized the cockpits. Canopy and windshield defogging, defrosting, and deicing were accomplished by a system utilizing heated air. The defrosting system was integrated with the pressurizing system to provide concurrent air circulation.

Airframe General Description

The airframe consisted of the fuselage forward and aft sections. The fuselage forward section included the nose, cockpit, windshield and canopy, equipment bays, refueling receptacle, nose landing gear compartment, fuel tanks 1 through 3, and the chines. The fuselage aft section included fuel tanks 4 through 6, the fuselage removable fillets, drag chute compartments, tailcone compartment, main landing gear compartment, engine air inlets, nacelles, the inboard and outboard wings, elevens, and rudders.

Titanium was used in the airframe for primary structure and the fabrication of longerons, stringers, rings bulkheads, and skins. The titanium used was identified locally as A110, B120, or C120, differentiated by their relative strengths and heat tolerance capabilities. These alloys were produced in conventional forms such as bars, fillets, and plates and in developed shapes such as extrusions, forging, and castings. In the fuselage, the fuel tanks, pressure bulkheads, and skins are made of annealed B120 alloy. Spot welding was extensively used as a joining technique, and the common fasteners in this area are B120 rivets and 6AL-4 V bolts.

In the wing and nacelle area, B120 was used for wing skins and beam webs where temperatures will not exceed 500 degrees Fahrenheit. In this heat region, C120 extrusions were used for wing beam and rib caps. A110 was used in sheets and extrusions where temperatures are greater than 500 degrees Fahrenheit but do not exceed 900 degrees. Related fasteners consisted of B120 Monel, or A286 corrosion-resistant steel and C120 or A286 screws and bolts.

Fuselage Forward Section

The nose section consists of a plastic cone-shaped radome that incorporates a pitot mast and radar test horn forward, and a metal adapter ring aft. Four latches were incorporated in the ring to attach and secure the radome.

The radome houses the fire control system transmitter/receiver components and the ASG-18 radar antenna, which was protected by a hemispherical heat shield. Coaxial cables, two sets of pitot lines, alpha beta lines, and heater wires are contained in two bundles attached internally on either side of the radome, directly opposite each other along the waterline and the ILS antenna coaxial cables, which run along the overhead centerline. Forward, the attached pitot mast functions both as an antenna for the 16ATT radio and as a sensing device that converts pneumatic pressure into electrical signals for flight instruments and engine spike movement. On the bottom centerline of the radome, three holes were provided for drain and vent.

The antenna heat shield provided a protective surface and a seal to ensure a pressurized and air-conditioned environment for the radar antenna and its components.

Armament

Aircraft armament consisted of three GAR-9 air-to-air missiles, carried in individual, air-conditioned, insulated bays, two on the left-hand and one on the right-hand lower sides of the forward fuselage. Two hinged doors closed off each bay when solenoid operation actuated fore and aft pairs of hydraulic cylinders. Missile cooling was provided by an ethylene glycol circulating coolant system. Each missile was ejected by means of electrically fired, breech-contained cartridges that provide gas pressure to drive ejector pistons and release mechanically connected release support hooks.

Radar and Electronics Equipment Bay

A small bay was provided on either side in the bottom of the right- and left-hand chines, just forward of the missile or traffic and fire control equipment bays. The left-hand bay accommodated the VIP (video integrator and processor) radar and dispersement gear; the right-hand bay, the data link system, platform electronics, and related components. Each bay was stabilized, raised, and lowered by means of devices similar to those used for traffic and fire control bays.

Chines

Th chine is the continuous longitudinal member on either side of the fuselage and consisted of high-strength titanium skins over approximately equally spaced frames, which were secured to upper and lower support structure. As fuselage components, chines are replaceable but may require skin trim and hole transfer substitute.

Infrared seeker antennas were located in the forward end of both chines, approximately opposite the pilot's cockpit. The related infrared detector head sensors in these areas were cooled by a liquid nitrogen system employed Dewar flasks. Data link navigation equipment was located in the foremost right-hand chine bay.

Tail Cone

The tail cone installation consisted of a typical terminal stringer, ring, and skin panel construction. There was one access door in the tail cone on the top. This door provides access to the fuel system components required to vent, recover, or dump engine fuel.

Rudders

The rudders consisted of twin titanium alloy vertical tails mounted mid-span on the engine nacelles, canted inboard toward the fuselage. Each rudder swings 20 degrees of travel, either side of neutral on its respective rudder post, and consisted of typical titanium spars, ribs, and skins.

Ventral Fins

Three titanium ventral fins, two fixed and one retractable, were provided. A fixed fin was attached to the bottom of each nacelle on either side. The retractable center fin mounts at two points beneath the fuselage, just forward of the tail cone, and swung outboard toward the left-hand nacelle. From a unit located within the fuselage contour, hydraulic power was supplied to the center fin to extend or retract it during takeoff and landing.

Movable (Folding) Ventral Fin

A movable ventral fin was attached to the fuselage bottom, and consisted of a full-length box section comprising ribs, beams, and skin panels, with leading and trailing edges and a tip assembly that caps the fin bottom edge. Folding and fixed doors were secured to the attachment points and served to fair the attachment points when the fin is raised or lowered.

Fixed Ventral Fins

A fixed ventral fin was attached to the bottom side of each nacelle and consisted of a full-length box section comprising ribs, beams and skin panels, with leading and trailing edges and a tip assembly that caps the fin bottom edge.

D-21 Drone and the M-21 Mother Ship

The resourceful people contemplating adaptations for the A-12 did not stop with things the plane could carry internally. When compared to a fully developed spy plane, an unmanned craft—a drone—offered reconnaissance capabilities at lower cost, and without risking a pilot. It did not take long to visualize a drone that made use of the A-12's speed and altitude capabilities.

After the U-2 shoot down debacle in 1960, American intelligence officials were looking for another way to keep an eye on the sky over the Soviet Union. Red China was developing military scenarios that interested the United States. By October 1962, the CIA—which heretofore had shown little interest in the drone concept—gave Kelly Johnson the approval to start up a drone project known as TAGBOARD. That project had an important fiscal benefit—it would use an already paid-for aircraft as the drone's mother ship.

Kelly Johnson wanted a Mach 3 reconnaissance drone that was so streamlined and lightweight, a modified A-12 could carry it and still be capable of launching and reaching Mach 3 and 90,000 feet while maintaining a low RCS. Johnson was fortunate in that his creation, the D-21 drone, would have the lowest RCS ever built at the Skunk Works. The D-21 turned out to weigh only 17,000 pounds. It was built from titanium and composite materials, and was powered by one Marquardt ram jet engine, left over from the BOMARC missile program. The 40-foot-long "Q-12," as it was called early in the program, was ready on December 7, 1962, in mock-up form.

D-21

The D-21—"D" for daughter drone—was mated to the A-12 mother ship, duly designated M-21. The combination when mated together was known as the MD-21. Two A-12s were purpose-built for the program, instead of taking one or two off the flight line for the program. The D-21 was latched to a pylon, attached to the aft dorsal section of the M-21's fuselage. This short pylon was the source of trouble on two flights. The pylon would cause the MD-21 to "push over" instead of launching, and flying straight on. The M-21 carried a second crew member, the LCO or launch control officer, who used a periscope to monitor the D-21.

The D-21 was powered by a Marquardt RJ43-MA-B4 ramjet which in this case, was an upgrade from the J-58 engine. However, the drone then needed a host ship because ramjets don't operate well a low speed. Hence, the M-21. The D-21 was a lightweight vehicle and capable of Mach 3 at 90,000 ft. when launched from the back of the M-21 mothership. The CIA finally agreed to the Lockheed study of the drone which was called "TAGBOARD" on October 10, 1962. The basic idea was to have the drone over fly the USSR and China.

By June 24, 1964, D-21 #501, and the M-21, S/N 60-6940, were mated, but the first launch didn't take place until two years later, on March 6, 1966, due to a variety of problems. There was limited clearance between the D-21's wingtips and the M-21's vertical stabilizers, which meant that the moment of launch was a dicey affair. The Skunk Works used frangible nose and tail covers on the D-21 to reduce drag. The cover was blown off before launch. On the first launch attempt, however, pieces of the jettisoned inlet cover struck the D-21's wing, causing heavy damage. D-21 inlet covers were never tried again. The D-21's engine was started above Mach 1.0, which added more power to help the MD-21 combination overcome drag.

To say the least, flight testing for the D-21 was a dangerous and arduous task. There were many trials and many errors before the Lockheed crew got it right enough to fly. The very high drag of the D-21 caused immense grief to the M-21 and actually affected the M-21's implementation in flight. It wasn't going to be as easy as it looked.

The first launches were scheduled to begin in March of 1966. Bill Park was the chief test pilot for Lockheed. The D-21 was launched over the Pacific Ocean. That meant that the MD-21 started its speed run over Albuquerque, New Mexico, and headed out toward Point Mugu, California. After the D-21 engine was fired up and the MD-21 pitched down, the D-21 was released.

The D-21 began its early tests with minimal fuel, to keep weight down. Subsequent flights progressively added fuel until a full load was reached. On March 5, the D-21 was launched with a 25 percent fuel load, and by the next launch date in April, the D-21 was launched with half its fuel capacity. On July 16, 1966, the D-21 launched with 100 percent fuel, allowing a 1,600-mile flight, including maneuvers.

Disaster

On July 16, 1966, a third test was made of the D-21, with Bill Park and Ray Torick in the pilot and launch operator seats. The flight was successful. The D-21 made eight programmed turns to take photos of the Channel Islands, Santa Catalina and San Clemente. The photos were taken with the drone at 92,000 ft. and Mach 3. The only thing that happened was the package containing the film did not eject because of an electrical problem, one that was quickly fixed for the next test, however the next test was not so lucky for Park, Torick or the D-21.

On July 30, 1966 during a D-21 release at 1.0g, the D-21 passed through the mother ship's wake turbulence, resulting in an "asymmetrical unstart" of the ramjet engine. This caused D-21 #504 to roll right. The mother ship pitched up, which pilot Bill Park tried to correct, but the D-21 went aft of the pylon at Mach 3.25 and hit the M-21. It destroyed the M-21's right rudder, engine, and nacelle, and most of the outer right wing. The aircraft went out of control and crashed into the Pacific. Both Bill Park and the LCO, Ray Torick, ejected with their suits inflated and landed in the water. Park survived and was picked up in a life raft about 150 miles at sea. Torick, very sadly, came down closer to their ejection site. He removed the visor of his helmet while trying to swim. His pressure suit just loaded with water and he drowned in his pressure suit.

After Torick was recovered, according to Ben Rich in his book "Skunk Works", with Leo Janos, Keith Beswick, who was the flight director went to the local funeral home to cut Torick out of the pressure suit so he could be prepared for burial. This was more than Kelly Johnson could take. Johnson was so distraught by the accident that he canceled the program and gave the USAF back its development money. Johnson said, "I will not risk any more test pilots or Blackbirds. I don't have either to spare."

He wanted to return all the money used for development back to the government and the military. Even though the drone was really working. It was then that Johnson thought about the B-52 and hanging the drones off the wings of the big B-52.

Captain Hook

The M-21 Blackbird dropped out of the equation. President Johnson's Secretary of Defense, Cyrus Vance, authorized the B-52 as the D-21's new mother ship, and the USAF supplied two specially equipped B-52Hs. The B-52s were capable of 16 hours of flight, allowing the D-21s a 3,000-mile range. With such long-range, missions now a possibility. It was time to set sights on China.

In 1968, the "Captain Hook" test flights began. This allowed for the B-52 and the newly redesignated D-21B to become acquainted. The D-21B mounted under the wing of the B-52 by means of a pylon, was attached to the wing at the existing hard point. No structural modifications to the B-52 were necessary. The two control officers replaced the B-52's electronic warfare officer and gunner. A stellar inertial guidance system was added, along with an air conditioning system to keep the D-21 cool.

Test flights left Hawaii, flew over the Pacific Ocean and photographed Christmas and Midway Islands. The "Captain Hook" flights suffered only two failures in just over 14 months. By late 1969, the CIA began recommending missions to the Committee on National Security. Those recommendations were then sent on to President Nixon.

The decision was made to go to Lop Nor, China, 2,000 miles inland of the China-Mongolia border. Lop Nor, situated in a 2,000-foot depression, about 20 miles wide on a 4,000-foot plateau, was a primary interest point for U.S. intelligence. The Chinese were conducting missile testing there. John Paragonsky, who was then taking over for CIA chief Richard Bissell, really didn't like the idea of sending the D-21s in. Nonetheless, a B-52H was prepared and left Beale AFB carrying two D-21s, one under each wing. When the bomber reached the launch point, it released the D-21, which overflew the target beyond range of the Chinese radar. The mission, however, bore no fruit. As Kelly Johnson described it, *"Damn thing came out of China, but was lost. It wasn't spotted or shot down, but it must have malfunctioned and crashed on us."* The Chinese radar never did pick up the drone, and Johnson and his team concluded that the drone's guidance was off.

About 11 months later, President Nixon approved another launching over Lop Nor. The drone flew well, but the film package was dropped and lost at sea. In March 1971, President Nixon approved a third flight. The drone once again flew well and performed excellently, but the film package was lost when it dropped into the sea after it was almost recovered shipside. Two weeks later, yet another flight was tracked for 1,900 miles into China, then was lost.

Cancellation

By 1971, the Defense Department told Johnson that the program was canceled. The Department of Defense ordered all tooling destroyed. Kelly Johnson was angry and frustrated. He blamed the USAF for holding the drones for nine months at Beale AFB before missions were activated. Johnson complained that the drones were unnecessarily taken apart and serviced, merely to justify USAF salaries. Johnson believed the Skunk Works should have been maintaining the drones all along, not the USAF.

The airframes, 17 of them, were moved to the Military Aircraft Storage and Disposition Center (now the Aerospace Maintenance and Regeneration Center—AMRC), or the "boneyard," at Davis-Mothan AFB in Arizona. The drones were later discovered completely by accident, when strong winds blew their concealing tarps off. A group of individuals on a tour of the base spotted them cocooned and hanging out by a back fence. The news immediately got out. After the USAF admitted their existence, the airframes had been dispersed to various museums, via the U.S. Air Force Museum—Program Coordination office at Wright-Patterson AFB, Dayton, Ohio. The rest were sent to NASA for use in a possible high-speed test research. There were even rumors that the D-21s were being used for the liquid hydrogen project, "Aurora". This nomenclature actually turned out to be a code name for the B-2 bomber.

As with most things that fly in the "darkness of secret programs," eventually they come into the light. When they do, they come to rest in museums. That is true of the A-12, the YF-12A, the MD-21, the D-21, and the SR-71. It will be true of black projects that are flying now. How much we can discern by looking at them isn't always everything they "know." At least we can marvel at the fact that they were flying when we didn't even know they existed.

There is a little side note to the history of the D-21. Back in May of 1975 in *"Progress Report #2 High Stealth Conceptual Studies"*, Kelly Johnson had another idea that blossomed from the D-21. Its name was *"Little Harvey"* (named after the invisible rabbit from the classic movie with James Stewart called "Harvey"). You could say that the "Little Harvey" based on results from the D-21 drone operations, was responsible for the F-117 stealth fighter. Johnson believed that the smooth edges and chine could offer both speed and stealth. There was an argument between Johnson and Ben Rich, Lockheed's aerodynamicist that a faceted body (Known as the "Hopeless Diamond") would work much better when bouncing radar off. Kelly Johnson even said to Ben Rich, *"Our old D-21 drone has a lower radar cross-section than that goddamn diamond."* However, it was one fight that Johnson lost and he didn't lose many as we see in the F-117 Nighthawk's faceted body.

End of a Phenomenal Era

SR-71—The USAF's answer to reconnaissance

The SR-71(SENIOR CROWN) quickly took the spotlight the A-12 had deserved, but characteristically avoided. The U.S. Air Force was bringing the SR-71 more toward the light, so it could carry on its program in a "gray" world. As much as the A-12 had revolutionized aircraft design, and had given America an unparalleled tool to use in overhead reconnaissance, it rapidly disappeared into the classified history books.

Although neither totally black nor white, the SR-71 flew on for an almost flawless 25-year run. To casual observers, the A-12, YF-12, and SR-71 appeared to be the same thing, but they were really quite different aircraft. They shared such a strong family relationship, however, that their similarities provided a broad experience base. The SR-71's success, therefore, was largely based upon knowledge and experience gained during the relatively short operational span of the A-12.

The A-12 and the SR-71 grew from the same seed. The remarkable thing about both aircraft was the life that both aircraft had left in their airframes. When the A-12 was relegated to storage, some people held out hope that it might be brought back into service. Twenty years later, in the last desperate days of the SR-71, studies showed that its airframe was able to be supported and was fit for flight indefinitely. It leaves one to wonder just how much was wasted in retiring both types.

Some of the differences between the A-12 and the SR-71 are obvious. The SR-71, unlike the A-12, is a two-place aircraft. The position in the second cockpit, was held by the *RSO* better known as the Reconnaissance System Officer. The A-12 pilot used a periscope in the cockpit for navigation fixes. The periscope in the SR-71, which is in the forward cockpit, was also used for navigation, but in addition allowed the pilot to have a rear view, so he could look at the top of the fuselage, wings and nacelles, something that the A-12 pilot could not do.

The SR-71 is 107 feet, 5 inches long, compared with the A-12's 99 feet. The difference is mainly in the longer tail cone, or "stinger" of the SR-71. The nose section of the SR-71 is removable and houses many different components such as the Advanced Synthetic Aperture Radar System (ASARS) and Optical Bar Camera (OBC).

One of the more significant differences is the SR-71's use of the Digital Automatic Flight and Inlet Control System (DAFICS). This meant that the SR-71 was not plagued as much by inlet "unstarts." The system effectively gave the SR-71 better flight performance in certain regimes, through electronic control of the elevon and rudder servos.

While the SR-71 had a Mission Recorder System (MRS), which is an airborne integrated mission and maintenance data recording system that monitors and records the performance of the aircraft and the rest of the systems, the A-12 had only the less-sophisticated "Birdwatcher" system to rely on.

To look at these birds together, you would not notice much difference. Making comparisons of these planes with the two-place YF-12, one would note the truncated forward chines and the ventral fins on the latter aircraft.

In the 1970s, the SR-71 moved from the "black list" to the white pages of the budget, which were subject to closer congressional scrutiny. This extra attention ultimately spelled the end of the SR-71 program. As in more recent years, concerns about defense spending were mounting, while Congress and the USAF were wheeling and dealing to accommodate newer projects, such as the B-1 and upgrades for the aging B-52 until its replacement, already in development, was ready for service.

It was also becoming plain that the upkeep of satellites - -but not necessarily their development and construction- -was far less costly than the upkeep of nine SR-71s. Physically, the aircraft itself could have seen the twenty-first century with ease, as was proven by a 1990s NASA study of the feasibly of using the SR-71 for a high-speed commercial test bed.

While the SR-71 was available, it had never really carved out a space to call its own in the Air Force's scheme of things. That helped the politicians, both military and civilian, with their efforts to discontinue the program. Ultimately, the SR-71's early "blackness," which for years kept the plane out of the Air Force mainstream, was used to discredit its contributions, as security classifications did not allow public discussion. The Air Force realized the SR-71 had value as a bargaining chip whose funding could be traded for other "priority" projects.

While the mission of the SR-71 was fuzzily termed "aerial reconnaissance," it was better known as a "spy plane", used to keep an eye on America's adversaries, and some-times her friends. As the Air Force shifted the aircraft's focus toward more mundane tasks, such as "bomb damage assessment," the "espionage" aspects of the program were de-emphasized. It could be argued, that the SR-71 was in the dark for so long that when it finally came into the light, no one really knew or cared what the original program was all about. Those seeking to discredit the SR-71, used that lack of knowledge to maximum effect.

In the 1980s, an officer in charge of making decisions for the use of the USAF's inventory actually asked of the SR-71, "What does it really do?" The question illustrates a misunderstanding of the meaning of aerial reconnaissance. Actual knowledge of events and circumstances, and the ability to gather such knowledge on demand, are as vital to a nation's security as any piece of equipment. Decisions demand knowledge, and aerial reconnaissance is a unique and proven means of gathering it. Friends of the SR-71 were becoming fewer and farther apart, and there were not many people around who were willing to take its side.

By the summer of 1987, things were getting very tough for the program. The few remaining advocates knew they needed help on a bill to authorize continued funding for the SR-71. Larry Kettlewell, a congressional staffer who worked for the *Senate Select Committee on Intelligence*, picked up the flag and ran with it. Kettlewell was going to take on all comers to fight for the support of the SR-71. That meant matching wits with the USAF's Pentagon brass in general, and the Strategic Air Command in particular.

It was amazing how the USAF could tie itself up in knots, wasting energy and precious assets to defame an aircraft and a program that did nothing but good. Such is the way of USAF politics. It was typical of the service, at the time, that politics, not logistics, mattered more than a viable program that supported all the military services with top-level performance. Admittedly, the SR-71, like the A-12, was expensive to operate. However, considering that the SR-71 was never caught doing its job and had delivered the goods, the question, "What did this aircraft do?" made little sense.

Eventually, politics, parochialism, and money came into play. Twenty-five years after the A-12 had been "retired", the USAF decided it was time for the SR-71 to pass into the twilight. In hindsight, this decision ranks with some of the dumbest ideas the USAF as an organization has ever devised. It was a total waste of talent, equipment and money. With nothing to take over the program's load, the USAF relied on satellites which as good as they had become, still could not give real time reconnaissance.

Retirement of the Blackbirds

The decision to release the SR-71s as a program, was announced by the USAF in 1989. Met with disbelief by many people who had been part of the program, the SR-71 program had been successful, and the airframes still had plenty of time left on them. True, the SR-71 was very labor intensive, but no more so than many other aircraft out on the flight line. The system to maintain and keep the SR-71 in the air was already in place. The SR-71 proved itself repeatedly as ready to do the job when needed. She was always ready, willing, and able as were her pilots and crew.

One of the reasons the USAF felt it was no longer necessary to fund the SR-71 was the claim that there were overhead reconnaissance systems-satellites, in this context-that duplicated it. However, that assertion raised a question that seemed to have no satisfactory answer. How could a satellite, which relies on ground communications for positioning and has no immediate human input to direct it to instinctively look for something specific or to follow a lead, create a redundancy with the SR-71?

As for the SR-71 being too expensive to maintain, it was well known that some reconnaissance satellites have cost up to $1 billion, 10 years' worth of SR-71 operations. How many launch dates were missed due to bad weather? How many satellites were placed in bad orbits, or experienced mechanical problems with rockets that left a satellite on the launch pad for weeks? How many satellites were lost by missile explosions? It takes three hours to set up an SR-71 for a flight, in any weather, any time of the day or night. It was sad that the Chief of Staff of the USAF at the time could not account for that. The Chief of Staff at the time was General Lawrence D. Welch.

By 1989, the USAF got its long-time wish. The SR-71s were retired. There was a rumor that this had been a personal goal of the Chief of Staff of the USAF, who was quoted as saying, "It had been a thorn in my side for a long time and I now had the power to get rid of it." The official rationale was that it cost too much money and didn't provide real-time capability. General Welch had no love of the SR-71. Many said it was because he had washed out of the SR-71program, but there is no proof that this is the reason for his intense dislike.

One reason given for taking the A-12 off the line was that it had become redundant when the SR-71 became operational. Considering that the A-12 and the SR-71 were different in the many ways previously cited, and that one was flown by civilian pilots and the other by military pilots—and their missions were different—it's difficult to take that reasoning seriously. In the case against the SR-71, many of its problems had to do with the fact that both the B-1 and the B-2 were in money trouble. The funding had to come from somewhere, a fact that lay behind the USAF's claim that it was not canceling a program that had any further use.

Thanks to the many grass rooters who fought back with a campaign of petitions, phone calls, and telegrams to their Congressmen, the SR-71 was saved in the budget for 1988. But, the fact that the same Chief of Staff, General Welch, was waiting in the wings to kill the program once again, didn't help the morale of the people who had saved it. Congress managed to play with the numbers and language, so that at least six of the SR-71s were to be kept in flyable storage, along with the trainer model, at a cost of only $160,000. That left the program with the capability to regenerate the fleet within 60 days, if need be.

Yet the USAF would not spend the money to do this, so the aircraft were "left on the ramp" to rot. If the money was spent to keep the aircraft in proper storage, Congress would not have had to allocate $9 million to reactivate the aircraft later on. As to the assets of the SR-71, such as the swap-out noses carrying various accouterments, they went the way of many things left hung out to dry. Pieces of the hardware were taken by various agencies, never to be seen again. NASA took three of the aircraft, and what was left of the assets, to manage them as it saw fit. At least NASA found a use for the three that they saved, using them in Aerospike research.

The drive to shut down the SR-71 came back to haunt the USAF during the Gulf War, when General Norman Schwarzkopf was looking for reconnaissance of the type provided by the SR-71s. Experience during *Operation Desert Shield* showed some holes in intelligence that needed to be filled for the coming *Operation Desert Storm*. The USAF explained there was no way that it could possibly get the SR-71 fleet back up and running in such a short time. That seems questionable, as the aircraft had stopped flying just four months before *Desert Shield*. What ever reconnaissance problems the Allied Coalition forces experienced during the Gulf War, it seems the lack of operational SR-71s may have been partly responsible. U-2 derivatives, satellites, and methods that are more conventional were used, but they could not quite make up for the advantages the Blackbirds could afford them had they been put back into service.

Although it's purely speculation, another reason for cutting funding for the SR-71 program could have been that the Air Force was secretly flying something much better, and expected it to become operational soon. For want of a better designation, Area 51 watchers were calling that "something" by the name "Aurora." It is interesting to note that the D-21s drones, after being discovered by tourists at Davis Monthan AFB in Arizona, were given to NASA to use for high-speed testing, which never occurred. If the Air Force was indeed testing something, it soon seemed to disappear even deeper into the black world of extremely advanced aircraft.

A number of Blackbird's buffs, however, seemed to think that an ultra-advanced replacement, the SR-72, ran into some ultra advanced problems before it went operational. However, recent developments have the Lockheed Skunk Works announcing in a June 2017 *Aviation Week Magazine* article that the new aircraft is almost ready for demonstrator tests. The Mach 6 hypersonic strike and reconnaissance aircraft has matured into the technology Lockheed and DARPA (Defense Advanced Research Projects Agency) has been slaving over for the past twenty years.

While many waited for the SR-72 to come on board, she still has a long way to go, possibly having the demonstrator ready by 2020, which is still a dream. Yet, the United States is still depending on the venerable U-2 and satellites along with the Predator family of drones to do the job of reconnaissance. With the exception of the U-2, there are no pilot's eyes in the skies for aerial reconnaissance. The SR-71 was a powerful reconnaissance tool, hopefully the SR-72 will give the country back that much needed asset.

Resurrection?

The SR-71 was like a cat with nine lives, or at least one more life, because in 1995 it had one more shot at trying to stay alive. Orders came down from Congress to reactivate three of the aircraft, and it brought out a $100 million check. The USAF was scrambling, and needed to have the aircraft ready in 30 days, due to ever-increasing problems with Korea and the Middle East.

Along with the revitalized SR-71, there were some improvements had to be tested. Those improvements were started in 1990, just before the first shutdown. The *Advanced Synthetic Aperture Radar (ASAR)* had been completed, but not yet totally field-tested. The ASAR was brought in with the reactivation of the Sr-71. A new *Common Data Link* (CDL) was also operational, and brought with it real time imagery. There were other improvements. A clip-in kit to replace the three vans that were the *Operational Deployable Processing*

System used to process the ASARS data was added. The ASARS-1 was an all-around radar sensor in the nose section of the SR-71. It allowed the CDL to download to a receiving station. If the system went off line for some reason, the information was held in the aircraft until it was within range of another offload station.

Another advantage was the *Optical Bar Camera*. The OBC was a panoramic camera in the nose of the aircraft, that was capable of covering a 70-mile swath in one pass. It could use wet film, and had the same type of processing as the U-2. The new Technical Objective Camera (TEOC) was a point-and-shoot framing camera, and was a wet process camera. There were also new Electronic Counter Measures (ECM) packages: *Def A2, Def H,* and *Def C,* that were all new as of 1995. These were some of the "new toys" that the SR-71 brought to the job, in pursuit of its first and most important objective: to be there on time, and to deliver the goods without so much as a missile being fired at it.

NASA was also busy trying to utilize the SR-71. As always, NASA was looking for a high-speed test bed. It had worked its way through the XB-70, the YF-12, and now the SR-71. A program known as "*Aerospike*" was devised to test scramjet engines (supersonic ram jet engine). The program was not completely successful, but it did give the SR-71 some work other than reconnaissance. NASA slaved to keep the SRs up and in good flying condition, but by 1999, it was all over. NASA had to give up on the *Aerospike* program. The aircraft were sent to aviation museums to become static displays. Only the three left at NASA were flyable. One of them had to be made derelict and was cannibalized for parts. It was an ignominious end to a 25-year career that spanned the earth's skies. SR-71s brought back intelligence information untouched by anything thrown at them. The SR-71 was no more. Edwards AFB, the last home of the SR-71, looked rather like a ghost town.

It was sad to see the number of former SR-71 pilots dwindle down to a handful, and then down to the point where there were no military pilots certified left to fly the aircraft. That was another shortcoming on the part of the USAF, too. It had taken so long, with many simulator hours required to keep pilots current, one by one, they dropped out, retired, or were transferred to another program. The SR-71s were becoming ghosts in their own "ghost town." Det. 2, the group that was responsible for the SR-71s' flying status, was also ushered out of Edwards AFB in 1999, as were spare parts and other materials.

The program to provide real-time reconnaissance capability to the United States had run out of airspace. This came in the form of "cancellation." Funding was allocated by Congress, and almost like the XB-70 story, was withheld by the order of the president. Again, supporters wrote letters and made phone calls to congressional leaders to save the SR-71, but the Blackbird would fly no more.

While many will argue that the SR-71 program was better off dead and gone, and shouldn't have been brought back to begin with, there is still one large, blinding concept that needs to be reckoned with. What do we have to replace it? Many will argue that technology moves on, and there is no need for the SR-71 when there are satellites and unmanned aerial vehicles (UAV)s ready for production. The loss of a predator UAV over Iraq has left open the question of was it shot down or subject to mechanical failure. The current loss of a drone over Iran, which was flaunted by the Iranian government to the hilt is another reason why UAVs, while doing an awesome job, still can't replace a pilot in the cockpit in a fast, high flying aircraft. Many said that the SR-71 would eventually come into harm's way with the development of higher-speed, laser-guided missiles. That is yet to be seen.

Of course, there is the ongoing speculation about the elusive creatures that may be hiding in the deserts of Nevada, and are sighted at odd times in the middle of the night. Yet, those speculations do not replace what was a fine reconnaissance asset. The B-52 will live on in the Air Force inventory for a number of years yet; this 60-year-old veteran has proven that being old doesn't mean an aircraft system doesn't work. The B-52Hs, which are now serving at both Minot AFB, North Dakota and Barksdale AFB Louisiana, have been updated with glass cockpits, along with structural enhancements and re-enjoining that will allow them to fly well into the 2040s. The B-52, armed with cruise missiles and other weapons have seen action in *Desert Storm* and *Desert Fox*, and *Operation Iraqi Freedom* (the last war in Iraq), and managed to do some real harm in Iraqis, giving them sheer terror by flying at high altitude which meant they could not be seen or heard and unleashing all bombs on Iraqi troops. Many Iraqi troops just threw their guns down and gave up to the nearest U.S. regiment.

Threats come in all shapes and sizes, and at all times. Should we wait until bureaucracy can define a way to develop something to replace the Blackbird and leave our men and women in the military, and indeed this country, open to possible action by terrorist action, or attack?

One of the greatest aircraft ever known has become a static display at your local air museum. She'll never fly again. She was relegated to the role of hangar queen. The Blackbird will remain on display at various military and civilian museums, albeit not in very good condition at some, because no one will be able to understand her. The care and feeding of Blackbirds-even those that do not fly is an art form that is soon to vanish from our midst. The people who developed the aircraft are slowing "going west," as the program has. This piece of vital Air Force history will become nothing more than a curiosity for the casual museum visitor.

No, it was not because the aircraft wasn't good enough. It was not because all the pilots retired. It wasn't because the aircraft had too many hours on it, or the engines went bad, or her systems were outdated. It was because of politics: pure, unadulterated, Washington "I'm-going-to-protect-my-turf-and-the-hell-with-you", politics. It is sad, but it is true. It is difficult to conceive in today's world, with every despot and terrorist renegade nation looking to knock down the United States, that the protection of this nation has been left in the hands of the creature known as the "politician," military or civilian. It is even sadder to note that the USAF, which was the keeper of the A-12, YF-12, and the SR-71, allowed this to happen.

Why have Air Force and the CIA been at odds with each other about bragging rights to the reconnaissance mission since the inception of the U-2? There is no good answer. Both were given the same mission: the defense of the nation. Nevertheless, the posturing continued. The infighting, suggested above, could fill a book in itself.

Jeannette Remak and Joseph Ventolo, Jr.

Classification, Security, and the Unseen Government

Kelly Johnson tried to keep things as simple as possible. He had his own methods. That was particularly true as far as TOP SECRET stamps and employee background checks were concerned. Kelly really did not like to use security stamps. All they did was attract attention to something that was already under the tightest possible control. Employee checks were something he could not do much about, but he tried to build the A-12 with a minimum of fuss.

The CIA and the Air Force, however, believed more "fuss" was necessary. Hiding an aircraft can be very expensive, and Kelly Johnson knew that established security methods would choke the A-12's development. That was why the Skunk Works operated the way it did. The CIA and the USAF tried to impose their procedures and methods, because the A-12 caused some real security concerns, yet Kelly Johnson was able to retain some of his own security methods within the Skunk Works, while satisfying most of the bureaucracy's requirements.

Much later on, the battle to keep the A-12's secrets, or divulge them, heated up between the CIA and the USAF. By 1971, the CIA's A-12 OXCART program was long closed out. With all OXCART aircraft in storage and no longer being flown, high-altitude, high-speed aerial reconnaissance missions were being flown by the Air Force's SR-71. After OXCART ended, the CIA wrote a rather detailed secret history of the program. It was titled ***The Oxcart Story***, and listed as author one Thomas McIninch, apparently a pseudonym for the CIA project manager, John N. Parangosky. On April 22, 1971, the National Reconnaissance Office (NRO) forwarded a copy of the CIA's 25-page history to an Air Force office for review under a secret cover memorandum. The memo read:

MEMORANDUM

4/22/71
Col. [DELETED]

Attached is a copy of the Oxcart Story which will appear in Spring 71 issue of STUDIES in INTELLIGENCE at SECRET LEVEL.

It is being forwarded to you at the request of Col. [DELETED].

PLEASE RETURN IT TO me when you have read it.

[Signed]
[DELETED]
- SECRET -

Studies in Intelligence was a classified internal CIA publication circulated to members of the intelligence community. The CIA obviously felt it was time to let some of their colleagues in on the details of the program and, perhaps, do a little bragging. The Air Force was not having any of it. It strongly opposed publication of the history outside of any NRO or Air Force intelligence channels. On May 6, 1971, Col. [DELETED] responded in a classified memorandum in the following way:

DEPARTMENT OF THE AIR FORCE

HEADQUARTERS UNITED STATES AIR FORCE

WASHINGTON, D.C.

6 May 1971

MEMORANDUM FOR THE DIRECTOR: NRO STAFF

Jeannette Remak and Joseph Ventolo, Jr.

SUBJECT: The OXCART Story

I cannot concur with the CIA intention to publish subject story in a collateral security channel, which will obviously be disseminated outside of NRO agencies. As you know, the NRO has nine A-12s currently in storage at Palmdale, California. Program D is charged with maintaining the capability to recall this fleet should a national requirement generate such action. Furthermore, the article [DELETED] ADP covert methodology, and names of individuals with extensive backgrounds in covert reconnaissance. Should such an article be released outside of [DELETED] security channels, we run the risk of grave security compromise and the possibility of widespread scrutiny from various agencies of the U.S. government. I suggest that the CIA be told that this is not the time for his sort of publicity.

[Signed]
[DELETED]

These memos were indicative of several things. First, the CIA was finished with the A-12 and the OXCART program. CIA thought it would be a good idea to let the intelligence world in on what it had been doing. The agency did not believe the classified release of that information within the intelligence community would do any harm to its other programs, and it wanted to press ahead. The NRO was reluctant to support the internal release, and the Air Force was totally against it. Although fully aware that the history would remain secret and would be printed in a secret CIA publication, the Air Force was unwilling to let some other government agency encroach upon its already-weakened intelligence territory.

Among other things, the Air Force had supported the CIA's A-12 missions, and was saddled with *de facto* ownership of the A-12s, even though they had been part and parcel of a CIA operation. The USAF did not want the

CIA to take credit for the OXCART program, as long as the USAF could not talk about its secret responsibilities for the follow-up SR-71 missions. Since there had been no publicity about the A-12, on the occasion of its retirement, the Air Force wanted to be able to cash in on publicity for its SR-71 later on, when that program eventually became better known to the public.

As it turned out, that is what happened years later. When the USAF retired the SR-71 fleet in 1989-1990, the blue suiters broke records telling of its successful operations. Security being what it is, however, the Air Force restricted release of some of the significant missions credited to the SR-71s. The reason for this touchiness on releasing information on those missions? A good portion of those missions, had actually been flown by the CIA, in A-12s.

The SR-71, the last of the Blackbirds, was a consummate aircraft. The SR-71 was every-thing that Kelly Johnson, Ben Rich, and the Lockheed Skunk Works had hoped she would be: fast, accurate, always on time, and always delivering the goods. From the skies over Vietnam, North Korea, China, the Mediterranean, or Middle Eastern countries like Yemen, the SR-71 always brought home the goods and **never**, **ever**, was caught doing it.

The aerial reconnaissance that the SR-71 and her earlier and less well-known sister, the A-12, provided, has been worth its weight in gold, as well as its weight in the lives of the U.S. military men and women whom her photographic reconnaissance protected. Well, that's all gone now. Now, the United States, due partly to the shortsightedness of some of its political leaders, and their lack of understanding of the world situation, along with the actions of some USAF leaders with egos larger than the Grand Canyon has seen to that. Now, we rely on UAVs—slow, low-flying, radio controlled unmanned aerial reconnaissance vehicles. Given that they are now stacked with hell fire missiles, there is something to be said about that. However, can you ever really be sure what has been missed by a UAV pilot who is 3,000 miles from the scene of the action? We rely on the satellites that are subject to cloud cover, positioning, and the ever-possible software failure. There is no rational method to this madness; It's just politics. UAV has become the way to go, but does it really replace the pilot's eyes in the cockpit of a high altitude aircraft?'

Jeannette Remak and Joseph Ventolo, Jr.

Blackbirds for Museums

Where the OXCART and *HABU* spend their retirement is a story that goes back to the mid-1970s, when an informal competition began among several of the Air Force's major generals (two-star) to see which of them could create the most impressive air museum. By and large, these generals commanded the numbered Air Forces and the then-five Air Logistics Centers. Somewhere along the line, these general officers got the idea there should be more than one USAF Museum. They had all seen the National Museum of the U. S. Air Force at Wright-Patterson AFB, near Dayton, Ohio and they knew what a showcase it was for the Air Force.

Many of those commanders wanted something like it for their own bases. Several of the more brash generals attempted to convince their Pentagon superiors that the National Museum of the USAF ™ should be moved. (A new museum building had been built and donated to the Air Force, at Wright-Patterson AFB, and occupied not six years earlier.) One of them generously suggested the existing USAF Museum could stay where it was, but he wanted to establish what he called the "USAF Museum of the West" at March AFB, California. Another believed it would be a wonderful idea to establish a "USAF Museum of the South." Moreover, there were perennial calls for the Air Force to move its entire museum collection to the Air Force Academy at Colorado Springs. Not to be outdone, some Air Force commanders overseas wanted to set up museums on their foreign bases.

In their eagerness to rewrite history and establish showcases at their favorite bases, these "junior generals" apparently forgot that one major museum was already established, for the entire U.S. Air Force. It mattered little to them that it was at Wright-Patterson AFB for very good reasons. The base is near Dayton, Ohio, which, as most school children know, is the birthplace of powered aviation. The Wright Brothers invented the first successful powered airplane at Dayton. Although the first powered flight took place at Kill Devil Hills, North Carolina, the Wright Brothers proved the practicality of heavier-than-air flight at Huffman Prairie, near Dayton, Ohio. The first military aircraft was invented in Dayton, and its prototype initially was first tested at

Huffman Prairie. Although early tests were done at Kill Devil Hills in 1908, Wright-Patterson AFB's Huffman Prairie remains the site of the site of world's first *true* airport, where military flight was proven.

Air Force Pentagon leadership, being what it is, supported all sides of the question, and none of these proposals were turned down out of hand. Members of the "Generals club" dealt with one another more subtly than that. The Air Force's leaders certainly were not going to split up their showcase museum and move it. Yet, they didn't want their brethren to be made out as fools, either. In true military fashion, they threw their fellow generals a face-saving bone. The two-star commanders were permitted to set up their own subordinate museums and aircraft parks at bases of their own choosing. They would be allowed to use USAF Museum assets to populate them. To the USAF Museum at Wright-Patterson, fell the task of locating airplanes and other artifacts to place in the new museums and aircraft parks. It put the USAF Museum in a very difficult position, because it was not staffed to monitor all necessary transactions. Orders are orders, and an office was set up within the USAF Museum to oversee all of these placements.

The subordinate museums got interested in Blackbirds when the USAF Museum acquired YF-12A S/N 60-6935 in November 1979, after it had completed its test program for NASA. Not only that, but the USAF Museum was also supplying aircraft on loan to qualified private, nonprofit museums. So it was, by the early 1980s, the USAF Museum was looking for more Blackbirds for its growing collection of airplanes. Since the SR-71s were still in operational service, interest turned to the single-seat A-12 Blackbirds, at that time still referred to as the A-11, owned by the Air Force. The A-12s, which were phased out, were in storage at Palmdale, California.

On July 29, 1983, the Director of the USAF Museum wrote to the Air Force's Pentagon office in charge of tracking obsolete, out-of-service aircraft (AF/PRPRC). He mentioned that "nine A-11 [sic] aircraft in storage at Palmdale were reflected in the recent MASDC D003 report of 30 June 1983." He asked that if any of those aircraft ever became excess to Air Force or U.S. government operational needs, the USAF Museum be considered a recipient of any or all of them for display use. Again, in August 1984, the Director asked the Pentagon to place "A-11s" with the USAF Museum, for external placement if they became excess to Air Force needs.

At that time, nobody dreamed that in 1990, just six years later, the SR-71s would be retired from Air Force operational service. Except for the few retained in storage, most of them were turned over to the USAF Museum program for placement in museums around the country. One was donated to the National Air and Space Museum, and another was flown to the USAF Museum for its collection. In addition, five SR-71s were distributed to museums or display sites in California. Seven others found homes in museums or aircraft parks in Arizona, Florida, Georgia, Kansas, Nebraska, Texas, and Utah. The SR-71 was canceled for good. The runways and the hangars at Edwards were emptied, and the last two SRs sat out on the apron, slowly being taken apart, while a third one was dispatched to a museum.

At about the same time the SR-71s were being retired, a number of A-12s were released to the USAF Museum program for placement. Three went to museums in California, and one each went to display sites in Alabama, Minnesota, New York, and Texas. One A-12 derivative, the M-21 mother ship used to launch the D-21 drone, was sent to a museum in Seattle, Washington. There, this one-of-a-kind aircraft, with the D-21 mounted on its back, forms an excellent indoor exhibit. Thus came the "end of the line" for the A-12, YF-12, MD-21 and the SR-71, brilliant veterans of the reconnaissance war.

Epilogue

As we end this book, a final thought should be given to the members of the OXCART program and their amazing aircraft. They did it all in the dark. This was no media event to be sure. No glitz, no glamour, and no acknowledgements other than the back pats of their brothers-in-arms. It took many years for this program to come to light and only now are we able to give them some of the thanks and glory that they deserve.

When we first became interested in the rare, mysterious A-12s, we had little idea that our interest would lead to a two decade obsession! Over that time, we discovered that OXCART's history included deeds, ingenuity, daring, danger, courage, sacrifice, and patriotism. The people of OXCART/SENIOR CROWN/TAGBOARD accomplished extraordinary things in extraordinary secrecy. They designed, built, maintained, and flew machines of extraordinary capabilities under such closely-guarded secrecy that, even now, there are many details and events they cannot reveal.

We both have been privileged to become acquainted with many of the men and women of OXCART in 2005 at the Roadrunners Internationale reunion in Las Vegas, and was honored to address the group at one of their sessions. Through the years we have grown closer to the family members of Jack Weeks and of course T.D. Barnes, the leader of the Roadrunners Internationale.

In this group are perhaps the largest collection of individuals on Earth who can legitimately claim, ***"What I did helped win the Cold War."*** Only, they can't tell anybody exactly how they did it. We hope we have helped them to get their story out there.

We must now think of something else the preservation of this unique Cold War history. We would like to think we've had a hand in that. Many of the OXCART A-12s are now on display in museums around the country, as are their progeny, the SR-71s, the remaining YF-12, and several D-21 drones. Some of these historical Cold War relics are receiving less than proper care and have been deteriorating. The public who paid for them needs to insist that they be preserved as valued artifacts that help tell the story of those who served silently, in the dark, to help keep America free. In saying that the National Museum of the United States Air Force™ which is responsible for the loan agreements to the various other museums where blackbirds reside, need to make sure that their artifacts are taken care. Until recently that may have been a big order because there was not much published on the OXCART- Lockheed Blackbirds. However, now there is no excuse. The National Museum must enforce its polices that all aircraft are indeed cared for and the host museum must be held accountable for yearly compliance to their contact agreements. The author has also written a manual for the display and restorative care of the Blackbirds in all Aviation museums, so there is no reason for the satellite museums to say there is no true method of how to care for these exotic aircraft. Many of which have been left outside to rack and ruin, a very poor level of respect for those "Silent Warriors" that gave the ultimate sacrifice for this Nation during the Cold War.

OXCART and all that encompassed it including the magnificent Blackbirds, needs to remain in the light. The accomplishments of OXCART and the programs of the YF-12, M-21/D-21 and the SR-71show that Area 51 didn't belong to little green men, but to a group of individuals that worked in silence, created a magnificent program and an aircraft that was years ahead of her time. It needs to remain in the light to give testament to what can be accomplished, even when no one knows about it, and can be successful. The Cold War history is now being preserved at the Atomic Museum in Nevada.

When you look at a Blackbird, either in a book or a museum, try to imagine some of her magnificent history and remember a little of Edgar Allen Poe's poem:

"Dream-Land"

By a route obscure and lonely
Haunted by ill angels only,
Where an Eidolon, named Night,
On a black throne reigns upright,
I have reached these lands but newly
From an ultimate dim Thule—
From a wild weird clime that lieth, sublime,
Out of Space — out of Time.

Appendices

TOP SECRET
OXCART

BYE-2737-66

EXPERIENCE RECORD

AIRCRAFT

First Flight	26 April 1962
Total Flights	2078
Total Hours	3186:39
Total Flights at Mach 3.0	485
Total Hours at Mach 3.0	244:39
Longest Flight at Mach 3.0	3:50
Speed - Max	Mach 3.29
Altitude - Max	90,000 ft.

J-58 ENGINES

Total Engine Flights	5194
Total Engine Hours	8370
Total Engine Flights at Mach 3.0	1914
Total Engine Flight Hours at Mach 3.0	939
Total Ground Test Hours	23,111
Total Mach 3.0 Environmental Ground Test Hours	6505
Total 150 Hour Qualification Tests	6

INS

Total Flights	1081
Total Flight Operating Hours	2361
Total Operating Time	30,754

SAS - AUTO PILOT

Total Flights	2433
Total Flight Hours	3690
Total Operating Hours	35,271

CAMERAS

	I	II
Total Flights	145	59
Total Flight Operating Hours	109	49
Total Flights Above Mach 3.0	43	33
Total Hours at Mach 3.0	39	33
Longest Flight at Mach 3.0	1.5	2.0

OXCART
TOP SECRET

2

HANDLE VIA BYEMAN CONTROL SYSTEM

A. The A-12's total flight times, engines, pilots and cameras.

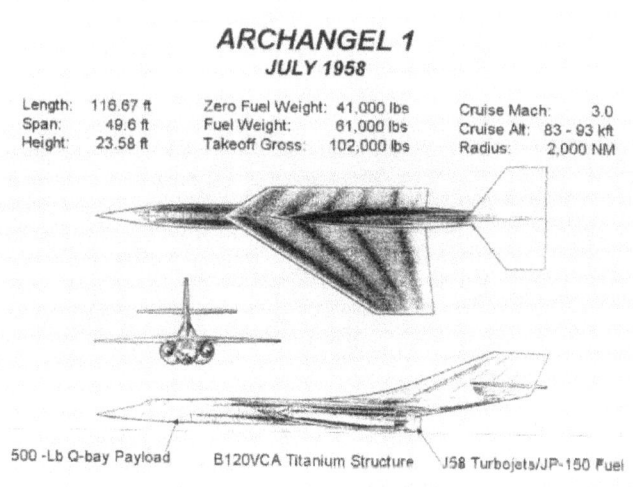

B. Archangel I draft dated July 1958. This was the "gleam in the eye" Kelly Johnson had for the soon to be A-12.

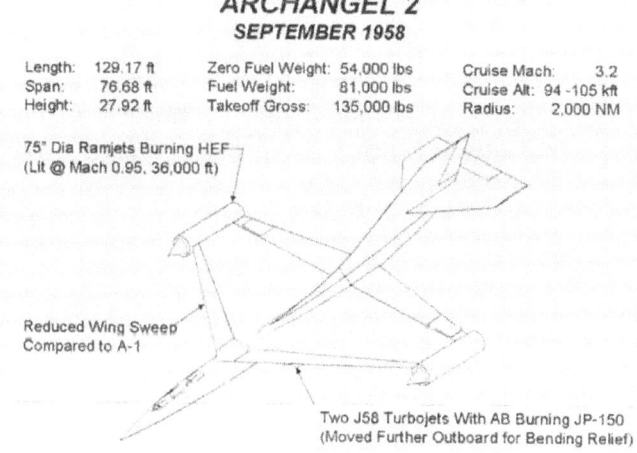

C. Archangel II – The Changes in Archangel II show where the changes in wing formation and the nacelles were applied.

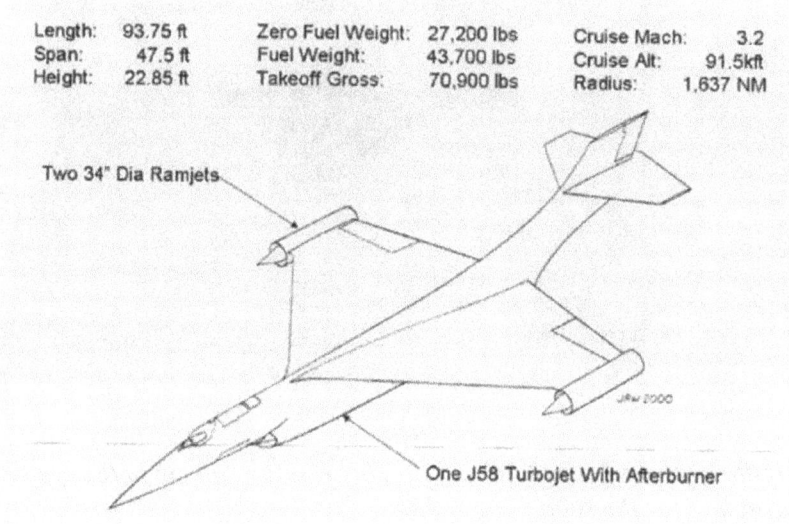

D. The A-7 thru A-9 series never made it off the drawing board as we have seen. However, it is a good look into what Kelly Johnson was thinking and trying to solve various aerodynamic issues. On the A-7 he added the two ramjets and the J-58 engine beneath the fuselage with an afterburner.

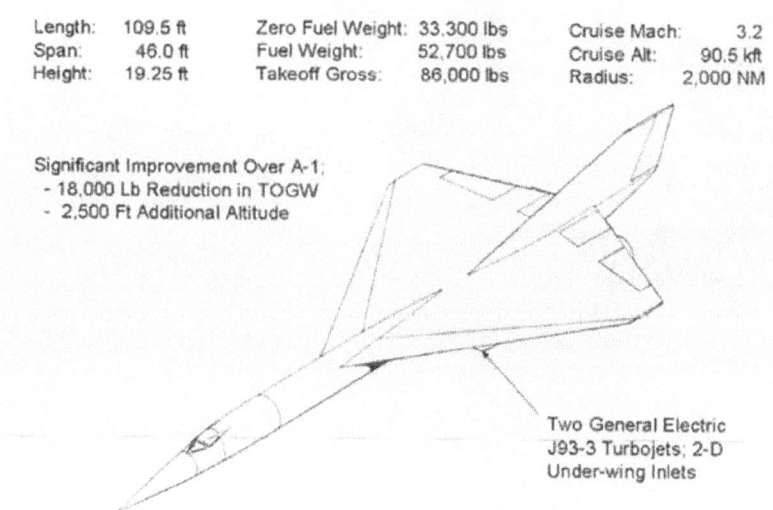

E. This plan for the A-10 of 1959 shows that Kelly Johnson had extended the wing closer to the cockpit than to the center of the aircraft. The tail extension almost meets the wing extension.

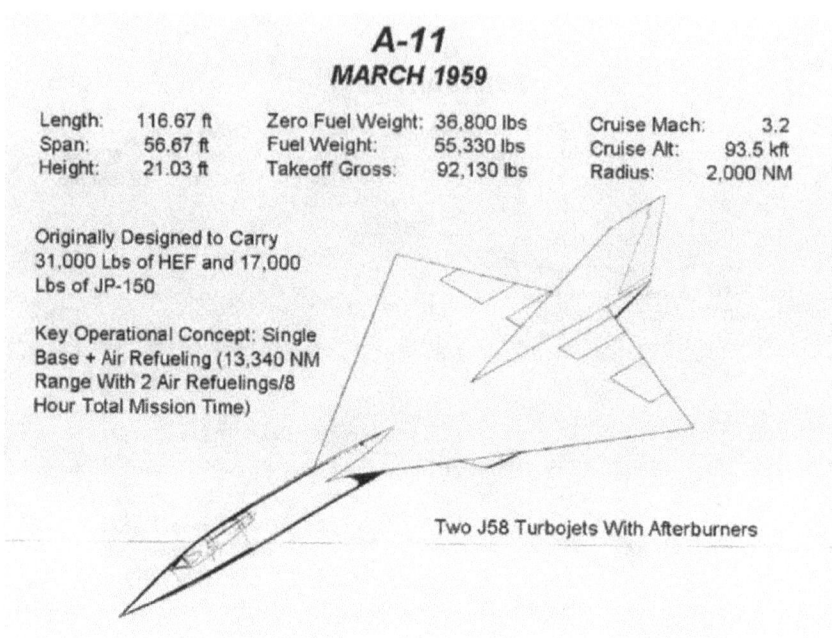

F.   The A-11 Planform when compared to the A-12 is truly different. The A-11 was a sleeker aircraft, but in the end, could not manage the weight ratios that were needed.

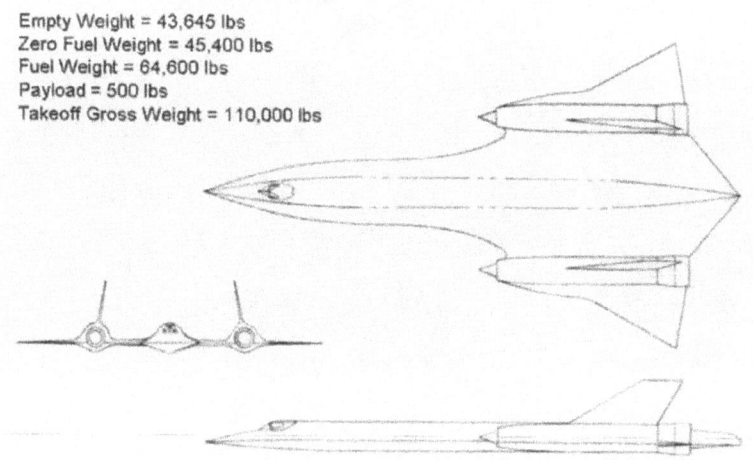

G. The planform for the finally realized A-12 There are some differences in weight and other figures when she finally came on board. There is a more blended body via the chines that have been added. The engine nacelles have been brought further into the wing. She has a basically more rounded shape, due to the use of the chines, unlike the A-10 which had a more diamond shape.

CONVAIR KINGFISH
JULY 1959

Cruise Mach: 3.2
Cruise Altitude: 85 - 94 kft
Total Range: 3,400 NM

Powerplants: Two J58 w/AB

Length: 73.6 ft
Span: 60.0 ft
Height: 18.3 ft

H. The Convair KINGFISHER that was the competitor for the A-12.

Page III-4
FIGURE 1

A-11 MISSION SUMMARY

	Weight Lbs.	Fuel Lbs.	Dist. N.Miles	Alt. Ft.
T. O.	84,800	1,700	0	S.L.
Climb	83,100	9,000	220	S.L.
Cruise Out	74,100	19,600	1,780	88,700
Target	54,500	-	-	94,300
Cruise Back	54,500	15,900	2,000	100,000
Reserve (30 min.)	38,600	1,800	-	35,000
ZFW	36,800	-	-	-

Radius   2,000 N. Mi. (180° turn at target)

Fuel   48,000 lbs. Total
         (31,000 lbs. HEF used in afterburner,
         17,000 lbs. JP150 used in primary)

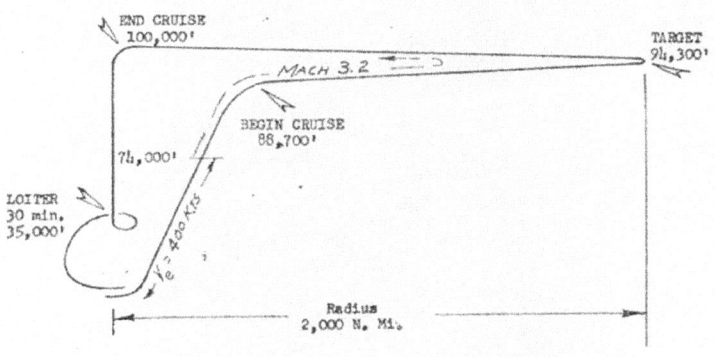

I. The A-11 Mission Summary as planned by Kelly Johnson.

Page VI-4

Lockheed AIRCRAFT CORPORATION
CALIFORNIA DIVISION

BORON FUELS (CONT.)

	HEF-2	HEF-3 Until 12-31-61
b. Increase in viscosity		After being held for 30 min. at 400°F, the viscosity shall not have increased more than 2 cs at 77°F.
Heating Value (77°F) Refined as the reaction yielding Amorphous B_2O_3 and H_2 vapor	24,100 Btu/lb nom. 23,600 Btu/lb min.	25,800 Btu/lb. nominal 25,500 Btu/lb min. 26,200 Btu/lb max.
Specific Gravity (77°F)	0.70 nominal 0.65 minimum	0.82 nominal 0.80 minimum
Viscosity at 77°F	1.5 cs nominal 3.0 cs maximum	7 cs nominal 9 cs maximum
at -40°F	To be investigated.	150 cs maximum
Vapor Pressure 77°F	1.2 psia nominal 3.0 psia maximum	0.01 psia nominal maximum to be investigated.
Freezing Point	-76°F	-76°F
Spontaneous Ignition Temperature	Pyrophoric	260°F nominal 250°F minimum
Compatibility with JP-6 Fuel	Incompatible	Compatible under N_2 atmosphere
Storage Stability	Zero solids formed after 3 months storage in an inert atmosphere at temperatures in the range of -65°F to +160°F.	Zero solids formed after 6 months storage in an inert atmosphere at temperatures in the range of -65°F to +160°F.
Flash Point	Pyrophoric	160°F minimum
Boiling Point		468°F to 510°F

J. Breakdown of the Boron Fuel System

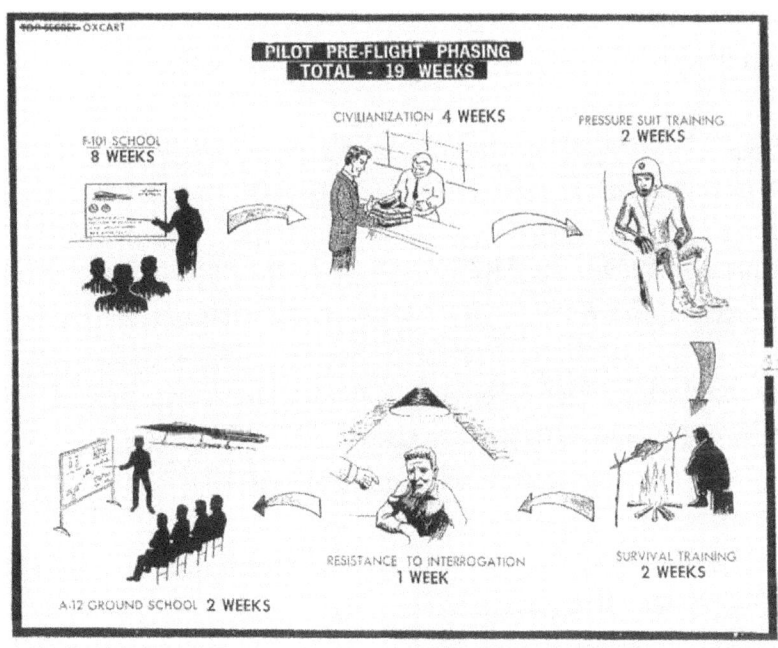

K. Training schedule for the new "Sheep-Dipped" A-12 Pilots.

L. Significant dates for the Lockheed Legacy:

October 18, 1956—The USAF cancels the REX engine. This hydrogen fueled engine was to be the basis for the CL-400. This hydrogen fueled engine was to be the basis for the CL-400-Project SUNTAN.

December 24, 1957—The Pratt and Whitney J-58 engine goes live for the first time in a test.

April 21, 1958—Kelly Johnson, for the very first time writes the name "ARCHANGEL" in his diary.

December 1958—The CIA delves into high speed reconnaissance aircraft for the first time by asking for funding for the ARCHANGEL.

August 29, 1959—Both Convair and Lockheed agree to the proposals for the first high speed, high altitude aircraft.

September 14, 1959—The ARCHANGEL becomes the CIA's answer to high speed reconnaissance aircraft as the study is now approved.

January 26, 1960—The order goes out to Lockheed to build 12 of the ARCHANGEL, now known as OXCART aircraft. The name was supposed to be a "joke" because of the mach 3 speed the aircraft would attain.

May 1, 1960—As Eisenhower prepares for a summit with the USSR, the unthinkable happens, Francis Gary Powers in his U-2 is brought down by a SAM missile over Sverdlosk, USSR. He is picked up by local farmers and turned into the USSR police. Powers was NOT supposed to survive the shoot down and would spend 10 years in Soviet prison. The CIA was not pleased with him to say the least. Eisenhower had to admit to the USSR and Krushchev that the U.S. had been spying. The summit was canceled leaving Eisenhower with proverbial egg on his face.

February 1962—Under cover in a wide angle, canvas transport, the first of the A-12s leave the Lockheed Burbank plant for the long trip to Area 51- Nevada, her new home.

April 26, 1962—The A-12 leaves the bonds of earth for the first time down a runway at the new Area 51 facility. Test Pilot Lou Schalk flew the aircraft which was designated Article #121 for the CIA and 60-6924 for the USAF.

April 30, 1962— Lou Schalk takes the A-12 #121 for her first official maiden flight with a bevy of CIA, USAF, Lockheed other official onlookers at Area 51 to cheer her on.

May 2, 1962—A-12 #121 goes supersonic for the first time reaching Mach 1.1.

June 1962—The USAF gets its first mock up look at its dream aircraft, the SR-71. This would be a two seater aircraft based on the A-12 with room for more ELINT and bigger cameras, not to mention other tracking goodies. She would not be as fast as the A-12 and the A-12 cameras would prove to be better.

October 1962—It wasn't too long after the A-12 had come into her own that the $1 million dollar Letter of Intent for the USAF's YF-12 Interceptor aircraft was signed by the USAF and Lockheed.

October 5, 1962—Due to a shortage of the J-58 engines, Pratt and Whitney were trying to catch up with production. The A-12 had to fly with one J-75 engine and one J-58 engine till production was up to speed. This occurred at the Area 51 complex.

October 10, 1962—Lockheed and Kelly Johnson received the okay to go ahead with the D-21 drone study also known as the Q-12. This would include the use of the A-12 as the mother ship. She would be known as the M-21.

December 28, 1962—The SR-71 becomes a reality and the USAF and Lockheed sign a contract to build six of the aircraft. This also signals the end of the A-12 program.

January 15, 1963—Pratt and Whitney make delivery of the J-58 engines which allows the A-12 to fly for the first time with 2-J-58 engines. By the end of January 10 engines were available.

May 24, 1963—The first A-12 crashes in Wendover, Utah. Article #123, 606926 is lost, but CIA pilot Ken Collins survives.

July 20, 1963—For the first time ever, the A-12 becomes the only aircraft to reach Mach 3.

August 7, 1963—The first YF-12 #606934 makes her debut with pilot Jim Eastham at the controls. The difference with the YF-12 was noticeable at once. The YF-12 had truncated nose section and was a two seater.

November 22, 1963—Mach 3.2 is achieved by the A-12 at an altitude of 78,000 ft. This actually occurred as John F. Kennedy was being assassinated in Dallas, Texas.

February 29, 1964—President Lyndon Baines Johnson tells the world of the A-11, a high speed, high altitude aircraft that the U.S. had been developing in secret. The mistake that Johnson made was first, the A-11 was actually the YF-12, and second, the error of the A-11 hid the existence of the super secret A-12 for the CIA. No one knew the A-12 even existed till she came out of storage with the Nat'l Museum of the USAF program coordination office to be put out to museums in the early 1990s

April 1, 1964—A-12 (606940) recently re-conformed to the M-21 made its first flight at Area 51.

April 16, 1964—The YF-12 Interceptor launches the AIM-47 Falcon missile for the first time. This was redesigned missile known as the XAIM-47.

June 1964—The last of the A-12s (606939) was delivered to Area 51.

June 19, 1964—The first mating of the D-21(501) and the M-21 was made at Area 51 hangars.

July 25, 1964—President Lyndon Johnson proudly announced the SR-71 to the world. Since no one knew about the A-12, there were many things that were hidden. The CIA was going out of the aerial reconnaissance business with the end of the A-12. The SR-71 was strictly a USAF bird. One that should have been protected better than she was. Due to politics and general nastiness, the U.S. lost one of the greatest reconnaissance tools it ever had.

Oct 29, 1964—The SR-71 prototype (61-7950), was delivered to the Palmdale Plant 42 used by the USAF from the Lockheed Burbank plant.

December 22, 1964—SR-71 (61-7950) made her first flight with Lockheed's test pilot Bob Gilliland at the Palmdale facility.

December 22, 1964—At the other side of the apron, back at Area 51 on the same day December 22, 1964, the M-21 loaded with the D-21 made her first flight with Lockheed test pilot Bill Park.

January 27, 1965—The A-12 made herself a new record by flying for one hour and 40 minutes 3,000 miles at the speed of Mach 3.1.

May 1, 1965—The only two YF-12 created (606934 and 606935) made two new records for speed and altitude over Edwards AFB, California. Both aircraft were stationed there.

March 5, 1966—M-21 (606941) launched the first D-21 (503), flying 150 nautical miles during the test.

July 30, 1966—M-21(606941) and D-21 (504) were destroyed during an accident where the D-21 hit the M-21 during launch procedure. Pilot Ray Torick was killed, drowning in his flight suit while in the water after ejection. This caused Kelly Johnson to stop the program as he did not want to lose any more pilots. He would go on to use B-52 as the mothership for the D-21, called "Captain Hook" program.

December 28, 1966—After a number of meetings including a test flight of the SR-71 and the A-12 called "NICE GIRL" to determine which aircraft would be more substantial, the decision to terminate the A-12 so that there would not be "redundancy" in the programs was made. The strange part to this decision is that both aircraft really had different missions. The A-12 was strictly reconnaissance, while the SR-71 was able to do ELINT and EWS work. However, politics reigned and the A-12 was retired while she still had a huge amount of life left. So, determined was Kelly Johnson to keep the A-12 flying, he had even proposed selling them to Iran (at that time the Shah was still in power and very much an ally). The plan did not go through, thankfully.

May 11, 1967—Operation CAROUSEL starts the move of the A-12s and crews to Kadena AFB, Okinawa

May 22, 1967—Operation Carousel continues with the first of the A-12s (606937) being flown to Kadena AFB in Okinawa, Japan. The CIA pilot flying was Mele Vojvodich.

May 31, 1967—Black Shield program was started with the first operational flights over North Vietnam. The flight lasted 3 hours and 45 minutes at Mach 3.1. A-12 606937 was the aircraft that had the honors. The mission number was BX001 and the photo take was considered good.

July 2, 1967—The first of the SR-71 missions was flown by SR-71A (61-7972). Unfortunately, there was a glitch with the INS (Inertial Navigation System) caused the aircraft to cross over to Mexican airspace.

November 3, 1967—NICE GIRL—was the fly off program which decided the fate of the A-12. Both aircraft did a great job and result were non-conclusive. However, the decision to kill the A-12 program was made.

January 5, 1968—YF-12 production line is officially closed down by Lockheed via official notice by the USAF. Only three YF-12s were made. One was lost in an accident-60-6936 was the YF-12 that was lost in a non-fatal accident.

January 26, 1968—Jack Weeks and A-12 #131—BX-6847-mission, made the first flight over North Korea after the USS PUEBLO had been taken by the North Koreans. Weeks, managed to find the PUEBLO frozen in Wonson Harbor in his photographic take. It was a difficult flight due to some technical problems with the aircraft, but Weeks made it back to base successfully.

Feb 5, 1968—Kelly Johnson is told to destroy all the tooling for the A-12, YF-12 and SR-71. However, the story goes, he sent it all in a freight car to Nevada and sent it to Area 51. He never did destroy the tooling.

March 8, 1968—The first of the SR-71s arrive at Kadena AFB arrive to replace the A-12s. Both aircraft were flying missions at the time.

March 21, 1968—SR-71 (61-7976) had the first of the missions flown over Vietnam.

May 8, 1968—The last mission of the A-12 was flown by CIA pilot Jack Layton. The mission number was BX 6858.

November 9, 1969—CAPTAIN HOOK program was now in play with the D-21 being launched from the B-52H mother ship.

December 11, 1969—YF_12 (606935) was now part of NASA's test flight team. This was the first flight.

March 20, 1971—The last of the CAPTAIN HOOK missions, this one over Lop Nor, China was launched from the B-52H. The mission was not successful. According to Kelly Johnson:" Damn thing came out of China, but was lost. It wasn't spotted or shot down, but it must have malfunctioned and crashed on us.".

Oct 12, 1973—The SR-71A made its first flight over the Mid-east in support of the Yom Kippur War.

September 1, 1974—New York to London speed record for the SR-71, 1 hour and 56 minutes with Pilot J. Sullivan and RSO N. Widdenfield.

September 13, 1974—Second record set, SR-71 to Los Angeles 3 hours and 47 minutes with pilot Buck Adams and RSO-Bill Machorek.

July 27, 1976—SR-71 speed record 2,092 mph Pilot P Bledsoe and RSO J. Fuller.

July 28, 1976—SR-71 Speed record 2,193 mph with pilot F. Loersz and G. Morgan.

July 28, 1976—High altitude record for SR-71 85,068 ft. with pilot R. Helt and RSO. L. Elliot.

Nov 16, 1978—First SR-71 flight over Cuba.

November 7, 1979—At Wright-Patterson AFB, the YF-12 #935 becomes a permanent exhibition, after landing at the base, to be moved over to the National Museum of the USAF™.

August 26,1981—North Korea launched two SA-2 missiles at and SR-71 in flight over the DMZ zone, Vietnam.

November 7,1984—SR-71 flew over Nicaragua on a mission due to political unrest in the nation.

April 13, 1986—SR-71s fly post strike reconnaissance over Libya to conduct mission after Operation El Dorado Canyon.

July 22, 1987—SR-71 flies the first operational mission over the Gulf in the Mideast.

October 1, 1989—SR-71 missions are suspended while waiting to hear about budget meetings.

November 22, 1989—All USAF SR-71 operations are terminated.

January 26, 1990—SR-71 is decommissioned at its home, Beale AFB.

January 5, 1995—SR-71 are reactivated. Aircraft #967 is the first.

April 16, 1995—the SR-71 is again decommissioned this time it's final.

October 10, 1997—In a line-tem veto then President Bill Clinton consigns the SR-71 to history by vetoing the SR-71 program in total.

October 6, 1999—The 9th Strategic Reconnaissance Wing is deactivated.

Jeannette Remak and Joseph Ventolo, Jr.

ROUTING
INIT ACT
Approved for Release 2013/11 19
SECRET
OXCART

OXC-0262-67
Copy 6 of 5

26 January 1967

HOLD FOR:
T.H.
FILE

MEMORANDUM FOR THE RECORD

SUBJECT: Review of Accident Board Recommendations (Article 125) Regarding Life Support Equipment.

1. The following recommendations have had action taken as indicated.

   a. <u>Remove head-rest spacers. Reverse nuts and bolts on front of seat which secure rotary actuator straps.</u> These recommendations have been satisfied as of 12 January 1967. (Ref CABLE 4632 IN 99524). However, investigation must be re-established to develop a means of insuring all crew members can reach the headrest regardless of torso height (ref Accident Board recommendations from Accident Report on aircraft 2003). LAC has proposed a parachute modification to aid in allowing the head to reach the headrest and this proposal is being evaluated in terms of parachute integrity by the parachute manufacturer at the present time. In addition, this modified parachute must be fitted to each driver and accurate comparative measurements made to determine its effectiveness in allowing the head to reach the headrest. I have discussed this approach with Ed Martin at LAC and Jim Seitler from Firewel (Prime contractor on parachute) and will attempt to schedule such an evaluation in the immediate future.

   b. <u>Expedite emergency faceplate heating and protective cover for the controller.</u> A prototype controller cover was built and tested by LAC and 20 items are now in production. Verification tests will be required when these become available to insure that no restriction to ventilation has resulted. In addition, the item will require further consideration by Area 51 personnel as to its possible effectiveness in preventing damage to the controller and or connections. In these respects the item must remain an evaluation item for the time being. The

OXCART
SECRET
Approved for Release 2013/11 19

M. These are the results of the accident report on Article #125- - in which CIA pilot Walt Ray was killed on impact trying to eject from his A-12. These are the corrections that were made to the ejection seat system.

Black Lightning

Approved for Release: 2013/11 19
SECRET
OXCART

OXC-0262-67

emergency faceplate heating provisions have been under development by LAC. The number, size, and type of batteries required have been established and location and wiring has been mocked-up. This prototype package should be ready for evaluation at Area 51 by the week of 30 January 1967 according to telecon with Ed Martin on 24 January 1967. In addition to Area 51 personnel evaluation, I have instructed the Firewel Co. (prime contractor on parachute system) to submit an evaluation on this item since the LAC proposal is to locate the batteries in the cover for the oxygen initiator pan of the parachute back pack. Whirl tower and or high speed drop tests may be required on this item before final approval can be given, to insure that proper parachute sequencing is not impaired by this modification.

c. Lap belt automatic release mechanism rework to prevent tension or side load binding. Develop a readily accessible manual release lever.

LAC is presently investigating these items to determine what corrective measures can be made. RCAF tests and modifications of the MA-6 lap belt are being reviewed and LAC is conducting their own series of tests at this time. A test report is to be provided the undersigned upon completion.

d. Apply smooth surfaces to headrest underside and top of stabilization parachute pack.

I have directed the prime parachute contractor to evaluate smooth materials for the pack as part of the parachute modification referred to in paragraph 1 a above. A smooth coating for the headrest underside is being investigated by LAC.

e. Reposition Rotary Actuator to provide maximum forward thrust to man/parachute.

LAC has initiated a redesign of the ejection seat headrest to include repositioning of the rotary actuator.

OXCART
SECRET

OXC-0262-67

f. **Shoulder harness loops sewn to prevent slipping over automatic latch level housing.**

This minor modification can be made by LAC personnel at Area 51. At the same time LAC is sewing the shoulder harness strap to the inertia reel strap to preclude the bunching-up of the shoulder strap into a rope-like configuration. Th s modification, which was discussed during the week of 9 January, will also aid in providing a smoother area between the headrest and stabilization parachute.

g. **D-Ring cable-cutter installation.**

This recommendation will require extensive consideration before a decision can be made to proceed or not. Because of the design of the OXCART ejection D-ring T-handle combination a simple inclusion of the D-ring cable cutter from the SR-7 stabilized seat, which does not have the secondary T-handle within the D-ring, is not possible. Either the T-handle would have to be relocated or an entirely new type of cable cutter would have to be developed. Consideration must also be given to the possibility of a D-ring impacting the helmet visor or suit after being cu free at high altitude. I do not feel that the D-ring played any significantly adverse role in this accident and there is no indication of D-ring difficulties in any previous ejection with this system.

h. **All future modifications to the ejection system must receive thorough testing and qualification prior to issuance of TCTO kits or service bulletins.**

There is no question as to the validity of this recommendation, since the headrest spacers were, from all indications, installed wi hout prior testing and qualification. With this recommendation in mind I have started a review of previous accident board recommendations and ejection syste life support modifications resulting from such recommendations to insure that all pertinent items have received or will receive adequate and appropriate evaluation and qualification testing prior to incorporation.

Black Lightning

OXC-0262-67

2. One further subject shou d be discussed here although it was not mentioned in the accident board's recommendations. The brackets securing the rotary actuator straps on the front of the ejection seat from aircraft #125 and the seat used for seat separa ion tests had the attaching nuts on the inside of the sent bucket facing the seat kit with the smooth screw heads on the outside of the seat. The ejection seat originally had these brackets installed with the screw heads inside the bucket, so it is apparent that during subsequent handling, nspections, repairs, etc., the screws were reversed. Also, on the seat used for tests which was removed from an OXCART aircraft, the uppermost portion of the knee guards were found to be reversed right for left. Although this latter item has no direct bearing on #125 nor would it probably influence the function of the knee guards it does reflect, along with the strap bracket screw reversal, that errors or oversights are occurring during ground handling of ejection system components. Re-emphasis on careful workmanship, quality control, and adequate supervision as well as specific, detailed instructions may be called for at this time for all personnel involved with egress systems both at Area 51 and LAC facilities.

[handwritten: Was this in accident board?]

BRUCE E. BASSETT
CAPT. USAF BSC
ASD R&D OSA

ASD R&D OSA/BEBassett:gd (26 January 1967)
Distribution:
Cy 1 - ASD R&D OSA
   2 - D R&D OSA
   3 - D SA
   4 - D O OSA
   5 - D   OSA
   6 - OXC OSA
   7 - chrono
   8 - RB OSA

N. SR-71 Speed Records:

September 1, 1974—New York to London with Pilot Major James V. Sullivan and RSO Major Noel F. Widdifield, 3,490 miles in 1 hour and 54 minutes 56.4 seconds in SR-71A 64-17972

September 13, 1974—London to Los Angeles with pilot Captain Harold B. Adams, RSO Captain William C. Machorek: 5,645 miles in 3 hours and 47 minutes, 35.8 seconds, in SR-71A 64-17972

July 27/28,1976—High altitude flight 85,068.997 ft. with pilot Captain Robert C. Helt, and RSO Major Larry A. Elliot in SR-71A-61-7962.

July 27/28, 1976—Straight course speed- 2,193.167 mph with pilot Captain Eldon W. Joersz and RSO Major George T. Morgan in SR-71A #61-7958.

July 27/28, 1976—Closed course speed—2,092.294 mph with Pilot Major Adolphus H. Bledsoe Jr. and RSO Major John T. Fuller in SR-71A #61-7958.

O. CIA MEMO

CIA memo 12-21-66
Memo of record
AM Meeting 12-21-66

OXCART program Donald Steininger of Don Horning's office had full understanding of Agency's position on OXCART

Memo for Record 10-23- 63
OXCART magnitude of Security problem:

1. 4th anniversary of "reduction go ahead" for OXCART vehicle. During intervening years the initial covert development of 10 OXCART aircraft has expanded into a group of separate developments of far greater magnitude an complexity than anticipated,

2. Project KEDLOCK-TAGBOARD –EARNING? Individually representing a sizable development have origins in OXCART.

At the same time with increased developments, OXCART operational readiness date slipped. On the premise that OXCART mission operational mission date slipped. On the premise that the OXCART mission must be concealed the associated projects identified the above have remained under the security cognizance and control of the CIA through Project OXCART HQ., Purpose of memo to outline in summary areas of growth which are of continuing security significance Procurements resulting from new developments cause increase in security areas.

A. Clearance: (redact) actively participating in OXCART, KEDLOCK clearances were given to (redact) personnel. OXCART clearances rose in October 1960, August 1961, March 1962, August 1963.

All government personnel cleared for OXCART were aware of the CIA participation. 5% of the cleared industrial personnel are aware of the CIA participation.

During past 6 months average requests for clearance for OXCART and KEDLOCK were given to OXCART HQ.

Breakdown of US Govt OXCART clearance by CIA:

Industrial contractors:

Oct 1960, OXCART HQ had granted clearances to individuals within (redact) industrial firms,

Full OXCART clearance (awareness of the CIA) granted to individuals within proximity of firms. Security cognizance of project activities within these facilities was maintained (redact) assigned to OXCART HQ. Each facility was visited 3-4 times per year for a review of personnel and physical security procedures.

Security cognizance within other industrial firms (where there is no knowledge of the CIA) was maintained by OXCART HQ through prime contractor security offices.

Hardware production:

For original order of 10 OXCART vehicles in 1960 production orders are now in for the following vehicles:

    OXCART—10 A-12s
    KEDLOCK—3 (AF-12)
    EARNINGS—31 (R-12s) SR-71
    TAGBOARD—20 (D-21)

Industrial speculation was aroused by large procurement needed to support this many aircraft constitutes a vulnerable area.

Personnel build up at the flight test location (Area 51) also greatly exceeded expectations. The latest increase happened by decision to conduct KEDLOCK flight test program at Area 51 (YF-12) Manned increase by December 1963:

Growth followed:

    January 1961
    August 1962
    April 1963

August 1963

Separation of (redact) Personnel from their permanent homes and transportation of the majority of them to (Area 51) constitutes a primary area of security concern. Every effort is being made to thoroughly brief each person before he departs for Area 51 and access to all aircraft entering Area 51 was strictly controlled by the CIA security officers assigned at the Burbank California. Lockheed Area 51 terminal points.

It was extraordinary that to date the existence of A-12 and state of development had received no compromising notoriety from the news media.

OXCART Awareness was generated with 4 principal causes:

    a. Industrial competition: aircraft industry highly competitive in general and aware of "Skunk Works" activity in Burbank. Kelly Johnson was notorious by reputation, conspicuous in his unavailability to the industry and invariably associated with "Skunk Works" giving rise to considerable speculation about a new vehicle at Lockheed.

    b. Large purchase orders already generated in support of OXCART associated projects presented an enormous development recognized within small vendor facilities and large contractor plants to sophisticated buyers and salesmen.

    c. Increasing concern is the problem of conflicting priorities currently being encountered within many sub-contractors facilities. Small vendor manufacturing parts for OXCART, B-70 and TFX are experiencing difficulties in explaining low delivery to the B-70 and TFX people. B-70 and TFX representatives visiting vendors observed similar hardware being made for "another customer".

TECHNICAL:

There were several speculative references in Aviation periodicals to "U-2" follow on" and Johnson's Skunk Works. No substantial articles of a compromising nature have appeared.

Information received at OXCART HQ that Robert Hotz editor of Aviation Week is aware of the existence of the OXCART and the nature of her.

Sighting of the A-12 vehicle:

Flight lines utilized by the A-12 vehicle during test flights transverse the flight lanes of commercial aircraft and military aircraft with possible exposure of the A-12 vehicle. When proximity is such that safety is involved and the non-OXCART pilot expresses a desire to file a "near miss "report with the FAA or if it is non OXCART pilot verbally reports an un-identified exotic aircraft procedures were activated to interview and debrief the pilot.

Successful concealment of OXCART was attributed to the individual responsibility of thousands of people participating and particularly to cooperation of contributing industrial organization.

All effort was made to re-scrutinize the need to know of all project participants both in govt and industry. Primary concern of SS/OSA during that year was continued to protect OXCART mission and compartment OXCART from KEDLOCK—EARNING and TAGBOARD.

Memo of record 8-10-67
OXCART DEACTIVATION MEETING:

    a. Meeting held in the comptroller office of OSA to discuss funding needed from the NRO to deactivate the first 4 OXCART aircraft.

b. Status of OXCART deactivation and what funds would be required to prepare the aircraft and storage facility and for deactivation

c. Kelly Johnson stated first two aircraft #122 and 134 which were to be stored in late August were handled in small hangar at Palmdale (building 3211). Johnson stated that partitioning and the sprinkler system would be done. Remaining aircraft stored at main hangar at Palmdale and that was needed to make it ready. The first two would be ready in September. This was to be all inclusive costs on a one time basis. (Col Geary) felt the quote was reasonable and he asked how much it would cost to prepare the aircraft. It was stated that there would be no "pickling" of the engines and they would be kept inside the aircraft. Aircraft #134 would be trucked in requiring more expenditure to place it at Palmdale. Aircraft #122 was flown in and only needed minimum care.

d. Short discussion of U-2 U2R programs followed. The first R is to be test flown on the 28th of August 1967 and two of Perkins Elmer cameras needed overhaul.

MEMO: Exec Director Comptroller Chief info processing Appendix A to CIA 5 yr.

A and P plan DDS&T to 5 year ADP plan.

OSA project ISSINGLASS cut OSA plans for OXCART were reactivated and support #1 priority. Requirements for ADP central services to support intelligence directorate and support directorate were changing.

Memo: Deputy Director for Plans aircraft accident investigation. MEMO from DDP to DDST&T and DDS Nov 1, 1967.

Subject: informal reviews of Aircraft / Incident Investigation accidents or incidents by DDP Special Ops Division Accident.

1. DDST and OSA (office special) programs & USAF vital interest. In addition to their in reports we normally follow procedures outlined below in accidents/incidents evolving OSA aircraft

2. USAF aircraft assigned to OSA activities. The incidents accident is investigated and a report rendered by a Board of USAF personnel

3. According to USAF regulations 127-4 "Investigation and reporting of USAF aircraft accidents/ incidents. OXCART—incidents /accidents involving the OXCART aircraft were investigated and reported upon by a specialty augmented board of cleared USAF personnel (familiar with technical equipment in use) especially USAF Office of inspector general with AF-12 127-4.

4. U-2

CIA-Jan 3,1968 –MEMO director of NRO OXCART SR-71 OPS

1. 5 options of OXCART/SR-71 ops are forwarded.

2. Recognized some comments on additional requirements may be minor nature, but listed for identification and info purposes.

3. No specific mention is made of cost or lead team factors. Formally discussed @JRC level meeting held at Pentagon Dec 30,1967.

OPTION B: Joint ops of both aircraft in Kadena using common facilities and resources.

1. Space in Kadena AB complex would be most critical both for personnel and equipment due to lack of commonality of oxcart /SR-71 systems and maintenance concerns. (SR-71 uses field maintenance concept i.e. work orders material control etc. OXCART contractor maintenance concept. Additional shop space needed to support SR-71 projects.

2. Power facilities in shops and hangars are peculiar to OXCART. Must be redone for SR-71.

3. Additional POL and storage requirements (OXCART requirement) plus 80% of OXCART requirement for SR-71) necessary for concurrent operation of both fleets.

4. Additional housing, messing, facilities and transportation for SR-71 personnel was needed.

5. Extra SR-71 operational command control and flight planning space was needed.

6. Physiological equipment area would have to be increased to support 6-10 additional SAC flight crew personnel equipment.

7. Security restriction dictate that SAC personnel (approximately 1200) (3 TDY teams of 400 each) to be O-3 cleared.

8. Co-mingling of the two aircraft could degrade the cover story and cause possible political problems.

9. No additional tankers would be needed on assumption that only single operational mission (OXCART or SR-71) would be flown on a single day.

10. There would be a definite benefit gained by the SR-71 project having immediate access to OXCART experience and know how.

11. This option would give OXCART backup of the SR-71 insuring against and reconnaissance intelligence gap.

OPTION C: Simultaneous operation of the A-12/SR-71 from Kadena without the use of common facilities and resources except on non-interference basis.

1. This option required use of the minor modifications to the two corrosion control hangars presently at Kadena to provide shop and hangar space.

2. Additional POL storage space (65% increase over current OXCART requirement) would be necessary.

3. Additional housing mess, transportation facilities as well as an enlarged physiological equipment area was needed.

4. Space for SR-71 operational command control and flight planning would have to be provided.

5. Co-mingling of the 2 aircraft could cause cover story and political problems.

6. Based on single mission per day (OXCART or SR-71) no additional tankers needed.

7. SR-71 project would have a benefit in immediate access to OXCART experience.

8. Both SR-71 and OXCART on Kadena would insure against any gap in reconnaissance intelligence collection.

OPTION D: Operation of the SR-71 from another base in far east with A-12 staying at Kadena for a period of up to three months after start of SR-71 operation.

Cost and led time needed for this option discussed at JRC working group meeting at Pentagon Dec 30, 1967.

OPTION E: Operation of both aircraft from same base using common facilities and or operating separately. Overlap phasing of aircraft considered this option.

1. Option required minor modification and utilization of the 2 corrosion control hangars at Kadena for shop and hangar space.

2. Additional requirements include;

    A. POL storage space

    B. expanded physiological equipment area for additional crew equipment.

    C. Housing, mess and transportation facilities.

    D. Space for SR-71 command control and flight planning.

3. Where possible common items of supply would be utilized.

4. Use of present OXCART communication facilities on non-interference basis was possible. Additional communications facilities were needed.

5. OXCART back up of SR-71 insures against intelligence gap.

6. SR-71 project will benefit from ON THE SPOT OXCART experience and know how.

7. This option provided for orderly transition of SR-71 to assume the military mission of North Vietnam reconnaissance without serious degradation of OXCART capability.

8. Use of OXCART against other possible southeast Asia reconnaissance requirements was possible under this option

OPTION A: Update of current plan for phase in of SR-71, no overlap of A-12.

1. Ground support equipment. Test and shop equipment that is to remain in place for SR-71 support had already been identified and tagged supply spares and hardware also tagged. Items to be returned to Area 51 after redeployment have been identified.

2. SAC had already surveyed assets and Kadena for SR-71 operations permitting facility transition from OXCART to SR-71 operations.

3. Housing used by OXCART was available for SR-71 personnel based on scheduled OXCART withdrawal.

4. Kadena Air Base support was geared to accept influx of SR-71 program, per previously coordinated plan.

5. No additional major construction needed. SR-71 used current OXCART facilities.

6. Orderly OXCART redeployment and SR-71 deployment plan with necessary supporting plans published and were current.

7. No problems from a security standpoint which have not been previously considered and for which provisions were made.

8. Possibility exists of intelligence collection gap between dates of OXCART operational cessation and actual reconnaissance operation date of SR-71.

MEMO –Sept 6, 1966 AM meeting

DD/I noted a number of recent intelligence publications complied to update for Secretary Rusk.

DD/I stated that he would prepare a memo for the director's signature transmitting publication. Director asked that the estimate of the number of insurgents.

DD/I reported meeting with Webb of NASA regarding political economic factor on Soviet space program.

Director requested the DD/S&T to prepare a memo for his meeting with Secretary McNamara on technical consideration of OXCART over-flights of Cuba, DDS&T suggested director agreed, the ONE prepare a paper commenting on the Cuban /Soviet reactions to such overflights.

CIA June 24, 1968

Fiscal year 1968/69 funds: Memo for Comptroller, Directorate of Science and Technology CIA dated 5/28/1968

Memo review OXCART phase out for 1969 estimate.
Total close out OXCART picture number of considerations that make it impossible to determine what total cost to government was.

OXCART contractors were told of termination and asked for estimate of closeout costs. Comments relate to assumption set in memos and represent qualifications of estimates:

A. Assumption 1: We are prepared to support TAGBOARD during period and support cost.

B. Assumption 2: All OXCART aircraft in storage

C. Assumption 3: Few contractor personnel at Area 51 engaged in "clean up "operation. Estimate included them as part of base population to be fed and housed. We cannot at this time estimate costs for the settlement of contracts with employers. We would presume that most of this would be charged to FY68 allocation for OXCART closeout.

D. Assumption 5: Kadena AB was closed and property disposition was complete. Any further shipment of residual assets will be USAF air lift under present support agreement. No budget for this.

E. Assumption 6: Actually included in estimate

F. Assumption 7: Estimates for contractor personnel limited to cost of supporting then all at Area 51 during July and August. There is no estimate of total cost.

G. Assumption 8: expenses like this included in total estimate.

H. Assumption 9: We interpret "IN STORAGE COSTS" to mean cost of Palmdale facility storage. These costs should be budgeted by USAF since OXCART aircraft are now their responsibility.

Memo September 12, 1967
OXCART phase out planning (SCOPE COTTON)

Retrieval of an OXCART mission capability extending beyond Nov 30, 1967 was problematic as support posture became degraded. Oct 1, 1967 decision was needed if extension of operational left of program was to happen:

ACTIONS PENDING:

A. Scope Cotton: planning notes that procured OXCART spares and hardware and repair of assets was not done if production lead times and delivery dates extended past Oct 31, 1967.

This proviso remained in effect. A related factor concerns the 90 days support pkg concept for support of 5 slated aircraft. In the event inventories prior to storage indicate certain line item quantities will not attain the 90 day objective if was not intended that new procurement be indicated for these items. This applied to all aircraft and systems spare part. Without ability to acquire additional spares or to repair aircraft and systems components, the OXCART program is entirely dependent on "living off the shelf" with a consequent serious attrition and degradation of support required items:

Examples:

a. engines non in repair cycle
b. after June 18, 1967
c. inverters
d. spike actuators / indicators
e. poor actuators / indicators
f. INS computer
g. INS gyro platforms
h. SAS components
i. Temperature control amplifiers
j. Camera systems non in current contractor repair facility.
k. Film stock-all orders completed based on November 20, 1967 close out date.

B. Storage of the OXCART fleet began when aircraft #122 was flown to Palmdale facility on September 16, 1967. #122 was turned over to the National Reconnaissance Office storage custodian who was assigned the responsibility for the receipt of OXCART aircraft and associated air craft.

C. Joint SAC /Agency team enroute to Kadena AB to cuduct a survey of the OXCART facility and equipment to develop the final plan for SAC deployment and agency transfer of assets. Transition date will be immediately subsequent to the conclusion of team's survey.

A SAC team composed of 5 specialists stayed a Kadena to begin implementing the transition phase.

D. Operation (Redat) redeployment of Black Shield task force was done and will be place in effect with the first aircraft alerted to redeploy approximate November 8, 1967.Tje actual departures the first aircraft #121 from Kadena is scheduled on November 14th with second and third aircraft leaving 16 and 18 of November respectively.

E. No personnel actions were started to replace military, CIA or contractor personnel scheduled to depart as their portions of the program terminated. Contractors personnel have been notified that a close out date is imminent. Each vendor was in process of closeout throughout the industry and no longer available to the Office of Special Activities. List of military personnel schedule for movement will be forwarded to USAF Oct.1st for transfer. Under NRO guidelines the phase down of the OXCART program continues to be implemented toward the deactivation.

DEC 11, 1967:

NRO funds:

Aircraft maintenance and overhaul, engine maintenance, and overhaul Maintenance, mods, and overhaul of airborne systems (including cameras, navigation and counter-measure equipment.

Operation and maintenance of Area 51 pilot salaries and equipment support:

USAF support via NRO free.

CIA support funds
    Salaries
    Travel ground communications
    Cable rentals.

One major Lockheed contract provided all spare parts (except those associated with engine and sensors)

Maintenance performed all the minor adjustments to the total overhaul for the aircraft and the flight test support.

Approximately 20 members were assigned to maintenance crew required to keep ONE aircraft serviced and operational. These were the best aircraft mechanics in the world and success in keeping aircraft flying with high degree of reliability belongs to them.

Three Pratt and Whitney provide for everything from daily service of engine to complete engine teardown at P7W factory in Florida. Increase of engine life between a major overhaul got 90 flight hours before engine tear down was needed.

There were only seven aircraft flying but a total of 42 engines were in inventory. Each aircraft had two engines and needed reserves to allow overhaul and assure reasonable stock against failure.

Maintenance work on the remainder of aircraft systems involved highly skilled technicians which encompassed 22 companies.

Equipment was the most advanced in the world and needed great care (example) a camera system could not go out without a check. Camera failure meant mission failure.

Six aircraft and trainer. The aircraft was no longer a research and development vehicle but an operational aircraft which brought a great deal of experience with it.

Present schedule: three aircraft would return from Kadena to Area 51 in early Feb and maintain an operational ability though March 31 and storage of all aircraft by April 1968.

Industrial competition:

Aircraft industry was very competitive and aware that the Skunkworks.

PHOTOGRAPHIC FILM PROCESSING: NRO system concept proposal March 20, 1968

All equipment uses "wet" process needing chemicals equipment skilled personnel "large qty of water and power. Time consuming, operations involved in production of duplicates.

Problem recognized and defined in Air Systems Command Technical Objective 934 07 (TO 1-69-34)

IF a suitable processing system could be devised to provide a transferable near dry process system providing higher quality produced in a fraction of the time used now, then al services USAF, NAVY (which had problem with fresh water), Army, would use it.

Establishing a facility for producing quality material in a large investment and cost for maintenance for operations.

One main problem, regardless of where film is recovered in the western Pacific (ie) if it has to be transported to facility for processing.

Downloading film from the aircraft to a local packaging facility site, unpacking the material and processing is all taking considerable time. There should be a suitable system for quality film processing at aircraft recovery site, where a small team of personnel could produce the immediate photo intelligence report in minimum time.

Some recovery sites may not have water or power available for a conventional system, a dry processing system was looked for. After looking at many off the shelf systems in research and development, the best place to start was Kodak and the use of the Kodak BIMAT film which used the diffusion transfer process. In this process the chemicals are carried in the emulsion of the film, and brought into intimate contact with exposed but unprocessed negative. After short period of time to allow process to get to completions, the two negatives are separated.

The results are:

1. processed high quality negative film
2. positive transparency in BIMAT film

Both materials contain residual chemicals and were slightly tacky to the touch.

Only solution that Kodak had supplied commercially to date to eliminate the tackiness so the film may be handled is to put a clear sheet of material over the BIMAT film and wither apply a clear sheet of film over the processed negative or wash the processed negative in a continuous manner. The disadvantages with this system are that the negative with the cover laminate impressed on it can't be used for printing and that is if the film is to be conventionally washed and dried, too much time spent processing and producing a usable negative.

CIA insisted on specification to Kodak that some other method be taken to provide a dry original negative without either the laminated cover sheet or conventional wet processing involved. In response –Kodak produced what they have labeled "DESIMAT tape". That was the most significant proposal and responsible for making it work.

Footnote:

BIMAT was not new and there were many in CIA that were skeptical about its ability to produce a high quality negative. To satisfy all concerned, CIA used regularly scheduled training mission in the U-2 from Edwards AFB detachment and employed the Delta III camera system. CIA had a forward camera film developed at Edwards on a VERSAMAT (BW) processor asking for best job the aft camera was forwarded to Kodak for BIMAT processing with conventional washing and drying. The two films were delivered to NPIC for an evaluation and ultimately to Kodak for evaluation. The conclusions reached were that BIMAT can produce a negative at least equal in quality to conventional processing.

The tacky film, processed is brought into contact with "DESIMAT tape" and reeled together on a single reel.

After suitable amount of time, 15 seconds process may be reversed and the DESIMAT tape delaminated from the original negative providing a dry partially cleaned processed original negative from which prints and duplicates could be made.

Two items noted at this point:

1. original negative is not archivable at this stage.
2. The image will deteriorate after a period of time unless steps are taken to permanently fix the film in the conventional manner. Not really important since the film can be handled without measurable deterioration for a week or more, then permanently fix them at a conventional lab later.

It was conceivable that film could be processed without large quantities of water. The photo interpreter needed a high quality dupe positive for his work and a method was needed to produce a dry original negative employed in dry processing such a positive.

Kodak developed DRIMAT film which wasn't that different from BIMAT since it contains a chemically imbibed processing emulsion.

Unlike BIMAT and DRIMAT developed little or no density within itself. DRIMAT provided an ideal material for rapid processing of exposed printed duplicates since the clear DRIMAT film supplies the processing agent and simultaneously acts as a clear cover sheet for exposed duplicate stock film material,

Kodak designed and proven part of the equipment to accomplish the processing system.

First piece of equipment developed was called TRISPAN machine consisting of 3 spindles each capable of holding film reel with drive mechanism. Two of the spindles were supply spindles holding original film negative and BIMAT film, 3rd spindle held take up reel that received the lamented film from reel one and two. The same machine can be reversed after processing is completed on reel 3 and film delaminated and returned to reel one and two in a tacky condition. After delamination, the TRISPIN can leaving exposed film on reel on substitute DESIMAT tape on Reel 2 and start lamination and de lamination (as shown) find)

This would provide on reel one after delamination a dry un-laminated processed original negative ready for duplication positives.

BIMAT film was handled the same way using TRISPIN to laminate the clear cover sheet to BIMAT film. No delamination in needed.

INDEX

1

1129th Special Activities Squadron, 92, 187, 230

1st Weather Reconnaissance Squadron, 53

A

A-11, 77, 78, 79, 80, 83, 84, 85, 120, 121, 172, 173, 174, 272, 281, 284, 289

A-12, 8, 10, 11, 12, 1, 4, 6, 44, 67, 70, 72, 73, 74, 76, 77, 78, 79, 80, 85, 86, 87, 88, 91, 92, 95, 97, 98, 99, 100, 101, 102, 103, 104, 105, 106, 107, 108, 109, 110, 111, 112, 113, 114, 115, 116, 117, 118, 119, 121, 122, 124, 125, 127, 129, 134, 135, 139, 140, 141, 142, 143, 144, 145, 146, 147, 148, 149, 150, 155, 157, 158, 159, 162, 163, 164, 165, 166, 167, 168, 169, 170, 171, 172, 174, 175, 176, 177, 178, 180, 181, 182, 183, 184, 186, 187, 188, 190, 191, 193, 194, 196, 198, 199, 200, 201, 203, 204, 206, 207, 208, 209, 210, 216, 217, 218, 222, 223, 225, 226, 228, 229, 230, 231, 232, 233, 234, 235, 237, 238, 239, 242, 243, 245, 251, 252, 256, 257, 258, 260, 261, 266, 267, 269, 270, 272, 273, 277, 278, 281, 282, 283, 286, 287, 288, 289, 290, 291, 292, 295, 302, 303, 306, 307, 308

A-12 Blackbird, 10, 1, 6, 107, 125

AD Sky Raiders, 30

AF-12, 102, 203, 239, 240, 301, 305

Air Force, 9, 10, 11, 14, 17, 18, 25, 27, 28, 32, 33, 34, 36, 39, 44, 45, 47, 50, 53, 57, 60, 70, 71, 75, 93, 94, 163, 172, 173, 174, 175, 185, 186, 187, 191, 196, 208, 218, 233, 237, 243, 256, 257, 259, 262, 265, 266, 267, 268, 269, 270, 271, 272, 273

Alamo Township, 52

Allan Dulles, 31, 35, 38, 48, 71

Angel of Paradise Ranch, 50, 56

AQUATONE, 9, 5, 49, 50, 57, 76, 93

Archangel, 10, 11, 12, 6, 73, 74, 75, 76, 77, 78, 83, 87, 99, 278

ARDC, 44, 59

Area 51, 9, 10, 11, 12, 52, 77, 91, 93, 94, 95, 98, 99, 104, 107, 108, 109, 110, 111, 112, 116, 117, 118, 119, 127, 128, 132, 135, 155, 165, 167, 168, 170, 171, 172, 173, 175, 176, 177, 181, 183, 190, 191, 200, 201, 204, 208, 226, 227, 230, 231, 232, 240, 262, 275, 287, 288, 289, 290, 292, 301, 302, 308, 309, 312, 313, 326

Article 341, 55, 56

B

B-24 Liberator, 8

B-29 Superfortress, 12

B-57 Canberra, 32, 45

B-58 Hustler, 35, 74, 228

BAIRD ATOMIC 6642-1 Periscope, 157

Bell Aircraft, 33, 44, 45

Ben Rich, 77, 90, 92, 136, 254, 256, 270

BIG HAMMER, 166

Bill Park, 176, 199, 232, 253, 290

BIRDWATCHER, 159, 226

Black Knight, 33

Black Shield, 165, 167, 189, 193, 208, 209, 210, 211, 215, 220, 222, 226, 291, 311

Boeing RB-50, 27

C

C-124, 52

Cadillac II, 8

Captain Hook, 126, 254, 291

Central Intelligence Agency, 9, 10, 5, 14, 16, 17, 31, 60, 71

CHALICE, 76

CIA, 5, 7, 9, 10, 11, 12, 1, 4, 5, 6, 14, 15, 17, 31, 35, 36, 37, 38, 39, 40, 41, 43, 44, 48, 49, 50, 51, 52, 53, 55, 57, 58, 60, 62, 65, 66, 67, 68, 69, 70, 71, 73, 74, 76, 77, 78, 87, 88, 89, 92, 93, 94, 95, 97, 102, 104, 112, 113, 114, 119, 127, 131, 140, 141, 163, 167, 169, 170, 171, 174, 175, 177, 179, 180, 181, 182, 187, 188, 193, 194, 195, 197, 198, 199, 200, 201, 202, 204, 205, 206, 207, 209, 218, 220, 221, 222, 225, 226, 228, 229, 230, 232, 233, 234, 237, 239, 251, 252, 254, 255, 266, 267, 268, 269, 270, 287, 288, 289, 290, 291, 292, 295, 299, 300, 301, 302, 304, 305, 309, 311, 312, 315

CL-282, 9, 41, 43, 44, 46, 47, 48, 163

CL-325, 69

CL-400, 70, 71, 72, 129, 286

Clarence "Kelly" Johnson, 108

Coldwall, 240

Convair, 27, 28, 71, 74, 75, 76, 228, 283, 287

CORONA, 4, 6, 58, 60, 61, 62, 63, 64, 65, 76, 163

Cuban missile crisis, 182

Curtis LeMay, 9

Cygnus, 2, 6, 93, 170, 187, 188, 190, 191, 230

D

D-21, 2, 117, 123, 126, 128, 135, 138, 251, 252, 253, 254, 255, 256, 273, 274, 275, 288, 289, 290, 292, 301

D-21B, 254

David Clark Company, 53

Davis Monthan AFB, 137, 262

Desert Storm, 262, 265

Dirty Bird, 57

DISCOVERER, 63

Dorsey Kamerer, 50

Dragon Lady, 5, 57, 58, 93

Dwight David Eisenhower, 58

E

Eastman Kodak, 61, 62, 64, 165

Edwards AFB, 126, 130, 137, 173, 191, 241, 264, 265, 290, 315

Edwin Land, 31, 36, 40, 41, 48, 71, 163

EG&G (Edgerton, Germeshauser and Grier), 77

Emerald, 27

F

"FERRET", 27

F-104, 45, 46, 72, 75, 82, 116, 124, 142, 176

F-108 Rapier, 237, 238, 239

F 12B, 240, 241

F-13, 9, 14

F-7A, 8

F-86 Sabre, 22, 29

Fairchild Aircraft, 33, 45

FOXBAT, 242

Francis Gary Powers, 5, 59, 65, 67, 166, 287

G

G2A, 74

GAR-9, 238, 239, 240, 243, 245, 246, 249

General Dynamics, 35, 71, 228

General Electric YJ-93, 83

General Henry H. "Hap" Arnold, 39

General Hoyt Vandenberg, 37

General James H. Doolittle, 40

General Maxwell Taylor, 197

General Norman Schwarzkopf, 262

General Paul Bacalis, 221

Glenn L. Martin Company, 32, 67

GOR, 33, 59

Groom Lake, 9, 50, 52, 89, 93, 114

GUSTO, 10, 6, 74, 76, 88

H

Hastalloy"X", 100

HEF fuel, 84

HYCON B, 166

I

Ilyushin–28 Beagle, 26

Issinglass, 228

J

J-58, 6, 76, 83, 84, 85, 109, 118, 130, 137, 141, 142, 149, 150, 151, 155, 156, 171, 199, 201, 227, 243, 245, 252, 279, 286, 288

Jack Weeks, 88, 114, 131, 180, 187, 221, 222, 223, 225, 230, 274, 292

James Killian, 36, 163

Jim Eastham, 289

JOE I, 19

JOE II atomic bomb, 27

John "Hank" Meiredierk, 97

John F. Kennedy, 171, 289

John McCone, 180, 197

JP-7 fuel, 127, 184

JT-11D-20, 149

K

Kadena AB, 97, 305, 309, 311

KEDLOCK, 239, 300, 301, 303

Ken Collins, 175, 227, 289

KEYHOLE, 63

Killian Technological Capabilities Panel, 48

Kirkland AFB, 180

L

"L", 160

LA-11, 20

LA-7, 30

LA-9, 20

LANYARD, 65

Lavochkin, 20, 30

Lloyd Bucher, 219

Lockheed Advanced Development Company, 91

Lop Nor, 57, 255, 292

Lou Schalk, 135, 171, 287, 288

M

M-21, 123, 135, 237, 251, 252, 253, 254, 273, 275, 288, 289, 290

Manhattan Project, 19, 93

Marquandt, 138

Mele Vojvodich, 22, 26, 179, 226, 291

MiG 15, 18, 20, 30, 210, 217

N

National Security Act of 1947, 14

Nellis AFB, 179

Nice Girl, 233

Northrop F-15A, 10

O

Okinawa, Japan, 206, 291

Operation Bordertown, 34

OPERATION CAROUSEL, 208

Operation Eardrum, 13

Operation Sea Lion, 34

Operation SKYLARK, 198, 199

Osmond Ritland, 3, 60, 62

OSS (Office of Strategic Services), 14

P

P2V Neptunes, 4

P4M Mercator, 31

P-51 Mustangs, 9, 21

P-61 Black Widow, 10, 32

P-80, 44, 89

PBY Catalinas, 7

Perkin-Elmer Company, 163

Pratt & Whitney J-**57**, 47

Pratt & Whitney J-58 engine, 149

Pratt & Whitney R-4360 WASP, 10

President's Scientific Advisory Board, 36

Project 51, 94

Project Rheinberry, 228

Project SUNTAN, 70, 71, 286

Q

QB-47, 241

R

Ray Torick, 253, 290

RB-36F, 28

RB-36H, 28

RB-45C Tornado, 22

Republic X-12, 10

RF-101 Voodoo, 32

RF-84K, 28

Richard Bissell, 4, 48, 49, 50, 60, 62, 70, 71, 76, 87, 93, 141, 193, 255

Richard Helms, 207, 220

Richard Leghorn, 3, 42

Roadrunners, 7, 11, 12, 108, 112, 113, 114, 190, 274

Robert Gates, 61

Robert McNamara, 196

Ronald "Jack" Layton, 226

S

SAM SA-2 missile, 66

"Scope Crown E" program, 167

Senator Stuart Symington, 38

Shaker Vane, 240

Sharlene Weeks, 7, 230

Silas Mason Company, 51

Silent Warriors, 31, 275

SILVER JAVELIN, 193, 201

SR-71, 10, 11, 1, 79, 85, 87, 99, 124, 127, 129, 130, 131, 132, 133, 136, 137, 143, 145, 161, 167, 168, 177, 186, 188, 191, 230, 231, 232, 233, 235, 237, 241, 242, 256, 257, 258, 259, 260, 261, 262, 263, 264, 265, 266, 267, 270, 273, 288, 290, 291, 292, 293, 294, 299, 301, 305, 306, 307, 308

Sverdlosk USSR, 166

T

TAGBOARD, 123, 251, 252, 274, 300, 301, 303, 309

Thomas McIninch, 267

Titanium Metals Corporation, 101, 102

Tony LeVier, 50, 55, 56, 113

Tupolev TU-4, 13

U

USAAF, 7, 8, 12, 13, 89

USS *Pueblo*, 217

V

VD-3 squadron, 8

VMD-254, 8

Vought F-8 Crusader, 149

W

Walt Ray, 295

WB-57s, 34

Wright R-3350, 13

WS-117L program, 59, 60, 61

X

XAIM-47, 240, 241, 289

XB-70 Valkyrie, 83, 85, 88, 105, 106, 237, 241

XF-12 *Rainbow*, 10, 11

XR-11, 10, 11

Y

Yakolev YAK-25 Flashlight, 27

YF-12, 2, 85, 98, 111, 122, 132, 133, 134, 145, 173, 191, 192, 237, 238, 241, 242, 257, 258, 264, 266, 273, 274, 275, 288, 289, 290, 292, 293, 301

YF-12C, 242

Bibliography

Air Force Magazine, Air Force Association, Arlington Va.

Apple, Nick P. and Gurney, Gene, The National Museum of the USAF™ The Central Printing Co., Dayton, Oh. 1991.

Ashley, Holt Engineering Analysis of Flight Vehicles, Dover NY, 1974.
Aviation Week & Space Technology Magazine, McGraw Hill Companies New York, NY.

Ball, Robert, Fundamentals of Aircraft Combat Survivability Analysis and Design, AIAA Education Series, AIAA, NY, 1985.

Beschloss, Michael R., Eisenhower and the U-2 Affair, Harper Row, NY.,1986.

Branford, James, The Puzzle Palace, Penguin Books, NY. 1983.

Brugioni, Dino, Eyeball to Eyeball, Random House, New York, NY. 1981.

Burrows, William E., Deep Black, Berkeley Books, New York, NY, 1986.

Bucher, Commander Lloyd, Bucher, My Story, Doubleday Press, Garden City, NY. 1970.

CIA, The CIA and the Overhead Reconnaissance U-2 and OXCART Programs 1954-1974, Central Intelligence Agency.

CIA, The U-2's Intended Successor :Project OXCART 1956-1968, Central Intelligence Agency.

CIA, *25 year declassified material FOIA request, various documents, memos, cables,etc. CIA FOIA ,by Author*

CIA, *Declassified Material 2008-1017,OXCART-Lockheed Internal papers*, CIA via Roadrunners Internationale, 2017.

CIA, *Report-Oxcart A-12 Aircraft Experience Data and Systems Reliability*, Central Intelligence Agency.

Coffey, Thomas M., *Iron Eagle: The Turbulent Life of General Curtis LeMay*, Crown Publishers, Inc., New York, NY. 1986.

Cresswell, Mary Ann and Carl Berger. *United States Air Force History: An Annotated Bibliography*, Office of Air Force History, Washington, D.C. 1971.

Crickmore, Paul F., *Lockheed SR-71 Secret Missions Exposed*, Osprey Aerospace, 1993, Great Britain.

Crickmore, Paul F., *Lockheed Blackbird, Beyond the Secret Missions*, Osprey, 1994, Great Britain.

Darlington, David, *Area 51:The Dreamland Chronicles*, Henry Holt, NY. 1997.

Drendl, Lou, *Air War over South East Asia-Vol.3*, Squadron/Signal Publications, 1984.

Francillon, Rene' J., *Lockheed Aircraft Since 1913*, Naval Institute Press, Annapolis, MD, 1987.

Gorn, Michael H., *Harnessing the Genie: Science and Technology forecasting for the Air Force,1944-1986* (Air Force Historical Study), Office of Air Force History, Washington, D.C. 1988.

Graham, Richard H., *SR-71 Revealed: The Inside Story*, MBI Publishing Company, Osceola, WI.,1996.

Kaplan, Fred, *The Wizards of Armageddon,* Stanford University Press, Stanford, CA., 1983.

Jackson, Robert, *High Cold War- Strategic Air Reconnaissance and Electronics Intelligence War*, Patrick Stephens Ltd., Haynes Publishing, Somerset, England,1998.

Jenkins, Dennis R., *Lockheed SR-71/YF-12 Blackbirds*, (Warbird Tech Series, Vol.10) Specialty Press Publishers, North Branch, MN,1997.

Johnson, Kelly and Maggie Smith, *More Than My Share of it All,* Smithsonian, Washington D.C., London, 1985.

Landis, Tony and Jenkins, Dennis R. *WARBIRD Tech Lockheed Blackbirds,* Specialty Press, MN. 2004.

Lert, Fredric, *Wings of the CIA*,Histoire and Collections, Paris, France, 1998.

LeMay, Gen. Curtis E., with Kantor MacKinlay, *Mission With LeMay: My Story*, Doubleday & Company Inc., Garden City, NY. 1965.

Lockheed Martin, *Lockheed Martin SR-71 Researcher's Handbook Vol. II.*

Mason, Herbert Molloy, Jr. *The United States Air Force: A Turbulent History*, Mason/Carter, New York, NY.,1976.

McInnich, Thomas, *The OXCART Story*, Central Intelligence Agency.

McNamara, Robert S. with Van DeMark, Brian, *In Retrospect: The Tragedy and Lessons of Vietnam*, Times Books, New York, NY. 1995.

Miller, David, *The Cold War-A Military History*, St. Martin's Press, New York, NY. 1998.

Miller, Jay, *Lockheed Martin's Skunk Works,* Midland Publishing Ltd.,Leicester, England, 1995.

Miller, Jay, *Lockheed Martin's Skunk Works, The First Fifty Years*, Aerofax, Arlington, Texas, 1993.

Miller, Jay, *Lockheed SR-71 (A-12/YF-12/AR-D21) Minigraph*, Aerofax, Arlington, Texas, 1985.

Neufeld, Jacob, Watson, George M.,Jr. and Chenoweth, David, Eds., *Technology and the Air Force: A Retrospective Assessment,* Air Force History and Museums Programs, Washington, D.C. 1997.

Pedlow, Gregory W. and Welzenbach,Donald E., *The CIA and the U-2 Program, 1954-1974*, Center for the Study of Intelligence, CIA, Washington, D.C. 1998.

Peebles,Curtis, *Dark Eagles: A History of Top Secret U.S. Aircraft Programs*, Presidio Press, Novato, CA., 1995.

Ranelagh, John, *The Agency-The Rise and Fall of the CIA*, Touchstone Press, Simon and Schuster,New York, NY. 1986.

Remak, Jeannette and Ventolo, Joe, Jr., *XB-70 Valkyrie:The Ride to Valhalla,* MBI Publishing Company, Osceola, WI.,1998.

Rich, Ben R., and Janos, Leo, *Skunk Works: A Personal Memoir of My Years at Lockheed,* Little, Brown and Company, New York, NY. 1994.

Schlesinger, Arthur, *A Thousand Days: John F. Kennedy in the White House,* Riverside Press/Houghton-Mifflin Co., Cambridge, MA.,1965.

Shapley,Deborah, *Promise and Power:The Life and Times of Robert McNamara,* Little, Brown and Company,Boston, MA.,1993.

Sherry, Michael S.,*In the Shadow of War, the United States Since the 1930s,* Yale University Press, New Haven and London, 1995.

Stone, John, *Blackbird Time Line of Events,*1995.

Suhler, Paul, *From RAINBOW to GUSTO Stealth and Design of the Lockheed Blackbird,* American Institute of Aeronautics & Astronautics,2009, Washington,D.C.

Stone, Ronald B.,Ed. *North American Aircraft & Aerospace Museum Guide,* 8th Edition, Bruce/Beeson Publishers, Olathe, KS., 1998.

Swanborough, Gordon and Bowers, Peter M., *United States Military Aircraft Since 1909,* Smithsonian Institution Press,Washington, D.C., 1989.

Timnot,Y.M, *Advanced Air Breathing Propulsion,* Kreiger Publishing, Malabar, Florida, 1996.

United States Air Force Museum, Air Force Museum Foundation,Inc. Wright-Patterson, AFB, OH. 1985.

Walker, Lois E., and Wickham, Shelby E., *From Huffman Prairie to the Moon: The History of Wright-Patterson Air Force Base*, Headquarters, Air Force Logistics Command, Wright-Patterson AFB, OH., 1985.

Walker, Martin, *The Cold War- A History*, Henry Holt and Company, New York, NY.1995.

Watson, George M., *The Office of the Secretary of the Air Force, 1947-1965*, Center for Air Force History, Washington, D.C. 1993.

Wensberg, Peter C., *Land's Polaroid*, Houghton-Mifflin, Boston, 1987.

Wise, David and Ross, Thomas B., *The U-2 Affair*, Random House, New York, NY. 1962.

Wolf, Richard I., *The United States Air Force Basic Documents on Role and Missions* (Air Staff Historical Study), Office of Air Force History, Washington, D.C. 1987.

COMING SOON!

To Slip the Surly Bonds

by

Jeannette Remak

Sign up for free and bargain books

Join the Speaking Volumes mailing list

Text
ILOVEBOOKS
to 22828 to get started.

Message and data rates may apply.

www.ingramcontent.com/pod-product-compliance
Lightning Source LLC
Chambersburg PA
CBHW071619170426
43195CB00038B/1429